# Photoshop
# After the Shoot

# Photoshop® CS4
# After the Shoot

Mark Fitzgerald

Wiley Publishing, Inc.

## Photoshop® CS4 After the Shoot

Published by
**Wiley Publishing, Inc.**
10475 Crosspoint Blvd.
Indianapolis, IN 46256
www.wiley.com

Copyright © 2009 by Wiley Publishing, Inc., Indianapolis, Indiana

Published simultaneously in Canada

ISBN: 978-0-470-38986-7

Manufactured in the United States of America

10 9 8 7 6 5 4 3 2 1

For general information on our other products and services or to obtain technical support, please contact our Customer Care Department within the U.S. at (800) 762-2974, outside the U.S. at (317) 572-3993 or fax (317) 572-4002.

Wiley also publishes its books in a variety of electronic formats. Some content that appears in print may not be available in electronic books.

Library of Congress Control Number: 2008941627

WILEY

# About the Author

**Mark Fitzgerald** is a Photoshop trainer and workflow consultant who specializes in helping professional photographers thrive in the digital age. He has taught countless photographers how to smooth out their workflow and get the most from their images — through private training, classes, and workshops. Mark is an Adobe Certified Photoshop Expert and an Adobe Certified Photoshop Instructor. He and his wife, Julia (with their three dogs, Ruby, Hazel, and Sam), live in Portland, Oregon, where Mark owns a consulting business called The Digital Darkroom (www.ddroom.com).

# Credits

**Acquisitions Editor**
Courtney Allen

**Senior Project Editor**
Cricket Krengel

**Technical Editor**
George Maginnis

**Copy Editor**
Lauren Kennedy

**Editorial Manager**
Robyn B. Siesky

**Vice President & Group Executive Publisher**
Richard Swadley

**Vice President & Publisher**
Barry Pruett

**Business Manager**
Amy Knies

**Senior Marketing Manager**
Sandy Smith

**Media Development Project Manager**
Laura Moss-Hollister

**Media Development Assistant Project Manager**
Jenny Swisher

**Media Development Associate Producer**
Josh Frank

**Book Designer**
Kathie S. Rickard

**Project Coordinator**
Erin Smith

**Graphics and Production Specialists**
Ana Carrillo, Andrea Hornberger,
Kathie Rickard, Erin Zeltner

**Quality Control Technicians**
John Greenough, Catie Kelly

**Proofreading**
Lynda D'Arcangelo

**Indexing**
Broccoli Information Management

In memory of Jerry Auker,
a caring and giving person
who used photography to
change the lives of people
in his community
and beyond.

# Acknowledgments

I would like to thank my family, my friends, and most importantly, my clients for allowing me to disappear into my cave while writing this book. Your understanding and flexibility allowed me to focus on the task at hand.

I also want to thank the following photographers for letting me use their images:

- Bob Bahner, Bob Bahner Photography: www.bobbahnerphotography.com
- Dave Hutt, Dave Hutt Photography: www. davehuttphotography.com
- Cindy Kassab, Cindy Kassab Photography: www.cindykassab.com
- Kathi Lamm, Lamm Photography: www.lammphoto.com
- John McAnulty, Inner Focus Photography: www.pro.corbis.com (search for John McAnulty)
- Brannon McBroom, Brannon McBroom Photography: www.bmcbphotography.com
- Wayne McDonnell, Cavalier Images: www.cavalierimages.com
- Connie Morrison, Connie Morrison Photography: www.conniemorrison.com
- Jordan Sleeth, Jordan Sleeth Photography
- Jan Sonnenmair, Jan Sonnenmair Photographer: www.sonnenmair.com
- Denyce Weiler, Something Blue Photography: www.somethingbluephotography.com
- Gary Wilson, Gary Wilson Photo/Graphic: www.garywilsonphoto.com

Please visit the Web sites of these photographers to see more of their work.

Thanks to the editing team at Wiley: copyeditor Lauren Kennedy, who noticed so many small details that made big differences; technical editor George Maginnis, who stepped in on short notice to lend his extensive expertise; and Senior Project Editor Cricket Krengel, who expertly managed this project from start to finish. I can't imagine writing a technical book without the support of a talented team like this one.

I especially want to thank Courtney Allen, Acquisitions Editor for Wiley Publishing, who so kindly invited me into the Wiley fold. Without her, this book would not be a reality.

# Contents

# Contents

# Contents

# Contents

# Contents

# Contents

# Introduction

Congratulations on your timing! This is an excellent time to begin learning Photoshop. That's because the main emphasis with the development of Photoshop CS4 was to make the software easier to understand and to use. Much of this was accomplished by overhauling the user interface. Important commands and features that were formerly hidden deep inside the program have been brought to the surface where they're much easier to find. Many of these features are arranged so that they improve the image editing workflow. All of these improvements are designed to help new and existing users manage the complexity of this powerful image editing software.

Even with these improvements, though, Photoshop CS4 can seem overwhelming to the new user. That's because it contains a wide range of tools that are used by all sorts of imaging professionals. My goal in *Photoshop CS4 After the Shoot* is to help you identify the tools you need for photo editing and then show you how they fit into the workflow so that you can quickly begin using a time-tested editing system. Along the way, I explain common digital photography concepts and theory so that you gain a deeper understanding of the digital editing process. By the time you finish this book, you'll know which tools to use, when to use them, and why you're using them, so that you can begin to use Photoshop CS4 to quickly craft quality images from your photos.

## How to Use This Book

To get the most from this book, start at the beginning and go through it sequentially. Doing so allows you to experience the learning process in the way I envision it. In many cases, ideas in one chapter build on information introduced in previous chapters. This amplification process won't make as much sense if experienced out of order. Also, take the time to read each chapter, even if you think you already understand its subject. You never know when you'll turn up a nugget that will completely change the way you work with your images.

Download the practice files from the Web site (www.wiley.com/go/photoshopcs4ats). If you have a slow Internet connection, borrow a friend's connection to download them. After you go through a hands-on process with the book's files, take the time to explore those new processes with some of your own photos. I know from experience that working with personal files makes a big difference in the learning process. This is where you'll find the time to go as deep as you need to go while exploring the content of this book.

After you've been through the book from front to back, you can use it as a reference guide to help you solve image editing problems. When a specific issue pops up, find the relevant references in the book and review them as needed.

# Should You Use a Mac or a Windows System?

The subject of Mac versus Windows comes up in my workshops and private training quite often. When it does, I explain it like this: I have used both systems extensively and I've found that each has its pluses and minuses. Deciding between Mac and Windows is like choosing Canon or Nikon (or any other camera system). Both systems are great. Your decision as to which camera to buy should be based on how you like that particular system. Does it feel good in your hands? Are the controls easy to understand? Is it the same system your friends are using so that they can help you when you have questions? After you make a choice and begin buying lenses for one of those camera systems, you'll probably want to stay with it for a while — much like when you purchase software for a computer. Consider all of these factors when choosing a computer system.

No matter which system you decide to go with, be sure that it's up to snuff. If your system is more than three or four years old, you may be disappointed in the performance of Photoshop CS4. Ideally, you should have a machine with a fairly fast processor. A dual processor is even better because Photoshop is designed to take advantage of two processors. Photoshop is a real RAM hog, so you'll want to have at the very least 1GB of system memory and preferably 2GB. If you have these bases covered, then it won't matter if you're running a Mac or a Windows machine.

# Conventions Used In This Book

Because this book was written on two Macs, all the screenshots are from the Mac version of Photoshop CS4. That shouldn't make much difference, because almost everything is the same in the Mac and Windows versions of the software. If you're using a Windows machine, the only real differences are the keyboard modifier keys.

Macs use the Option (Alt) key and the Command (Apple) key as modifiers, and Windows systems use the Alt key and the Ctrl key for the same functions. (This is all the more confusing because a standard Mac keyboard has a Control key on it that has a completely different function.)

- Mac Option (Alt) key = Windows Alt key

- Mac Command (Apple) key = Windows Ctrl key

Because every modern Mac keyboard I've seen has an Alt label on the Option key, I refer to this key as Alt, which should be straightforward. When I need to mention the other set of modifier keys, I say ⌘/Ctrl. The only reason I'm putting the Mac command first is to be consistent with the screenshots.

# Which Version Of Photoshop Cs4 Should You Use?

Photoshop CS4 comes in two different versions: Photoshop CS4 and Photoshop CS4 Extended. The Extended version has some added capabilities for users who work with 3-D objects and for other people, such as scientists and engineers, who need to perform detailed analysis on their images. These features are in menus called Analysis and 3D. Because Photoshop CS4 Extended was used to write this book, you may notice these menus in some screenshots. Don't worry if you don't have them. Most of the photographers don't need the added features of the Extended version.

# One Last Thing

I tried very hard to make sure everything in this book is 100 percent accurate. If you notice any errors or omissions, please let me know by emailing me at books@ddroom.com. That way, I can fix them in future editions.

# 1

# Creating an Organized System

**W**hen photographers were mostly shooting film, their filing systems weren't very complicated. They labeled and stored sets of slides or negatives and proofs in places like boxes and filing cabinets. Though some photographers were more organized than others, the system was intuitive because it was similar to the way other important documents are organized and stored. As photographers began to capture digital files, this organizational system became less intuitive due to the virtual nature of the image files. This problem was compounded by the large number of original files generated by digital shooters, as well as the ease of creating derivative files that are nearly identical the original photo. In this chapter you learn about the different kinds of files digital photographers use and some of the strategies used to organize them. By the time you finish this chapter you'll be ready to create an organizational system that makes sense.

# Understanding File Formats

Think of file formats as different languages. When a book is printed in a particular language, only someone who reads the language can understand it. If the reader knows a second language, he can translate the book into that other language, making it available to other people. This is similar to the way file formats work in Photoshop. Certain file languages are used for different purposes. As an image moves through the digital workflow, it's translated into the language that's most appropriate for that particular portion of the workflow.

When discussing how file formats fit into the workflow, it's useful to divide them into three groups — image capture formats, editing formats, and output formats. Image capture file formats are the file types that come directly out of a digital camera. Editing formats are file types that are created during the editing process in Photoshop. Output formats are used for specific output purposes such as printing or Web display.

## Image capture formats

Digital photographers tend to capture images in one of these two file formats: JPEG and camera raw. The decision about which file format you use can have a huge impact on the possibilities of what you can do during the editing process.

### JPEG

The JPEG file type (JPG when used as a file extension) was designed to be a space-saving file format. It was created in 1992 by a committee called the Joint Photographic Experts Group (JPEG). The committee's goal was to establish a portable standard for compressing photographic files that would be universal for all kinds of editing software. This compression results in smaller, more portable files.

File compression is a system of analyzing a file and looking for common strings of data. When several identical stings are located, they're replaced by a single representative string with references to all the places where it appears in the image. Compression can substantially reduce file size, especially when images contain lots of the same tones, such as solid backgrounds.

There is a downside to JPEG compression. Though very small files can be created with high compression, JPEG compression is lossy, meaning that information is lost during the compression process. The amount of loss depends on the amount of compression. Additionally, whenever a file is resaved and compressed again, more data is lost. Eventually this cumulative data loss begins to affect the quality of the photo. The key is to limit the total loss by compressing a JPEG file as little as possible — not editing and resaving the file later on. That's why the JPEG file format is not considered an editing format.

To understand the effects of file compression, it helps to look at what happens to a JPEG file when it's saved in Photoshop. When saving a JPEG file in Photoshop, you're presented with the option to determine the amount of compression that's applied to the file. Greater amounts of compression yield smaller files sizes.

Take a look at this example to see it in action. Figure 1.1 shows the JPEG Options dialog box that appears when saving a JPEG file in Photoshop. In this case, an image that is 24.8MB becomes a 3.2MB JPEG with a compression quality of 12. If the compression on this file is lowered by two, to 10 instead of 12, the file size is reduced by two-thirds to 1.0MB without adversely affecting the image quality. However, if this file is repeatedly reopened and resaved with a level of 10, the quality of the photo is affected.

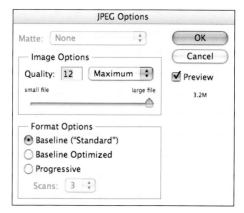

Figure 1.1

Figure 1.2 shows a photo of the beach. This photo was saved as a JPEG with a quality setting of 10. It's nearly indistinguishable from the original file JPEG file that was captured with the camera.

Figure 1.3 shows the same photo after opening and resaving it several times with a JPEG compression of 10. Notice that the gradient in the sky now shows what's called banding. This is caused by over-compression that has

eliminated many of the intermediate tones in the sky, causing tonal variations to show up as bands rather than gentle tonal graduations.

When you use JPEG as a capture format in your camera you have the option of choosing the level of compression for the photos as they're saved to the camera's media card. Oftentimes this is presented as a quality setting or a size setting. In both cases you want to choose the higher number—higher quality, or larger size. This reduces the number of images that can be saved to the media card, but it insures that the files have the highest quality with the least amount of compression.

JPEG is one of the most widely used file formats for digital imaging. Virtually any software that can open an image file can open a JPEG. What's more, nearly all the photographs you see on the Internet are JPEG files — at least the ones that look good. That's because JPEGs can be compressed to very small sizes, which is perfect for online delivery or e-mail where quality isn't as noticeable.

Figure 1.2

**Figure 1.3**

## Camera raw

Camera raw (raw) files can be created with digital single lens reflex (dSLR) cameras and some high-end point-and-shoot cameras. These files get their name from the kind of information they contain.

To understand raw files it's useful to compare them to the JPEG capture format. When you point your camera at a scene and press the shutter button, the camera's image sensor captures a huge amount of information. If you have the camera set to capture JPEG files, the camera's onboard processor processes all that information into a JPEG file. The processor looks at all the settings you have set on your camera — sharpness, white balance, color space, contrast, and so on. Then it applies all these settings and creates the JPEG file from a small sliver of the data that the camera's sensor recorded. The rest of the information — most of what was captured — is ignored and deleted. Even if the JPEG is of the highest quality (meaning the least compression), it represents only a fraction of what the camera actually saw.

JPEG capture is easy because it allows the camera to make lots of decisions very quickly, based on the settings you have dialed into your camera. If you're working in a very controlled environment, or under extreme deadlines, this can be a fast way to get things done. The problem is that you don't get to look at all the information before it gets thrown away. You have to live with the data the camera selected to create the JPEG files.

Shooting in raw is the solution to this problem. It allows you to save most of the information that a camera's sensor is capable of capturing. After you have this information in a file, you can selectively choose which information becomes part of the editing file by converting the data from the raw file into an editing file format that Photoshop can use. This adds an additional step to the workflow because you have to make some decisions that the camera would normally make when shooting JPEG, but the flexibility is worth the added step.

## see also

Raw files are covered in detail in Chapter 4.

## Editing formats

As I mentioned earlier, the JPEG file format isn't the best choice for editing because of the destructive nature of lossy compression. Another reason the JPEG format isn't a useful editing format is the inability to save layers in a JPEG file. A layer is just that — a segment of image information that's stacked on top of the original image. This ability to isolate different aspects of the image allows a great deal of control over the image as a whole. Because of that, the two primary file formats for editing are TIFF and PSD.

### TIFF

TIFF (or TIF when used as a file extension) stands for Tagged Image File Format. TIFF is a flexible format that's supported by most image-editing and graphics software.

Normally, a TIFF file is larger than a PSD file (Photoshop's native format) that's saved from the same image. That's because PSD files are compressed a bit by default to make them smaller when they're saved. However, compression can also be applied to a TIFF file. This compression results in much smaller files size than PSD files. Just be aware that compressed TIFF files take longer to save and to open.

With a TIFF file, compression doesn't happen automatically; it's an option. You must select it in the TIFF Options dialog box, as shown in

Figure 1.4, when the TIFF file format is chosen in the File → Save As dialog box. Photoshop offers three different types of TIFF file compression: LZW, ZIP, and JPEG. The main difference among these three compression methods is that LZW and ZIP are lossless compression methods (no data is lost during compression), and JPEG is a lossy method of compression similar to the compression used on JPEG files that was discussed earlier.

**Figure 1.4**

When compressing a TIFF file, stick with lossless compression by selecting LZW or ZIP. They're fairly equal in performance, and Photoshop opens either of them. However, be aware that ZIP is not supported in older software. I compress TIFF files only when I'm planning to e-mail or transfer them electronically to someone and I want to save space. Many people also compress all TIFF files to save room on their drives.

As mentioned earlier, an option with TIFF files in Photoshop is the ability to save layers. This seems pretty cool, except that few image-editing applications can open all the layers of a layered TIFF file. If I'm saving a layered file and planning to use Photoshop to edit it — even if it began as a TIFF — I save it as a PSD file. If you're worried about hard drive space, go ahead and save your layered files in the compressed TIFF format.

## see also

Layers are discussed in Chapter 6.

### PSD

PSD is Photoshop's proprietary default file format (and stands for Photoshop document). It supports more Photoshop features than TIFF. One advantage of working with PSD is that Adobe products such as Illustrator can open PSD files and access all the saved features. This makes life easier for people who move among Adobe software applications.

Another advantage to using PSD is that all layer information is preserved and stored. When the image is opened, it goes to the state that it was in when it was last saved. All the layers are there, and the last active layer is still active. When you work extensively with layers, saving them becomes important.

## Output file formats

After you have done all the editing work, you need to generate some kind of file for output. This output often takes the form of a slide show, a print, or display on the Web. The JPEG file format is the most common file type for these uses. In fact, when it's time to have prints made, you'll find that most photolabs only accept JPEG files because the compressed files take up less room on their servers and move through their workflow faster. To create these output files, you'll need to save a version of your editing files as JPEGs using Photoshop's Save As command.

## note

If you print with an inkjet printer, you can print from any of the editing file formats.

Sometimes a TIFF is preferred when a file is being prepared for publication. This is because the publication workflow takes place in a CMYK (cyan, magenta, yellow, and black) color space, which cannot be used with the JPEG file format. When saving a layered TIFF file for this use, be sure to flatten it (Layer → Flatten Image) unless you have specific instructions from the graphic artist handling the project. Otherwise, she may not be able to see all layers of the image in her layout software.

# Organizing Different Kinds of Files

When you first get interested in digital imaging, you may not realize just how quickly the digital dream can become an organizational nightmare. In the days of shooting film, organization was just as important, but with digital photography, organization is more complicated for a couple of reasons. For one thing, if you aren't careful, the place where image files are stored isn't quite so intuitive. Sometimes, files end up in cryptic places requiring three software engineers to find them. For another, working with digital images tends to create lots and lots of derivative files, as well as output files, from some original files. When so many similar yet different files are created, organization takes on a whole new meaning. If all of these files are stored in the same folder it becomes difficult to identify a particular version of the image.

## Considering the non-destructive workflow

Earlier I mentioned that layers are used to keep your editing options open. This is the first step in creating a non-destructive workflow. The idea behind a non-destructive workflow is to keep your options open at all times so that it's easy to change individual elements of the editing process. Another way to limit the destructiveness of image editing is to avoid cropping and image-size adjustments in Photoshop whenever possible. If you make these changes and close the file, they become permanent.

The problem with this is that you need to flatten and crop files at some point. You usually do this when you're giving someone else a copy of the file, taking it to a lab to be printed, or uploading it to a Web site. To solve this problem in a non-destructive way, you save two separate files: an editing file (PSD) that retains all the flexibility possible in a PSD, and an output file (JPEG or TIFF) that has been sized, cropped, prepared for output, and flattened. Often, you'll prepare multiple output files from the same original image for different uses. These versions begin to add up, creating a level of complexity that was never a problem when shooting film.

## Three kinds of workflow files

When creating a non-destructive workflow it becomes necessary to organize three different kinds of files: originals files from the camera, edited master file that contain as much information as possible (usually in layers), and final files for printing or display. Both a master file and any related final files are derivatives of the same original file. Look more closely at these three kinds of workflow files:

- **Original files.** These are the capture files from your camera that should never be overwritten. Original files need to remain pristine so you can go back to them when necessary — for example, when you learn a new technique.

- **Master files.** These editing files contain all the flexibility and options that are built into the file as it's edited in Photoshop. These files are almost always saved as PSD files, though they can be saved as layered TIFF files.

- **Final files.** These output files have been prepared for some final usage, such as for print, Web, or e-mail. They have been cropped and sized to a final size and sharpened for output.

When all these different files from the same image are stored in the same place, they become difficult to manage. They all look similar in Bridge, (Photoshop's file browser), so you spend time sorting through them. To minimize confusion, these three file types need to be organized in two ways: They need to have unique names based on the original file's name, and they need to be in special folders.

## see also

Bridge is discussed in detail in Chapter 2.

## Creating a virtual filing cabinet

Imagine a filing cabinet for a moment. Your filing cabinet has three drawers. Each of those drawers is used to store folders that contain specific information. Sometimes a folder contains subfolders inside of it. If you think about it, this is much the same way filing occurs on a computer. Images are placed inside of folders and those folders are often placed inside of larger folders.

Figure 1.5 shows a typical filing strategy with the following file path: Photos → 2008 → Alice → individual files of Alice. The folder named Photos (in the first column) is my filing cabinet. It has three drawers named 2006, 2007, and 2008. Each of those drawers has a bunch of folders in it. The third column shows the folders inside of the 2008 drawer. The last column shows the individual images inside of the folder named Alice.

The previous example uses three levels of organization:

- **One main folder contains all images in subfolders.** This is incredibly useful when it comes to backing up photos because only one folder — with its subfolders — needs to be backed up.

- **Subfolders are created for each individual year.** This level of organization prevents you from having to sort through folders from previous years unless you want to.

- **Shoot/job folders are used to hold the files from an individual photo shoot.** This folder is often divided into subfolders containing different kinds of non-destructive workflow files: original, master, and final files.

Creating a filing system like this is the first step to becoming organized. The next step is to begin using a folder and file naming system that complements the kind of photography you do.

# Naming your folders and files

When it comes to naming folders — and the files stored inside them — there are two predominant lines of thought. One is to name folders with pertinent dates and the other is to use descriptive names that describe the photos in the folder. Take a look at both of these strategies to determine which is best for you.

## Using dates to name folders

Some photographers prefer to name all shoot/job folders with the date they were shot, or in some cases uploaded. That way every folder is listed in chronological order. The key to using this naming strategy is to use the right date format so that folders are sorted in the correct order. The preferred method is Year_Month_Day. This way every file is sorted in the correct order, beginning with the year, then the month, then the day. Some people like to make life easier by adding a descriptive name to the end of the date. For example, if I shoot some photos at the Oregon coast, I name my folder 2008_08_21_Oregon_Coast.

**Figure 1.5**

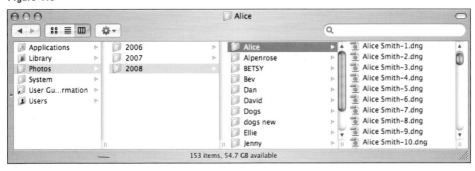

# note

I use an underscore (_), (Shift+−) to separate the numbers in the dates. This is better than leaving a space, especially when you plan to upload photos to the Web because most Web servers replace a space with %20. Some won't even accept files with a space in the name. You can also use a hyphen (-) or you can run the numbers together.

One of the main drawbacks to using this Year_Month_Day system is that it tends to spread out similar images too much. In its purest form, all photos are placed into dated folders that represent the day they were created. If I take a trip to Europe for two weeks and then download all my photos using the date naming system, I end up with a folder for every day. If I took pictures every day, then my vacation photos would be spread out into 14 folders. I prefer to see them all together. A better way to use this system in this case is to create a main folder with a general date — such as the date the files were uploaded — and then add all files to this one folder instead of placing them into individual daily folders.

# caution

Mac users can use a slash (/) in a folder name instead of a hyphen. However, Windows users may not be able to see the folder because / is an illegal character in a Windows environment. Web servers may also have a problem with the character, therefore it's best to not use this character in your naming strategy.

## Naming folders with descriptive names

Another strategy is to use a descriptive name to identify a shoot. With this strategy, the folder from my coast trip is named Oregon_Coast_08. If I took more than one trip to the coast in 2008, I would add the month after the year. An advantage to this strategy is that folder names have a more descriptive name. Another advantage is that all photos from the shoot are automatically located in one main folder.

The main disadvantage is that folders are sorted alphabetically by your system, instead of chronologically. If that's important to you, then this system may not be the best choice. Another disadvantage is that a single descriptive name doesn't always describe everything in the folder. This happens when you allow lots of images to collect on your camera's media card before uploading them. One way to solve this is to do multiple uploads from the camera's card — placing groups of images into individual folders with descriptive names. A better way to solve this is to regularly upload your photos so they don't accumulate on the card.

## Choosing a folder naming strategy

I know photographers who use both the date and descriptive systems to file images. The people who tend to use the date system are photographers who shoot lots of images, such as commercial and stock shooters. They also tend to be photographers who are highly organized because they often have to locate stored files over long periods of time. The photographers who tend to use the descriptive name method are mostly portrait and wedding photographers who are more oriented to locating jobs by the client's name.

Some photographers don't fall squarely into either of these camps. They tend to use a blend of the two naming systems. If the images in the folder can be categorized with a descriptive name — such as Hawaii 08, or Jones Wedding — then they use a name. When the images don't have a predominant theme, they use a general date for the name and then use keywords to identify the individual images.

No matter which system you choose, make sure that you're consistent in the way you use it.

# note

A keyword is a descriptive term that you attach to a photo file to describe something about it. For example, if I go to the coast I might use keywords such as beach, seagull, tide pool, and ocean to identify the contents of various photos. Later, if I search for the keyword seagulls, all photos with the seagull keyword attached to them will be found. You learn how to do this with Bridge in Chapter 2.

## Naming original files

Digital cameras automatically create filenames for every photo you shoot. Sometimes those names are quite cryptic. Filenames like those shown in Figure 1.6 don't tell me much about the photos they represent, even if I understand why the camera created that name in the first place. That's why I always like to change these names to descriptive names that tell me something about the image when naming original files. This is usually done as the original files are transferred from the camera's media card to the computer, as discussed in Chapter 3. I might use something like Jane_Doe_123 instead of the name created by the camera because it makes more sense on a couple of levels. First, if I ever need to find Jane's photos using the photo's names, I can do a system search with my computer's operating system for Jane_Doe. Without a descriptive name, this becomes impossible.

The second reason a descriptive filename makes sense is that eventually derivative files for editing and output will be created from some of the originals. It's easier to keep those files organized when you begin with a meaningful name. For example, suppose the original file is named ZOA6337.cr2 because that's what the camera automatically named it, the master file is named sarah_jones123.psd, and the final file for 8 × 10 printing is named girl_in_boat.jpg. This causes problems in two ways. First, if the files are all in the same folder and they're being sorted

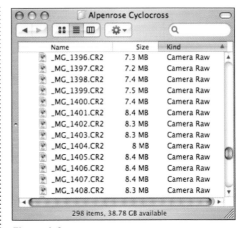

**Figure 1.6**

alphabetically, they're scattered all over the place among the other files. Second, if you learn some new tricks next year and decide to redo the girl_in_boat.jpg image, you may have trouble remembering from which original file it's derived.

I solve this problem by naming the original file as soon as it's copied from the media card to the computer. Then any new derivative file uses that name as a base. In the previous example, the original file becomes sarah_jones123.cr2, the master file becomes sarah_jones123_edited.psd, and the final file becomes sarah_jones123_8x10.jpg. This way, I know exactly what kind of file I'm looking at just by looking at the name. In the case of sarah_jones123_8x10.jpg I even know that it's been prepared for an 8 × 10 print.

After you establish a naming methodology, you must address the second level of file organization: filing different kinds of workflow files into the appropriate folders. Figure 1.7 shows how I organize my file folders. When I begin a new project, I create a folder for it. In this case, the parent folder is titled Sarah Jones. I create three subfolders inside of the Sarah Jones folder: Originals, Masters, and Finals. (You can also place the originals directly into the parent folder, eliminating the need for the Originals folder.)

**Figure 1.7**

My goal with this organizational system is to make it so intuitive that I know where everything is without looking. Even though I never do it, I want to be able to call my assistant back at my office and ask her to send a particular file to me if I need it. I can do that because I know exactly where the file should be, and so does she.

Your system doesn't have to look exactly like mine. If necessary, create something that makes more sense to you because you're the one who needs to understand it. The thing that's most important here is to get a system in place and begin using it now.

# Backing Up and Archiving

Why organize all your photos if you don't take the time to back up all your work? Digital photography offers all kinds of creative opportunities that have changed the way photographers work with images. Unlike film, though, digital files can disappear in an instant when a hard drive crashes. If proper archiving measures aren't used, a bad hard drive crash can be catastrophic. The following sections explore some archiving options and strategies.

## Hard drives

One of the easiest ways to create a backup is with a separate hard drive that backs up all image files. In its more sophisticated form, this is often an array of multiple hard drives that are set up to act as one. This kind of array is called a RAID (Redundant Array of Independent Disks). Several different schemes are used to protect file integrity on a RAID. Here are the two main ones:

- **Mirroring.** (Sometimes referred to as RAID1) Identical data is written to more than one disk. If a disk in this array crashes, identical data is recovered from the mirrored disk.

- **Striping.** (Sometimes referred to as RAID0) Information is spread out across multiple disks. This greatly enhances performance because several disks are doing the job of one disk when reading and writing. However, unless some form of redundancy is built into the system, there is no data protection as in mirroring. Setting up some form of redundancy allows for striped data to be recovered after a crash. One method of doing this is to have software that can reconstruct missing data from a crashed hard drive by analyzing data that wasn't lost on the other hard drives.

All the workings inside a RAID, mirroring and striping, happen in the background. The best part is that it happens automatically. The RAID just looks like a big hard drive to the computer's operating system. After a RAID is set up, it does its job whether you think about it or not. With the low cost of hard drives today, a RAID is a great option if you're dealing with lots of files.

A less sophisticated, yet equally effective hard drive solution is to have a secondary hard drive that's used for storing backup copies. These backups can be created automatically with specially designed software, or they can be created manually by dragging and dropping files. Of these two schemes, the automatic solution is by far the best. With backup software like ChronoSync by Econ Technologies (for Mac) and Microsoft Sync Toy (for Windows), multiple auto-backup scenarios are easy to set up so that you never have to think about them again.

# tip

I solved my crashing hard drive problem by purchasing an uninterruptable power supply (UPS). A UPS is little more than big battery that you plug your computer into. If the power goes out unexpectedly, the UPS kicks in, giving you time to close important files and shut down your computer. Most UPS units also do something else: they clean up the incoming power so it's more stable. That's what solved my crashing problem.

Hard drive storage is a great solution for storing backup files, but this also can lead to a false sense of security. A few years ago, shortly after relocating my office, I had three hard drives crash within months of each other. They were all from different manufactures, and they weren't in a RAID. One of those drives was my main drive that had lots of data files on it. One of the other drives was a backup drive of that same data. Unfortunately, I hadn't taken the time to restore all the backed-up data, so when the second drive crashed everything was gone.

A more extreme nightmare scenario with hard drives is fire and theft. Either of these events can wipe out years of work. You have to think about all these possibilities when you consider the storage of image files. I know several photographers who locate a backup drive or RAID in a hidden portion of their home or office in case of theft. With some of the wireless hard drive solutions appearing today, this is an even more viable option. In the case of fire, the best protection is to have a backup of important data that's stored off-site.

# tip

Many photographers are beginning to use online storage options for backing up image files. This can be a great solution, too. But if you use online storage, make sure it's not your only backup. You want to make sure your data is still there when you need it. As you may recall, a few years ago when the economy took a dive many Internet companies disappeared overnight without any warning.

## CDs and DVDs

Another system for backing up and archiving images is using CDs and DVDs. CDs and DVDs are cheap, and almost any computer can read them. If handled properly, they faithfully preserve data for many years.

CDs and DVDs are not as easy and seamless as using a hard drive, and they don't offer quick access to data. In my mind, they're best used as an adjunct to a hard drive backup — more of an archive that can be pulled out anytime a file needs to be resurrected. In a well-designed workflow, they should be used at two different times:

- **As soon as you finish transferring, sorting, and renaming a new job or project burn a CD (or DVD if necessary) of all original files and store it in a safe place.** In the case of a professional photographer, that would be in the job or client's folder.

- **After all work for the job or project is done, burn a DVD(s) of all related folders — originals, masters, and finals folders.** File this DVD with the first CD/DVD backup you created. If the job or project is important, burn a second copy and store it off-site. Now everything is completely covered. You will probably never need these discs, but it's comforting to know that they are there in case you do. If the job or project is a big one that takes lots of time, then intermediate DVD backups are a good idea. You can use rerecordable media for this.

# note

A debate is currently raging concerning the longevity of CDs and DVDs. Some people say that they can't be trusted, while others say they'll last 100 years. In my own experience, I've seen more hard drives fail than CDs or DVDs. However, some photographers recopy their CD/DVD archives every few years to ensure longevity.

When working with plastic discs, you need to observe some basic ground rules regarding handling. They scratch easily when dragged across rough surfaces, so they should be in some sort of acid-free sleeve at all times. It's important to use acid-free sleeves because acids in other types of plastic or paper sleeve can deteriorate the plastic that the discs are composed of. Keep these additional things in mind when working with CDs and DVDs:

- **Try to avoid writing on the top surface.** These discs are read by a laser beam that shines up from the bottom through the lower layers of plastic, reflects off the shiny layer on top, and bounces back down. If anything is done to degrade the reflective nature of the surface on the top of the disc, the laser won't be able to read it. Sometimes the acid in a pen's ink can destroy the shiny layer on top.

  If you have to write on a disc, try to do it on the inner circle where the plastic is clear. Another option is to purchase printable CDs and DVDs. These are designed to be printed on with an inkjet printer, so they have a more durable surface that you can write on.

- **Only use labels that are approved for CDs and DVDs.** These use adhesives that are acid-free. You really don't know what kind of adhesive is used on a standard mailing label. Besides the adhesive issue, mailing labels can cause a different set of problems. A couple of years ago, a client dropped off a CD with files he wanted me to work on. He labeled the CD with three small, rectangular mailing labels. Each label had a different set of information. I was unable to read this disc on any of my systems because when it was spinning at 10,000 RPM in the disc drive, the labels threw it out of balance.

- **Store disks in proper, acid-free sleeves or envelopes.** Keep them out of the sun, preferably in the dark. Store them lying flat if possible, rather than upright.

In a perfect world, hard drives and CDs/DVDs are used together with the hard drive acting as an up-to-date backup that can be easily accessed and the plastic discs acting as long-term storage. You don't need a sophisticated backup and archiving system, but you do need a system. Working without one is like a trapeze artist working without a net. When things come crashing down, it can be a real showstopper.

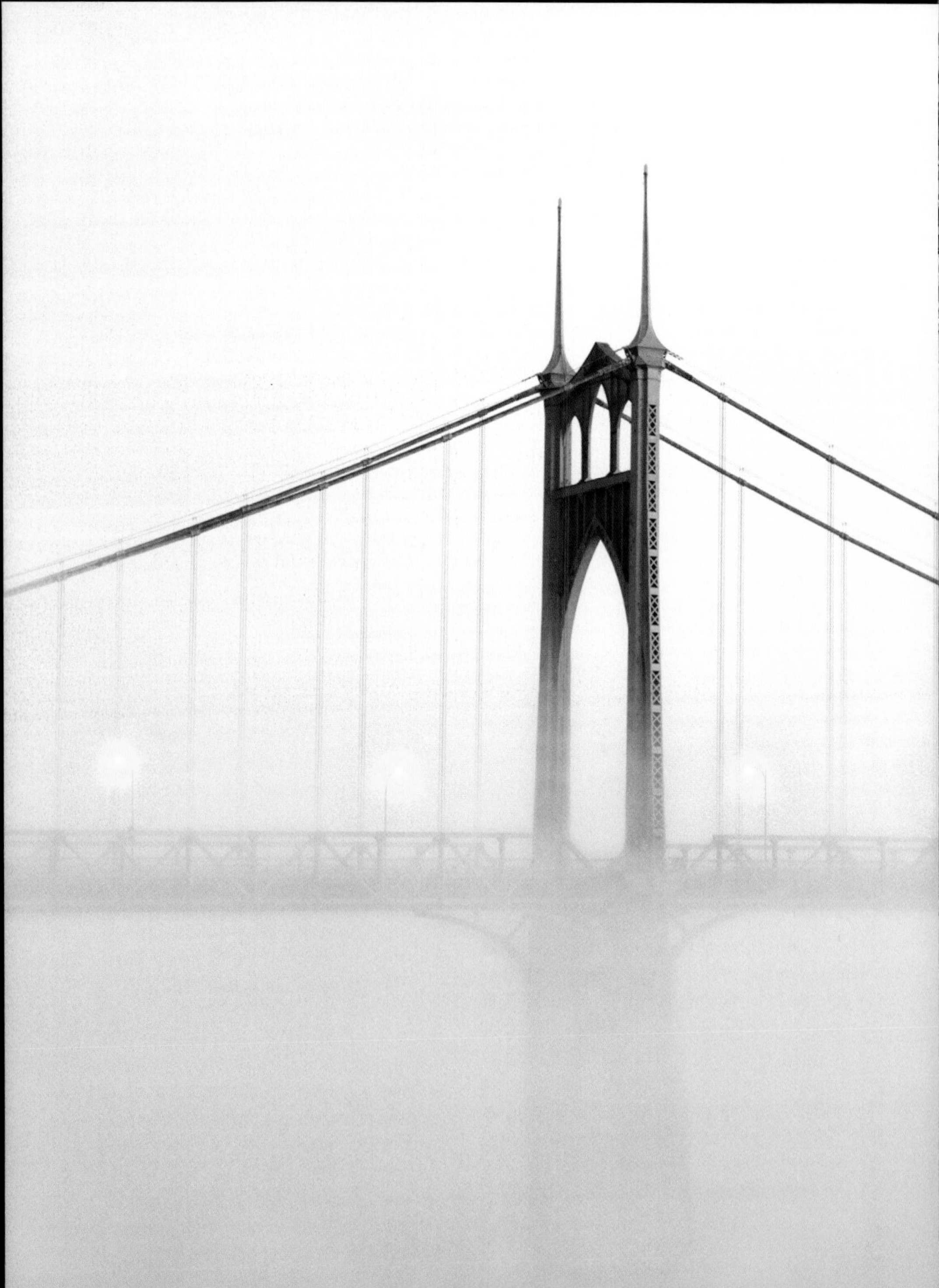

# 2

# Overview of Bridge

One of the biggest problems for digital photographers using early versions of Photoshop was the lack of a file browser. A file browser is a special program that allows you to visually sort and manage files so that you can choose which files to open by looking at the photos they represent. Without a file browser, it's hard to differentiate one file from one another because there are no visual clues as to which photo is contained in a particular file. Adobe introduced a file browser with Photoshop 7. When Photoshop CS2 was released, the file browser was overhauled and separated from Photoshop, allowing it to be opened independently of Photoshop. Adobe named the new file browser Bridge because it's used as a bridge between different Adobe applications. Bridge has lots of features designed to make organizing your photos more intuitive and efficient.

# Understanding the Default Workspace

Like most things related to Photoshop, there's more than one way to launch Bridge. Because it's a separate program, it can be launched from the Applications folder on a Mac, or from the Start menu in Windows. If Photoshop is already open, Bridge is launched by clicking the Launch Bridge button, which is next to the Photoshop Application icon on the Application bar, as shown in Figure 2.1. This icon can also be used to quickly jump from Photoshop to Bridge after it's already open.

**Figure 2.1**

## tip

You don't have to close Bridge when you begin working in Photoshop. It's better to leave it open in case you need another file. When both Bridge and Photoshop are open, you can move between them by clicking on their icons on your dock (Mac) or taskbar (Windows).

The default layout of Bridge CS4, called the Essentials workspace, is shown in Figure 2.2. It consists of groups of panels with a feature packed application bar at the top. In this view a central thumbnail viewing area, called the Content panel, is surrounded by an assortment

**Figure 2.2**

of other panels to the right and left: Favorites, Folders, Filter, Collections, Preview, Metadata, and Keywords. These panels are used to manage various aspects of photo files while viewing thumbnails of them in the Content panel.

# note

I'm using amber as an accent color in Bridge so you can see the highlighted areas better better. I show you how to change your own accent color in the preferences section of this chapter.

# The Content panel

The Content panel is the most important part of Bridge because it's where you see your photos displayed as thumbnails. These thumbnails are representations of the original image designed to allow you to quickly view the image without having to load the full file. You can change the display size of these thumbnails by using the thumbnails size slider, shown in Figure 2.3, below the Content panel.

Use the curved arrow buttons, shown in Figure 2.4, on the right of the Application bar to rotate selected thumbnails clockwise or counterclockwise.

**Figure 2.3**

**Figure 2.4**

A thumbnail's filename appears directly below the thumbnail. If you want to modify the name, click the current name to highlight it and then type the new name.

In addition to the filename, information about the each photo displays below its thumbnail. This information tells you something about certain properties of the file. Another way to see information about a file is to hover the cursor over it. When you do, a small window pops up (you can see it in Figure 2.2) displaying information that includes: dates, file size, dimensions, and applied keywords.

To open a file in Photoshop, double-click its thumbnail. To open multiple files, first select the thumbnails and then double-click one of them.

To select multiple contiguous files, (files that are next to each other), click the first file and then Shift+click on the last file. To select non-contiguous files, ⌘+click/Ctrl+click on each file. ⌘+click/Ctrl+click is also used to deselect individual selected files.

# Favorites and Folders panels

On the upper-left side are the Favorites and Folders panels stacked together. Panels that are stacked like this are called panel-sets. You move between them by clicking their tabs.

## Favorites panel

The Favorites panel, shown in Figure 2.5, is used to quickly jump to a favorite folder or location. Most of the default items listed in it are useful, but if there's one you don't need, you can right-click it and choose Remove from Favorites.

To add a new item to the Favorites panel, locate it in the Content area and drag it into the Favorites panel. On my main workstation I store all my photos on a dedicated hard drive. If I want to add that hard drive to the Favorites panel, I first click Computer in the Favorites. When I do, all my hard drives appear in the Content panel. I simply click my special drive and drag it into the Favorites panel to add it. You can do this with folders as well as hard drives.

## Folders panel

Though Favorites are handy, I usually use the Folders panel, shown in Figure 2.6, to navigate to the folder I need for a particular session.

**Figure 2.5**

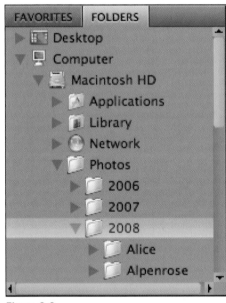

**Figure 2.6**

## note

Some older Macs have mice that don't have a right button. If you have one of these, use the Control key combined with a mouse click to get the same response as a right-click. If you have a Mac that was purchased in the last few years, you most likely have a two-button mouse. They look the same as the single button mouse so you may not be aware that you have two buttons. Even if you have one of these mice, by default the second button isn't set up to be a right-click.

This panel features a typical folder tree. If you take the time to organize your files and folders, as discussed in Chapter 1, it really pays off here. Click a folder to display its contents in the Content panel, or click the twirly to its left to display any subfolders in the Folders panel. A twirly is a triangular icon that is used to reveal hidden information. When it points to the side, the information is hidden. When the twirly points downward, the information is revealed.

## Filter and Collections panels

The Filter panel is one of the cooler things about Bridge. This panel intelligently collects information for all photos displayed in the Content panel, analyzing them for a number of criteria. It then dynamically displays all the criteria that apply and the number of files that are associated with those criteria.

# tip

Because the Filter list is context sensitive, its size changes depending on the selected folder. Sometimes you have to scroll down to see all applicable criteria.

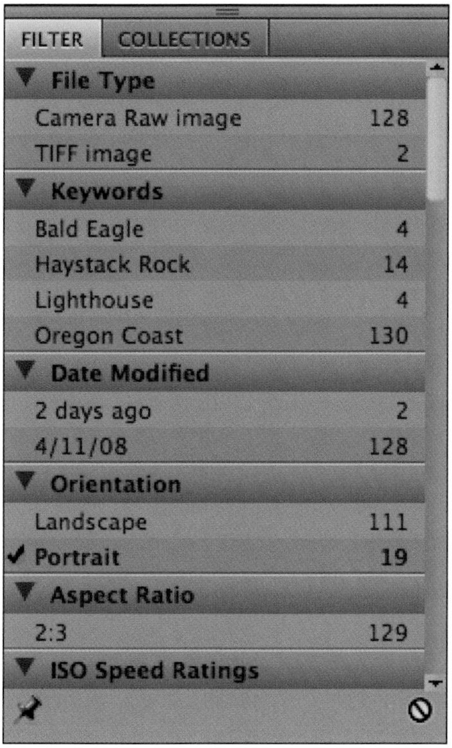

You can quickly filter for any criteria by clicking it. For example, in Figure 2.7 I clicked Portrait, in the Orientation section. This causes only the 19 vertical shots to display in the Content panel. If I wanted to see only the horizontal shots, I'd click the Landscape orientation instead. To turn a filter off, click the filtering criteria a second time to uncheck it.

The Collections panel is used to create virtual collections. When a photo is placed in a collection, the file itself isn't moved. Only a visual reference of it — more like an alias or shortcut — is placed into the collection. Collections are used in a number of ways to gather similar photos that reside in different folders without moving the

| FILTER | COLLECTIONS | |
|---|---|---|
| ▼ **File Type** | | |
| Camera Raw image | | 128 |
| TIFF image | | 2 |
| ▼ **Keywords** | | |
| Bald Eagle | | 4 |
| Haystack Rock | | 14 |
| Lighthouse | | 4 |
| Oregon Coast | | 130 |
| ▼ **Date Modified** | | |
| 2 days ago | | 2 |
| 4/11/08 | | 128 |
| ▼ **Orientation** | | |
| Landscape | | 111 |
| ✔ **Portrait** | | 19 |
| ▼ **Aspect Ratio** | | |
| 2:3 | | 129 |
| ▼ **ISO Speed Ratings** | | |

**Figure 2.7**

actual files. Say that I want to keep track of all my best photos. I right-click anywhere in the Collections panel and choose New Collection. When the dialog box opens, I name the collection "Portfolio." Now whenever I see one of my best images, I can drag it into the Portfolio collection, placing a reference of it into the collection without moving the actual file. Now when I want to see all my best photos, I click the Portfolio collection.

# see also

Collections are explored in more detail in Chapter 3.

# Preview panel

At the upper right of the workspace you see the Preview panel. This panel provides a preview of the selected thumbnail. If multiple thumbnails are selected, all of them appear in the Preview panel together. In the default workspace you're looking at here, the preview provided is quite small. I show you how to change that in a moment. Before I do, however, I want to show you one especially cool feature of the Preview panel.

When you hover over the previewed image, the cursor switches to display the Zoom tool icon (a magnifying glass with a plus sign). When you click the image with it, a magnifier called a Loupe opens, as shown in Figure 2.8. You can see in the figure that I'm using the Loupe to zoom in on the name plate of this antique tractor.

The Loupe displays the image at 100 percent magnification by default. You can use the scroll wheel on your mouse to zoom in closer once the tool is activated. Click and drag the zoomed window to reposition it, or click anywhere in the image to move it to that location. To turn the Loupe tool off, simply click inside the magnified area.

**Figure 2.8**

# Metadata and Keywords panels

Metadata literally means data about data. In this case it's standardized information contained in the image file that describes the properties relating to that file. The camera generates some metadata, such as exposure properties, when the photo is first created. You can add other metadata, such as filename, copyright information, and keywords, later during import or editing.

The Metadata panel, shown in Figure 2.9, is where you go to view all this information. The two graphical displays at the top of the panel give you basic file information. The graphic on the left displays exposure information, such as ISO and shutter speed. The graphic on the right displays file properties, like size and color space. To learn more about a file, use the various metadata fields below the display.

Figure 2.9

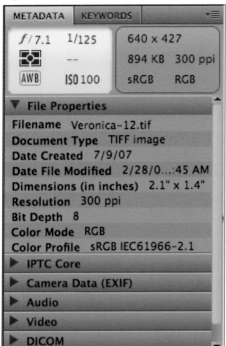

Each of these fields contains different types of metadata. Use the twirly next to the name to open or close its section. For the average user, most of these sections are unnecessary and can remain closed. However, a few of these metadata types are useful:

- **File Properties.** All of the basic file properties appear here, including file type and resolution.

- **IPTC Core.** This area allows you to record lots of information about the file, including copyright information, location information, and job identifiers. The pencil icon next to the IPTC Core metadata fields indicate that you can edit them. Click in a field and type to edit it.

- **Camera Data (EXIF).** This information tells you which camera settings were used to capture the image. This area is useful when you're trying to troubleshoot a problem. For example, if you have a blurry image, you would look here to see if the shutter speed you used was too slow for a handheld shot.

The Keywords panel, shown in Figure 2.10, shows all the current keywords that are in use for the selected photo, here shown in Figure 2.11. Any keywords that are applied to the photo have a check mark beside them. In Figure 2.10 you can see that the selected photo has keywords for three dogs; Hazel, Ruby, and Sam, and Seattle. That means three dogs are in the photo and it was shot in Seattle. To add an existing keyword, click inside the box to the left of it to add a check mark. Uncheck a keyword to remove it from the photo. Keywords can also be added and removed from multiple selected files.

Figure 2.10

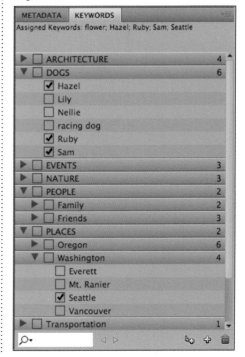

**Figure 2.11**

# tip

If multiple photos are selected the keywords that apply to all of them have a check mark in the box, and the keywords that apply to some of them, but not all, show a hyphen (-) in the box.

Try to keep keywords organized as you add them. Use container keywords to manage groups of sub keywords. For example, the keyword Dogs is a container keyword that holds all dog-related keywords.

# see also

Keywords are discussed in detail in Chapter 3.

## The Applications bar

The Applications bar at the top of the window places many of the most important commands within easy reach. I'm not going to cover each icon right now because I cover many of them soon. However, I do want to take a moment to point out some features on the left side of the Applications bar, shown in Figure 2.12.

- **Path bar.** The complete path to a file's location appears at the left of the bar. The path is like a map that shows the actual location of a file on the system, revealing all subfolders and the folders that contain them.

- **Go to Parent or Favorites.** Click this button to quickly access a menu of your favorites without displaying the Favorites panel.

Go to recent file or folder

Go to Parent or Favorites            Open in Camera Raw

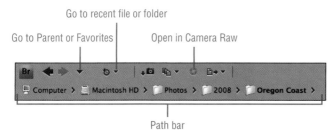

Path bar

**Figure 2.12**

- **Go to recent file or folder.** This cool feature allows you to quickly jump to a recently viewed file or folder.

- **Open in Camera Raw.** This button allows you to edit selected raw files in Adobe Camera Raw (ACR) without using Photoshop. (You could do this in earlier versions of Bridge, but it wasn't as obvious.) This is a faster way to make edits to raw files when you don't need to open the files in Photoshop.

Now that you are oriented to Bridge, get ready to use it by setting up some preferences.

## see also

Raw files are covered in detail in Chapter 4.

# Modifying the Bridge Workspace

One of the best things about Bridge is that you don't have to use the default workspace if you don't want to. You can modify the workspace by moving or removing panels, and you can change the size of individual panel sets or temporarily hide them. Here's how:

*1* Hover over a horizontal boundary line until the cursor changes to a double-headed arrow, as shown in Figure 2.13. Now you can click and drag the boundary line upward or downward to change the size of the panel set.

*2* Hover over a vertical boundary line until the cursor changes to a double-headed arrow again. Now you can click and drag the line to the left or right to change the width of the panels.

**Figure 2.13**

## tip

Press the Tab key to hide all side panels. Press it again to reveal them.

**3** **To move an entire panel, click and drag it by its name tab.** As you drag, notice that different target areas light up with blue lines. These lines indicate where the panel will be dropped when you release the mouse button. A box indicates that the panel will be added to the target panel set. The blue line indicates that the panel will be placed between existing panels or panel sets. You can even rearrange panels within panel sets by dragging them sideways.

**4** **To turn off a panel you do not use, uncheck it from the Window menu.** In Figure 2.14 you can see where I unchecked the Preview panel.

```
Window   Help
New Synchronized Window    ⌥⌘N
Workspace                      ▶
✓ Folders Panel
✓ Favorites Panel
✓ Metadata Panel
✓ Keywords Panel
✓ Filter Panel
  Preview Panel
  Inspector Panel
✓ Collections Panel
✓ Path Bar
  Minimize                    ⌘M
  Bring All To Front
  Bev
```

Figure 2.14

Take a few moments to experiment with different layouts. Whenever you want to start over, choose Window ➔ Workspace ➔ Reset Workspace to reset your workspace back to its default.

## Using workspace presets

In addition to the workspace preset named Essentials, there are other workspace presets you can choose:

- **Filmstrip.** Shows the thumbnails in a horizontal strip while increasing the size of the Preview panel.

- **Metadata.** Changes the display in the Content panel so that metadata about each file is displayed next to the image's thumbnail.

- **Output.** Uses the new Adobe Output Module (AOM) to allow you to create slideshows and Web galleries from photos and folders in Bridge without using Photoshop.

### see also

The AOM is covered in detail in Chapter 14.

- **Keywords.** Displays much of the same information as the Metadata workspace, along with any keywords attached to the file.

- **Preview.** Increases the size of the Preview panel while changing the Content panel to a vertical filmstrip. It's very similar to the Filmstrip workspace.

- **Light Table.** Displays only the Content panel, allowing you to concentrate on your thumbnails.

- **Folders.** Shows the Folders and Favorites panels on the left and hides the panels on the right to maximize the Content area.

# note

Notice that as you change workspaces some panels are omitted from the view. If a panel that you want to use isn't present, use the Window menu to add it.

There are a few different ways to access these workspaces. You can choose Window → Workspace, or you can use the keyboard shortcut shown to the right of each listing in the Workspace menu, shown in Figure 2.15. For example, the shortcut for the Essentials workspace is ⌘+F1/Ctrl+F1. You can also select workspace presets using the Workspace Switcher button on the Application bar, just to

# tip

To fill the screen with a single image, Choose View → Choose Full Screen Preview Space. Click on the full screen preview to zoom it to 100 percent. When you're done, press the Esc key.

the left of the search field. Click on the downward pointing triangle icon identified in Figure 2.15 to open a menu with all presets and preset options.

As you explore these presets, make a note of which ones you like and what you like about them. I personally use the Essentials, Preview, and Light Table workspaces the most, but they aren't quite laid out the way I like them. Because of that, I like to create my own versions of them.

## Creating custom workspace presets

You can easily create your own customized workspace. For example, the Preview workspace is designed to maximize the size of the preview panel, which is very handy. When you click one of the thumbnails, you get a large high quality preview. However, you can modify it to make it even more useful by removing the two panel sets on the left to increase the size of the Preview area.

**Figure 2.15**

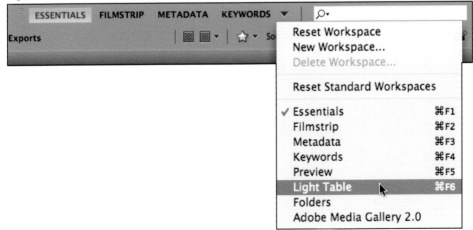

Follow these steps to create a custom workspace preset:

**1** Go to the Workspace menu and select the Preview preset, (⌘+F5/Ctrl+F5) to change your workspace to the default preview workspace.

**2** If you have made any changes to the layout of this workspace, go to the Workspace menu again and choose Reset Workspace to reset this particular workspace back to its default settings. If you haven't made any changes to the layout, then you shouldn't see any changes after resetting.

**3** Hover over the vertical line separating the left panel set and the narrow Content area. When you see the double-headed arrow click and drag it to the left until the left panel set is hidden, increasing the size of the Content area.

**4** Click the vertical line dividing the Content area and the Preview area and drag it to the left until you have one column of thumbnails. This expands the size of the Preview panel. Your workspace should now look very much like Figure 2.16.

**5** Choose Window → Workspace → New Workspace. The New Workspace dialog box opens.

**6** Change the name to suit your needs. In Figure 2.17, you can see I changed it to Preview 2. Notice that the new workspace is placed at the top of the list and that the keyboard shortcut, ⌘+F1/Ctrl+F1, is assigned to it and the other shortcuts are reassigned.

Figure 2.16

Figure 2.17

| | |
|---|---|
| Reset Workspace | |
| New Workspace... | |
| Delete Workspace... | |
| | |
| Reset Standard Workspaces | |
| | |
| ✓ Preview 2 | ⌘F1 |
| Essentials | ⌘F2 |
| Filmstrip | ⌘F3 |
| Metadata | ⌘F4 |
| Output | ⌘F5 |
| Keywords | ⌘F6 |
| Preview | |
| Light Table | |
| Folders | |

**7** **Select the Save Window Location as Part of Workspace option.** This ensures that everything looks the same when you come back to this workspace later.

**8** **Click Save.** The workspace is added to the front of the list on the Bridge toolbar.

Now you have a custom version of the Preview workspace. It stays this way until you choose Reset Workspace while this workspace is active

or Reset Standard Workspaces (which resets all of the default presets at once) from the Workspace menu.

# tip

When multiple images are displayed in the Preview panel, you can place a Loupe on each image by clicking them individually.

Think about creating your own custom workspace presets. Use the presets that come with Bridge as starting points. If you decide you don't want one of your custom workspaces, you can remove it by choosing Delete Workspace from the Workspace menu and then choosing the workspace you want to remove.

# tip

I usually create a second custom workspace preset called "Mark's Default" that's a modified version of the Essentials workspace. I remove the Preview panel and select the Folders panel so it's the most active panel in its group. Before saving the preset, I adjust the thumbnail size so that it's optimal for my screen.

# Setting Up Preferences

Now that you know something about Bridge, I want to show you how to use the Preferences dialog box to further modify the look and feel of the workspace.

**1** **Choose Bridge CS4 ⇀ Preferences/ Edit ⇀ Preferences to open the Preferences dialog box.** Notice that it has a menu of preference sets on the

left. Take a look at a few of the more relevant preferences now. Feel free to explore the rest of them when you're done here.

**2** **Choose the General preferences from the menu on the left if it isn't already selected.** When you do, the Preferences dialog box looks like Figure 2.18. Use the Appearance section to modify the brightness of the user interface and image backdrop areas.

Figure 2.18

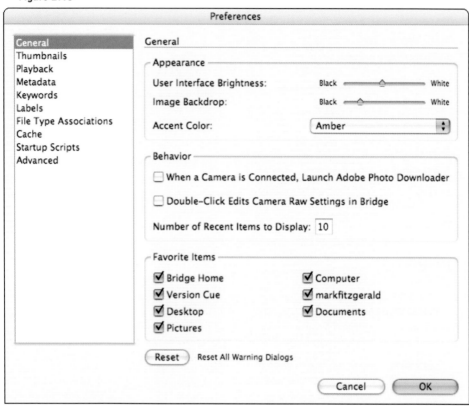

3 **Choose from the Accent Color dropdown menu to select a custom accent color.** As you can see in Figure 2.18, I chose Amber.

## note

Version Cue is part of several of the Adobe Creative Suites, which are different collections of Adobe software. If you have Photoshop CS4 installed as a stand-alone program, this option won't show in the Favorite Items list.

4 **If you want the Photo Downloader to open automatically when you connect your camera or card reader to your computer, check When a Camera is Connected, Launch Adobe Photo Downloader.** I usually check this.

5 **Uncheck any items that you don't use in the Favorites panel to remove them from it.** I unchecked Version Cue and Pictures, (called My Pictures on Windows) because I don't use the Pictures folder for storing photos. This saves room for the personal favorites I'll add later.

**6** **Choose the Thumbnails preference option from the menu on the left**. Use the Details section, shown in Figure 2.19, to choose which information appears below each thumbnail by selecting from the pull-down menus. You can display up to four lines of metadata information. Just be aware that more information takes more space to display beneath the thumbnails, which makes the thumbnails smaller.

**7** **When you're through setting your preferences, click OK.** Now Bridge is set up and ready to use.

For now, the rest of the preferences are best left at their default settings. Here's a list of what each is used for so that you know for future reference:

- **Playback.** These preferences are used to change audio and video playback properties.

- **Metadata.** Use these preferences to choose which metadata fields are displayed in the Metadata panel.

- **Keywords.** Used to change the way keywords are recorded as metadata.

**Figure 2.19**

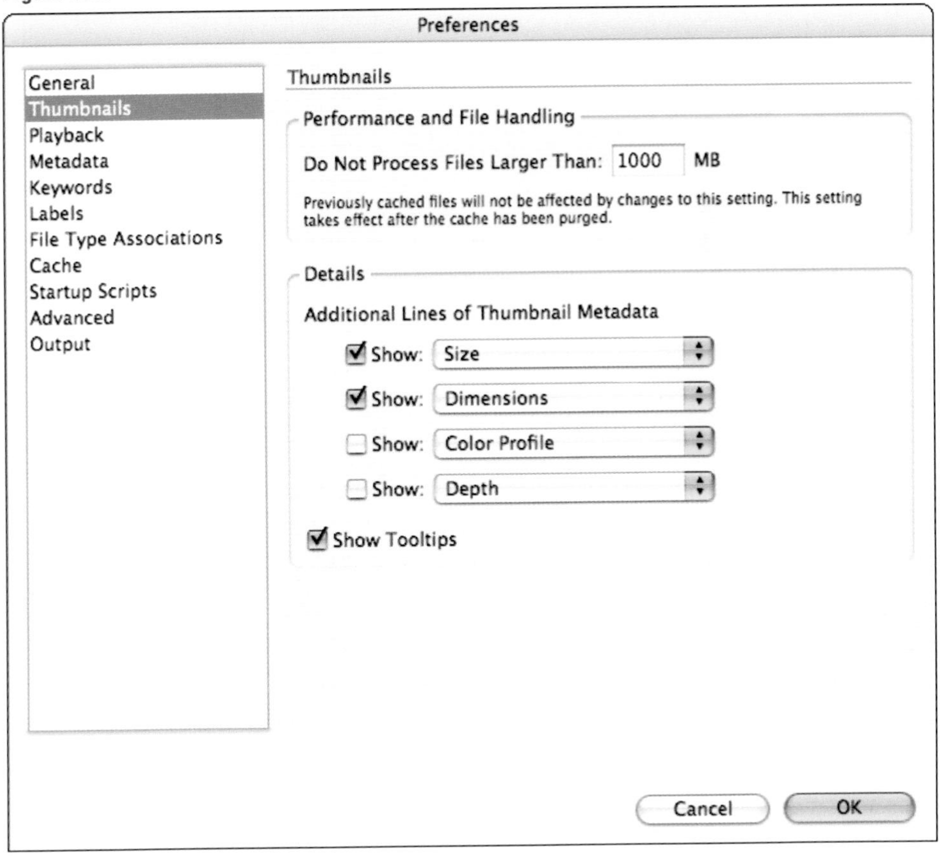

- **Labels.** Labels are used to rate photos. Some people choose to change the names of the labels to other titles, such as changing the red label to Reject. That way they know that any file with a red label is a reject. Un-checking Require the Command (Ctrl) Key to Apply Labels and Ratings makes it easier to apply labels because you only need to press one key. Rating photos is discussed in detail in Chapter 3. Leave these preferences at their defaults for now so it will be easier for you to follow that discussion. Then you can come back to see if you want to change any of these preferences.

- **File Type Associations.** Sometimes you want a particular type of file to always open in Photoshop, and sometimes you want a particular type of file to open in some other software. Use these preferences to change the main program that's associated with a particular file type by choosing from the pull-down menu next to the file type.

- **Cache.** These preferences are discussed in detail in the next section.

- **Startup Scripts.** Use these preferences to choose which scripts (mini programs) automatically start when Bridge is launched.

- **Advanced.** This is a collection of miscellaneous preferences. The option to notice here is the Start Bridge At Login option. When this is selected, Bridge launches when you login to your system. If you use Bridge on a daily basis, this is a good option to choose.

- **Output.** These options are used to set some properties for Bridge's Output Workspace, which is discussed in detail in Chapter 14.

# Working with the Cache

There's one last thing you need to look at before you begin using Bridge in the next chapter. When a folder of photo files is first viewed in Bridge, the software takes a close look at all of the files and collects information about them. This information is used to create the thumbnails and to populate the various panels, such as the Filter and Metadata panels. Because this information collection process takes time, it's best to do it once and then store the information in a more convenient place. Bridge accomplishes this by creating a cache.

The Oxford dictionary defines cache as, "a collection of items of the same type that are stored in a hidden place." Bridge's cache is used to store metadata information about each file in a central folder that's hidden from view. As I mentioned, this information consists of thumbnail information and camera-generated metadata. It also contains any rotation done to a file, rating information, editing metadata for RAW files, and 1:1 previews (100 percent magnification) that are generated when the Loupe tool is used.

## tip

It takes a moment for Bridge to build a cache the first time you view a folder. It's best to allow the process to take place before trying to work with the images; otherwise Bridge may run slowly. You'll know Bridge is ready when the spinning circle on the bottom left, next to the file count, disappears.

## see also

In Chapter 4 I show you a more efficient way to handle metadata for raw files.

Figure 2.20 shows the Cache preference set from the Bridge preferences (Bridge CS4 → Preferences/ Edit → Preferences.) If you check Keep 100% Previews in Cache, all of your 1:1 previews are stored so that you don't have to wait for them to rebuild the next time you zoom in. This speeds up things when you use the Loupe tool again on the same image, but it also increases the size of the cache.

Every time new files are viewed in Bridge, the cache grows. Over time, depending on how much you shoot, its size can become quite large. When this happens, it affects Bridge's performance. Though the files in the cache folder are hidden, there are some things you can do to optimize them.

Every once in a while it's a good idea to toss out all of those previews, as well as cached thumbnail previews, to save space and improve performance. To do this, click the Purge Cache button at the bottom of the Preferences dialog box. If you're not ready to toss everything, you can use the Compact Cache button to remove old items while retaining more recently cached information.

Sometimes the cache information for a particular folder gets corrupted, for example the thumbnails aren't displaying correctly. This is solved by choosing Tools → Cache → Purge Cache For Folder. The cache information for the selected folder is rebuilt the next time you view the contents of the folder in Bridge.

**Figure 2.20**

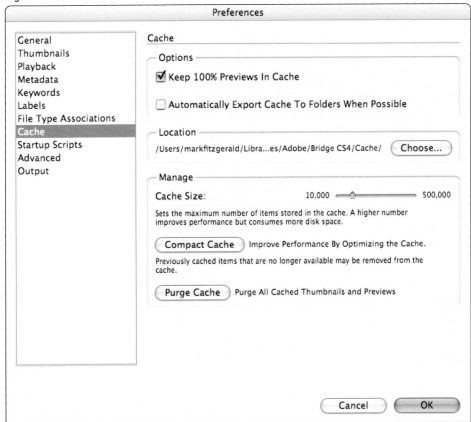

©Mark Fitzgerald

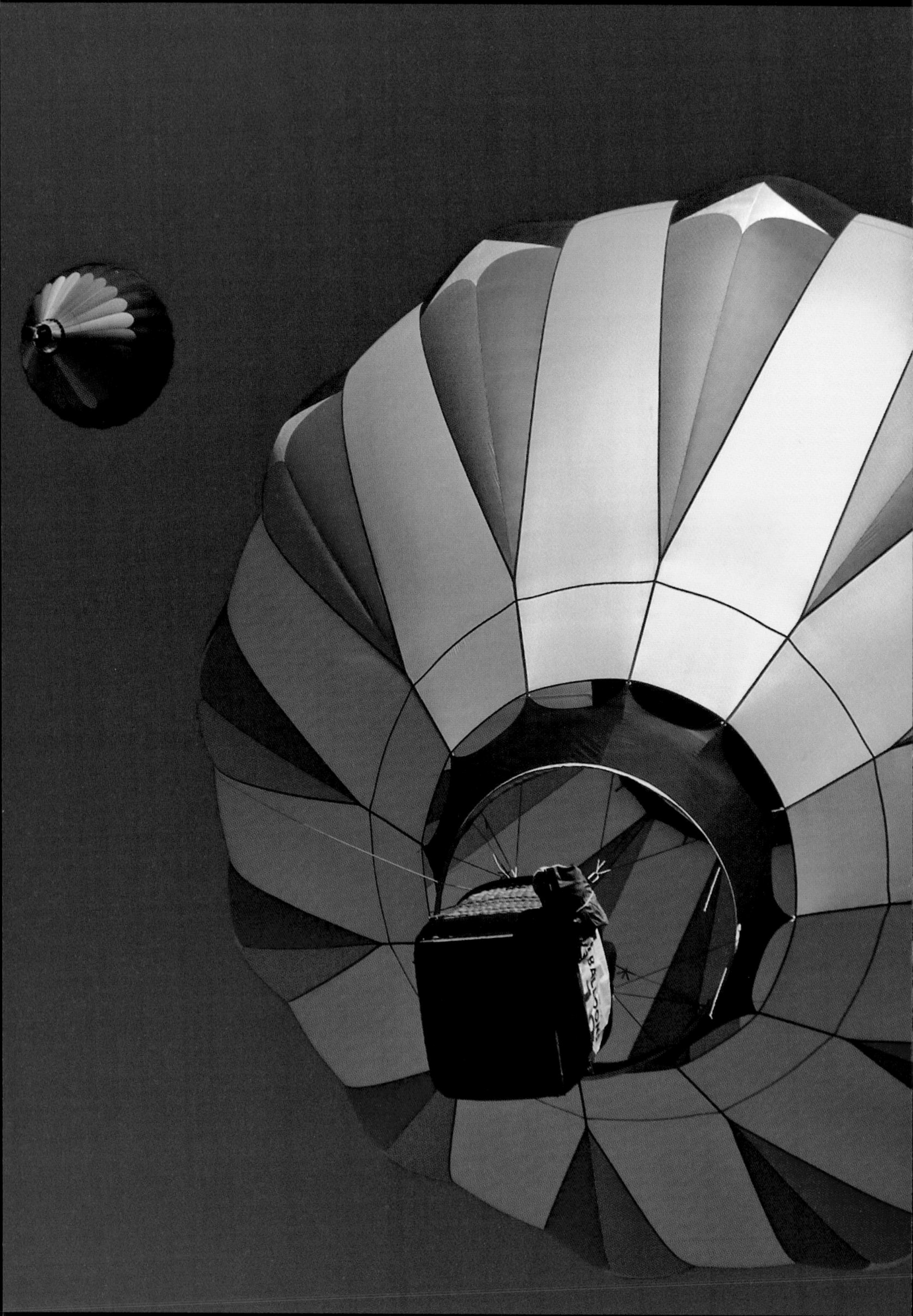

# 3

# Downloading and Organizing Your Photos

With what you learned in Chapter 2, you can begin using Bridge as a file browser right now. However, the true power of Bridge is when it's used for digital asset management (DAM). DAM is the system used to identify and organize digital assets such as photos. Some photographers purchase special DAM software because they have extensive collections that need managing, but for most photographers, Bridge is the perfect DAM solution. In this chapter you learn to use Bridge to download, organize, and sort your photos so that you're always able to find a photo when you need it.

Before you can begin to manage your photos, you need to get them onto your computer. Fortunately, Bridge not only helps you with the file download, but it also allows you to begin the asset management process while files are being downloaded.

# Downloading New Photos from Your Camera

Downloading photos from your camera's media card to your computer with Bridge has never been easier. If you turned on the preference to automatically launch the Photo Downloader when a camera or card reader is connected, (as discussed in Chapter 2), all you need to do is connect your camera or card reader and the downloader opens — even if Bridge isn't currently running. When the preference is turned off, you need to choose File → Get Photos from Camera. This opens the warning dialog box shown in Figure 3.1, which gives you another chance to make the downloader open automatically in the future. This is a good idea if you use Bridge for all your photo downloading because it speeds up the process.

**Figure 3.1**

When the Photo Downloader dialog box opens, if you don't see a group of thumbnails on the left, as shown Figure 3.2, click the Advanced Dialog button on the lower left, (where the Standard Dialog button is in Figure 3.2). This expands the Photo Downloader so that you can

**Figure 3.2**

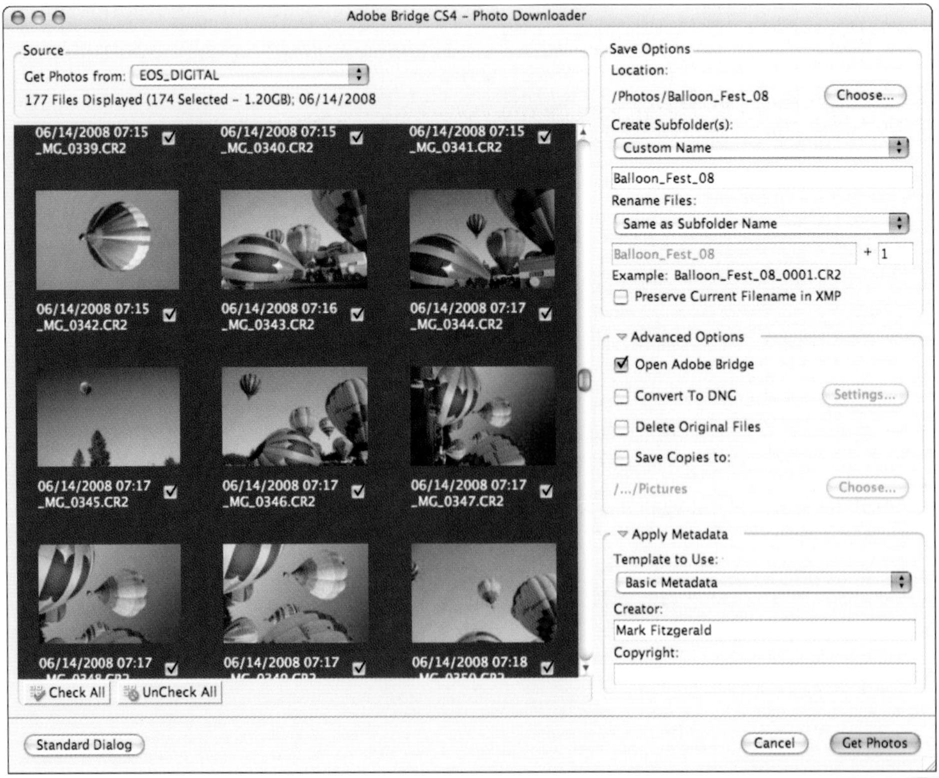

preview the images being downloaded from your camera or card. It also adds a section called Apply Metadata. If these options are already visible the Advanced Dialog button changes to a Standard Dialog button.

The Photo Downloader dialog box is the beginning of your asset management process. It combines a number of useful tasks with the downloading process. This saves time and makes your workflow more efficient, allowing you to spend your time reviewing your photos and identifying the winners and the losers. Review it section by section so that you know how to get the most from it.

- **Get Photos from.** This menu is in the Source section. It allows you to choose from multiple cameras or cards in a card reader.

- **Preview window.** Uncheck any photos you don't want to download. Do this with caution and only when you absolutely know that you won't want the shot — it's an accidental shot of the ground, for example. Otherwise it's best to wait to look more closely at the photos in Bridge before making decisions. You can also use the preview area to choose groups of photos for individual import sessions. This is useful for someone like a portrait photographer. If she has two client sessions on one media card, she can download each set individually with two different download sessions. That way each set of images is in the appropriate folder with the appropriate file names.

- **Location.** This first option in the Save Options section allows you to choose the hard drive location where the files are stored. On my laptop I use a folder named Photos to store all photo folders. I choose it here. (The subfolder shown in Figure 3.3 is added in the next section.)

## tip

The preferred method for transferring photo files to the computer is to use a media card reader. When a media card is inserted into one of these readers, the card appears as a hard drive on your system. Card readers don't require any special software, so they can be used on just about any computer.

- **Create Subfolder(s).** This section allows you to create a folder for the download files on the fly. This is where you choose between using a date or a descriptive name (as discussed in Chapter 2) for the folder by choosing from the menu shown in Figure 3.3. In this case, I chose Custom Name and typed the name into the text box below the menu. The other options allow you to choose the date the photos where shot (Today's Date), or different formats of the date of the download. Choose None if you're downloading to an existing folder.

- **Rename Files.** This menu allows you to choose the naming format you want to use. The options are similar to the subfolders options with a bit more variety. Choose Same as Subfolder Name if you want to use the same name. Choose Custom Name to create a name that doesn't fit any of the options.

Use the numerical box below the menu to choose the starting sequence number. Usually this will be 1, but it's nice to be able to change it when you're downloading photos to an existing folder. This happens when you have more than one media card for the shoot. When you download the second card, change the starting number to pick up where the numbering finished when you downloaded the first card.

**Figure 3.3**

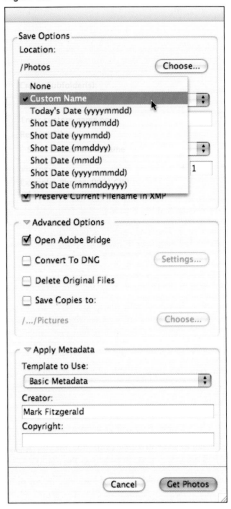

- **Preserve Current Filename in XMP.** This setting is used for raw files when XMP (Extensible Metadata Platform) sidecar files are used to hold the original file's metadata. Essentially this setting allows you to keep the original filename as part of the file's metadata. I don't see much use for this for most photographers and I personally don't choose this option. If you think that someday you'll want to know what the original names of your photos were, go ahead and check it.

- **Open Adobe Bridge.** When this is selected, Bridge launches, displaying the files after they're downloaded so that you can get to work on them. You usually want this checked, but it's nice to be able to turn it off.

- **Convert To DNG.** This option converts raw files to a special version of raw file format that was invented by Adobe. It's called DNG, which is short for digital negative.

## see also

DNG files, as well as XMP sidecar files, are discussed in detail in Chapter 4.

- **Delete Original Files.** Choosing this deletes the original files from the media card. I strongly recommend that you do not check this. It's best to make sure all files display properly in Bridge before taking this action.

- **Save Copies to.** This handy option allows you to automatically create backup files during download. It's most useful when you use a second hard drive to hold all of the backups. Select it and use the Choose button to select the backup hard drive..

## tip

Look at the Example section to preview what your new naming strategy looks like.

- **Template to Use.** This section is used to add some basic identifiers to each photo's metadata. Creator and copyright information is useful when you want people to know who owns the images because this information can be viewed in areas like Bridge's Metadata panel. When Basic Metadata is selected from the Templates to Use menu, you use the Creator text box to add your name. If the photos are copyrighted, use the Copyright text box to add the copyright information.

After all of the menus and text boxes are filled out appropriately, click the Get Photos button to begin the download process. Remember to give Bridge time to review the files and build its cache before you begin working with the photos. You'll know Bridge is ready when the spinning circle on the lower left of the workspace disappears and the file progress count next to it stops counting.

## tip

The best way to delete all files from your media card is to insert the card into your camera, and then use the camera's menus to format the card. This not only removes the existing photos, but it also insures that the card is optimized and ready to receive new files.

# Using Keywords to Identify Photo Content

During the download process you can add general keywords that describe the visual content of the photo. After the photos are transferred to the computer, it's a good idea to spend a few minutes adding additional keywords that describe the contents of smaller groups of files, or individual files. Sometimes keywording is an easy step to skip in the excitement to get a closer look at your photos. But if you take the time to do it, you'll be able to find any photo on your hard drive in moments by searching for the specific contents of the photo.

Here's an example of how keywording works: if I take a trip to Europe, when I download the photos to my computer, I apply the keyword Europe to all of the photos during the download process. Then I apply a London keyword to all photos shot in London and a Paris keyword to all of the Paris photos. I also add more general keywords titled England and France. I add a keyword for my wife to every photo with my wife

in it, and so on. Therefore, if I have a photo of my wife posing in front of a London taxi, the keywords associated with it are: Europe, London, Julia, and Taxi.

This allows me at any time in the future to find this specific photo by searching the folder, or my entire hard drive, for all of these keywords. This photo will also be found be a much broader search, such as all photos shot in Europe. This is DAM at it's best!

## tip

The trick to using keywords is to not get overly detailed in assigning them. That's because when you become serious about keywording, the Keywords panel gets crowded very quickly. Try to use only keywords that you think you'll use in the future.

## Organizing keywords

Before you begin creating keywords, it's important to consider how they'll be organized. Keyword organization is similar to folder organization. Main keywords are created to hold sub-keywords. Sub-keywords can contain other sub-keywords. These main keywords are called container keywords. I always type container keywords in all upper case so that they are easy to visually locate in the Keywords panel shown in Figure 3.4.

**Figure 3.4**

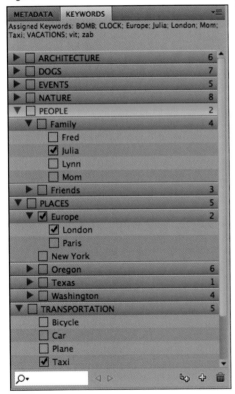

## tip

It's best to always use uppercase for the first letter in a sub-keyword name. That prevents you from creating two separate keywords — one with an uppercase initial letter and one with a lowercase initial letter.

The Keywords panel in Figure 3.4 shows keywords for photos of my wife in London. Notice the hierarchical organization of the container keywords and sub-keywords. For example, the hierarchy for the Julia keyword is PEOPLE > Family > Julia. This organizational structure allows you to do two things. First, you can collapse general areas that don't interest you, giving more space to the things you want to see. Secondly, you can quickly find a specific keyword because you know exactly where it should be.

## Creating and adding keywords

To create a new keyword, click the New Keyword button (it has a plus sign on it at the bottom right of the panel). The keyword is added directly above the currently selected keyword. To add a sub-keyword, select a keyword to contain it and click the New Sub Keyword button (to the left of the New Keyword button).

You can also create keywords and add them to the selected image(s) by typing them into the text box at the bottom of the panel. The new keywords are added to the Other Keywords container keyword in the keyword list. This is useful when you have lots of new keywords to add. Just type them all into the box, separating the keywords with commas. You can then drag-and-drop them into the appropriate locations in your organizational structure. If you're typing an existing keyword, it's added to the photo. Be sure to spell it correctly, though. Otherwise you end up with two different versions of the same keyword, which can be confusing. Bridge tries to help with this by highlighting keywords that match your spelling as you type.

# tip

Select a keyword and click the Delete Keyword button (trashcan) to remove it. To rename a keyword, right-click on it, and choose Rename.

## Searching for keywords

To find a photo using a keyword, type the keyword into the search field at the top of the screen on the right side of the Applications bar and press the Enter key. (These search terms are not case-sensitive.) This filters the current folder and any subfolders for the keyword. Click the magnifying glass icon to open a menu with additional options, including the most recent searches, as shown in Figure 3.5.

As Bridge performs the search, it populates the Content panel with the results of the search. To clear these results and return to the previous view, click the Cancel button (the one with the X on it at the top right of the Content panel).

If the search is too broad and you need to refine it, click the New Search button on the Content panel, to the left of the Cancel button. This opens the Find dialog box. This is useful for finding the photo of my wife with the taxi. Because I have so

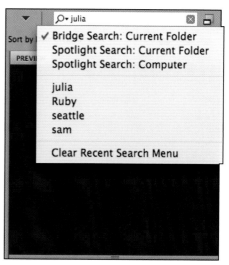

**Figure 3.5**

many photos of her, searching for the keyword Julia returns too many images. I use the Find dialog box shown in Figure 3.6 to refine my search so that I can quickly zero in on the specific image.

The Find dialog box shown in Figure 3.6 was configured by using the plus sign (+) to the right of the text boxes to add additional search criteria fields. Every time you click the plus sign, a new field is added. Then the pull-down menus on all fields are used to change the criteria to Keywords. This allows me to search for all three keywords at the same time. The key to making this search work is to select If all criteria are met from the Match pop-up menu. If this is set to If any criteria are met, the search will return all photos that contain any of the keywords.

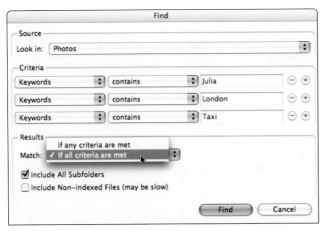

Figure 3.6

# Organizing and Classifying Photos

The process of selecting your favorite photos — as well as those that don't make the grade — is a straightforward procedure. You can accomplish this most easily using colored labels and stars.

## Using labels and stars

The process for organizing your photos is two-tiered. You do an initial reviewing pass using colored labels to mark above-average images and images that need to be deleted. Then you do a second pass on the above-average images to identify with star ratings the special photos that really stand out.

Follow these steps to quickly find your favorite images from a shoot:

**1** **Quickly go through all of the thumbnails and rotate any images that need rotating.** If auto-rotate is turned on in your camera, this step won't be necessary.

**2** **Click on the first thumbnail to make it the selected thumbnail.**

**3** **Change the workspace to Preview by choosing Preview from the Workspace menu on the Applications bar, or by choosing Window → Workspace → Preview (⌘+F6/Ctrl+F6).** If you saved a custom version of the Preview workspace, as discussed in Chapter 2, choose it instead.

**4** **Evaluate each image for exposure, composition, and focus.** The goal in this first viewing is to label above-average images and images that need to be deleted. An above-average image excels in at least one of these three criteria. An image to be deleted is one that has no redeeming qualities. Average images do not receive a label. Use the arrow keys to move among the thumbnails.

## tip

Remember to use the Loupe to zoom to 1:1 magnification to check focus.

**5** **Choose Label → Green (⌘+6/Ctrl+6) to mark and above average photo with a green label or choose Label → Red (⌘+6/Ctrl+6) to mark an image that needs to be deleted.** Feel free to apply green labels liberally. The point is to find all of the better images. You get a chance to look at them more closely in a moment. On the other hand, be selective with the red labels because all files with a red label will be deleted. This isn't something you should take lightly. Storing original files is fairly cheap and you never know when you might want an image or part of it. Label only the truly useless files, if you have any, with red labels.

**6** **Choose the Essentials workspace from the Workspace menu on the Applications bar, and then click the Red label option in the Labels section of the Filter Panel, shown in Figure 3.7.** The Content panel is populated with photos that have red labels on them.

Figure 3.7

**7** **Take one last look at the photos to ensure that you want to delete them.** If you change your mind on a photo, use ⌘+6/Ctrl+6 to remove the red label and remove it from the Content panel.

**8** **Select all the photos by choosing Edit → Select All (⌘+A/Ctrl+A) and press the Delete key.** The dialog box shown in Figure 3.8 opens.

**9** **Click Reject to remove the files from the view without deleting them or click Delete.** Note in the dialog that you can use ⌘+Delete/Ctrl+Delete to skip this dialog box when deleting photos. If you get a second warning dialog box informing you that the selected files are being moved to the trash, click OK.

**10** **Go back to the Filter panel and click Red again to stop filtering for red labels, and then click Green to filter for only green labels.** This populates the Content panel with all of your above-average photos. Now it's time to pick the best of the above average photos.

# tip

Always remember to turn a filter off by clicking it again when you're through with it. Otherwise some of your photos may not be visible in the Content panel.

Figure 3.8

**11** **Go back to the Preview workspace and go through the photos one by one.**

When you see a photo that meets two of the three evaluation criteria, give it a one-star rating using the Label menu or ⌘+1/Ctrl+1. When you see a photo that meets all three criteria, give it a two-star rating (⌘+2/Ctrl+2). Save three-star ratings for your best photos. These are photos that meet all three evaluation criteria and have an extra emotional impact. If you have a group of similar photos, select all of them in the Content panel to compare them in the Preview panel. Deselect a photo to eliminate it from the preview group.

Now you have evaluated all of the downloaded photos and can sort them instantly. Whenever you want to see the best photos from a shoot, you simply select the shoot's folder and use the Filter panel to filter for green labels or stars.

# note

Consider your rating system to be universal throughout your entire library of photos. That means a green label with a two-star rating has the same meaning whenever you use it. You may have noticed that you aren't using four- and five-star ratings. Save these rating levels for later so that you can expand your rating system as your skills grow.

# Renaming photos after downloading

Sometimes it's necessary to rename photos after they're downloaded. This happens when you delete lots of photos during the review process. It also happens when files don't get renamed during downloading. To rename a photo, or a group of photos, select them and choose Tools→Batch Rename (Shift+⌘+R/Shift+Ctrl+R) to open the Batch Rename dialog box, shown in Figure 3.9.

**Figure 3.9**

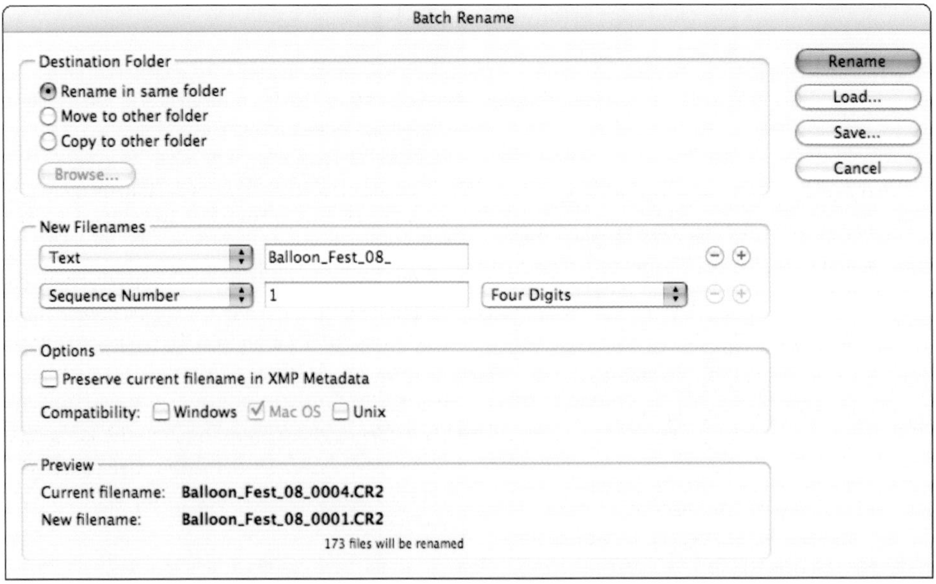

The Batch Rename dialog box is fairly straightforward. Use the menus in the New Filenames section to create the kind of filename you want to use. Use the plus signs (+) to add additional naming fields and use the menus and text boxes in those fields to add naming information. In Figure 3.9 I use the same naming scenario I used when I downloaded my photos because I'm renaming a folder of photos to remove gaps in the sequence numbers after deleting some files from the Balloon Fest shoot.

# caution

If you're using a date at the end of the name, be sure to add an underscore or a hyphen after the date in a file so the sequence numbers don't blend with the last number in the date.

## Creating a collection of your favorites

After all of your best photos are identified, it's useful to create a collection of them. Collections are virtual groups of files. When a photo is added to a collection, it isn't moved or copied. Instead, a visual reference to the photo is placed in the collection.

To create a collection of your above average photos, follow these steps:

**1** Go to the filter panel and click the green label to populate the Content panel with only green-labeled photos.

**2** Choose Edit → Select All (⌘+A/Ctrl+A) to select all photos.

**3** Go to the Collections panel and click the New Collection button at the bottom. A dialog box opens, confirming that you want to add the selected photos. When you click Yes, a new collection is added to the Collections panel, shown in Figure 3.10.

Collection

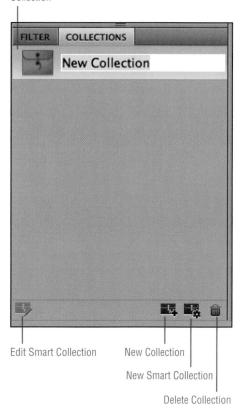

Edit Smart Collection    New Collection

New Smart Collection

Delete Collection

**Figure 3.10**

**4** Type a new name to identify the collection and press Enter.

You can add photos to the collection by dragging their respective thumbnails from the Content panel onto the collection in the Collections panel. Photos are removed by selecting them and clicking the Remove From Collection button that shows at the top of the Content panel when a collection is being viewed. If you want to change the Content panel back to the contents of the folder, use the Back button at the top of the screen, next to the Bridge App icon. (You can also use the back button on your mouse if it's equipped with one.)

Another way to create a collection is with a smart collection. A smart collection uses standard metadata to automatically sort a range of files. To create a smart collection, click the New Smart Collection button on the bottom of the Collections panel. Figure 3.11 shows the Smart Collection dialog box. Use the menus to filter for the kind of collection you want. In this example I am filtering my 2008 folder, which is all images I created during 2008. I am using a two-star rating for my criteria. The resulting collection contains all two-star photos created during 2008.

Use the Edit Smart Collection button to change the filtering scenario for the smart collection. When you click it, the Edit Smart Collection dialog opens, which is the same as the Smart Collection dialog box shown in Figure 3.11.

# note

When a thumbnail is dragged into a collection, a reference is added to the collection, but the image's thumbnail stays in its folder. When a thumbnail is dragged to another folder instead, it's permanently moved to that folder, along with the file.

# Using Slideshow and Review Mode

After you've identified your best images, it's fun to watch them in a slideshow. For example, you can create an impromptu slideshow by filtering for green labeled photos or selecting a collection, and then choosing View → Slideshow (⌘+L/ Ctrl+L).

The slideshow begins with the currently selected photo. It runs automatically, but you can use the Spacebar to pause it and restart it and the right and left arrow keys to advance it to the next or previous slide. Press Esc to cancel the slideshow. You can also zoom to 1:1 during the slideshow by clicking a slide. Click again to zoom back normal. When you click on an image the slideshow automatically pauses, so you have to press the spacebar to make it resume playing. Use the Slideshow Options (View → Slideshow Options) to change some of the slideshow display parameters, such as slide duration, captions, and transitions.

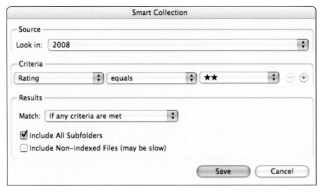

Figure 3.11

Review Mode is similar to slideshow, but much cooler. It's a new feature in Bridge CS4. To launch it, choose View→ Review Mode (⌘+B/Ctrl+B). All photos in the Content panel are selected and displayed, as shown in Figure 3.12.

The first image is displayed in the center of the screen. Click any of the images in the background to move them to the front. Use the right and left arrow buttons on the lower left to rotate the view one slide at a time. Use the downward pointing arrow to remove the front slide from the view. You can also use the right, left, and down arrows on your keyboard for these same functions. Use the buttons on the lower right to zoom in, create a collection, or close the Review Mode.

Balloon_Fest_08_0075.CR2

**Figure 3.12**

# Changing the Way Photos Are Sorted

Sometimes it's necessary to sort photos in ways that aren't possible using the Filter panel or keyword searches. For example, it's often useful to sort photos by file type, the dates they were modified, or even their color profiles. In Bridge this type of sorting is easy to accomplish.

By default, Bridge sorts photos by filename. To change the way files are sorted, choose View→ Sort and choose among the options in the pop-up menu. A faster way to change the sort is to use the Sort By menu on the Applications bar, shown in Figure 3.13. Clicking the upward pointing arrow to the right of the menu reverses the sort order from ascending to descending.

**Figure 3.13**

| Sort by Date Created ▾ ⌃ |
| --- |
| By Filename |
| By Type |
| ✓ By Date Created |
| By Date Modified |
| By Size |
| By Dimensions |
| By Resolution |
| By Color Profile |
| By Label |
| By Rating |
| Manually |

One of the most useful sorting methods is the Manual sort. This allows you to arrange the photos into any sequence by clicking and dragging them. Manual sorting is useful when you have images from an event that were shot on two different cameras. This happens often for wedding and event photographers. One would think that you could combine the two sets of files into one folder and sort them by date created to get the sequencing to line up. However, it's quite common for a camera's clock to be off — sometimes quite a bit. (Have you checked yours lately?) This can lead to a huge mess when the files are combined. To solve a problem like this, follow these steps:

**1** Combine all of the images you need to sort into a single folder.

**2** Choose View → Sort → Manually and drag the thumbnails into the correct order.

**3** Choose Edit → Select All (⌘+A/Ctrl+A) to select all of the files.

**4** Choose Tools → Batch Rename (Shift+⌘+R/Shift+Ctrl+R) to rename the files and preserve the new sequence.

If you're dealing with a large number of files, manually sorting can be tedious work. One way to make the job more efficient is to place each set of files into individual folders and then open a second Bridge window. To do this choose File → New Window (⌘+N/Ctrl+N). Set one Bridge window to display images from camera 1 and the other to display images from camera 2. Then begin dragging photos from camera 2's window into camera 1's window until they've all been moved into the appropriate chronological order. (Be sure to set the sort order to Manual in the window for Camera 1.)

## tip

If you are shooting an event with multiple cameras, be sure to synchronize each camera's clock just before the event. Doing so allows you to avoid the previous scenario. These clocks tend to drift, so to be safe, be sure to check them before every event.

# Working with Metadata

Metadata can be viewed and managed with the Metadata panel. However there are a couple of other ways to work with a file's metadata that you should know about.

## Creating a custom metadata template

Earlier in this chapter, you saw how basic copyright metadata is added to files during import. This is a very good practice to have in your workflow. Sometimes, though, you want to add a more comprehensive set of standard information to the metadata of new files as they're downloaded, or existing files. This is common for photojournalists and stock photographers.

The best way to do this is to create a metadata template by following these steps:

**1** **Choose Tools → Create Metadata Template.** The Create Metadata Template dialog box opens; click the twirly next to IPTC Core if the area is collapsed. IPTC Core (International Press Telecommunications Council) metadata is editable metadata that allows you to add an array of information about an image and its owner. Figure 3.14 shows a partial listing of the metadata fields in this area.

**2** **Type the appropriate information into the text boxes.** As you do, you'll notice that a check mark appears to the left of the field's title, indicating that the field is added.

**3** **Name your template using the Template Name textbox at the top of the dialog and click Save.**

## tip

If more than one photographer is using Bridge on the same workstation, each of you can create individual metadata templates.

Now whenever you want to add your metadata template to existing photos. To do this, you select the thumbnails and choose Tools → Replace Metadata or Append Metadata and choose your new template from the pop-up menu that appears when you hover over either choice. The difference between Replace and Append is that Replace does just that: it replaces any existing metadata fields with the metadata in the template. Choosing Append Metadata adds the new metadata to any existing fields. If you haven't added any metadata, go ahead and choose Replace Metadata so that "unknown" is removed from any fields where it may exist. This only affects metadata that's editable by you (the IPTC core section in the Metadata panel) and does not affect metadata added by the camera when the file was created.

Your new template can also be applied when new files are downloaded from your camera because the template you created now appears in the Template to Use menu of the Apply Metadata section of Bridge's Photo Downloader.

Figure 3.14

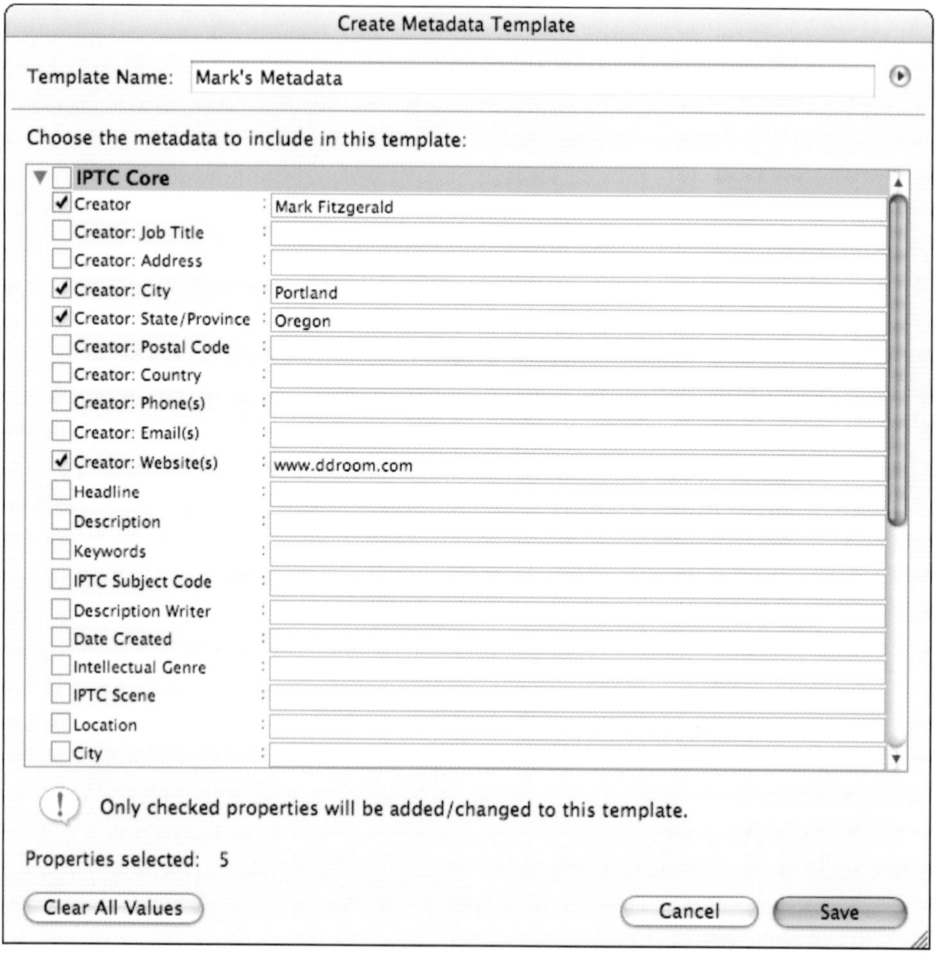

| Create Metadata Template | | |
|---|---|---|
| Template Name: Mark's Metadata | | |

Choose the metadata to include in this template:

▼ ☐ **IPTC Core**
| | |
|---|---|
| ☑ Creator | Mark Fitzgerald |
| ☐ Creator: Job Title | |
| ☐ Creator: Address | |
| ☑ Creator: City | Portland |
| ☑ Creator: State/Province | Oregon |
| ☐ Creator: Postal Code | |
| ☐ Creator: Country | |
| ☐ Creator: Phone(s) | |
| ☐ Creator: Email(s) | |
| ☑ Creator: Website(s) | www.ddroom.com |
| ☐ Headline | |
| ☐ Description | |
| ☐ Keywords | |
| ☐ IPTC Subject Code | |
| ☐ Description Writer | |
| ☐ Date Created | |
| ☐ Intellectual Genre | |
| ☐ IPTC Scene | |
| ☐ Location | |
| ☐ City | |

( ! ) Only checked properties will be added/changed to this template.

Properties selected: 5

[ Clear All Values ]          [ Cancel ]   [ Save ]

# Using the File Info command

There's another way to view and work with metadata that's a bit esoteric, but it's very powerful, so you should be familiar with it. It's called File Info. To use it, select a file or multiple files, and then choose File → File Info (Alt+Shift+⌘+I/Alt+Shift+Ctrl+I) — (one of the dreaded four-key shortcuts). When the dialog box opens as shown in Figure 3.14, you can use it to view and change most metadata associated with the file by clicking the various tabs at the top. In Figure 3.15 the Description area is being displayed. (Use the arrow at the top right or left to scroll the tabs sideway so that you can see all of them.) If a single file is selected, it's name is displayed at the top of the box. When multiple files are selected, the title bar is blank.

**Figure 3.15**

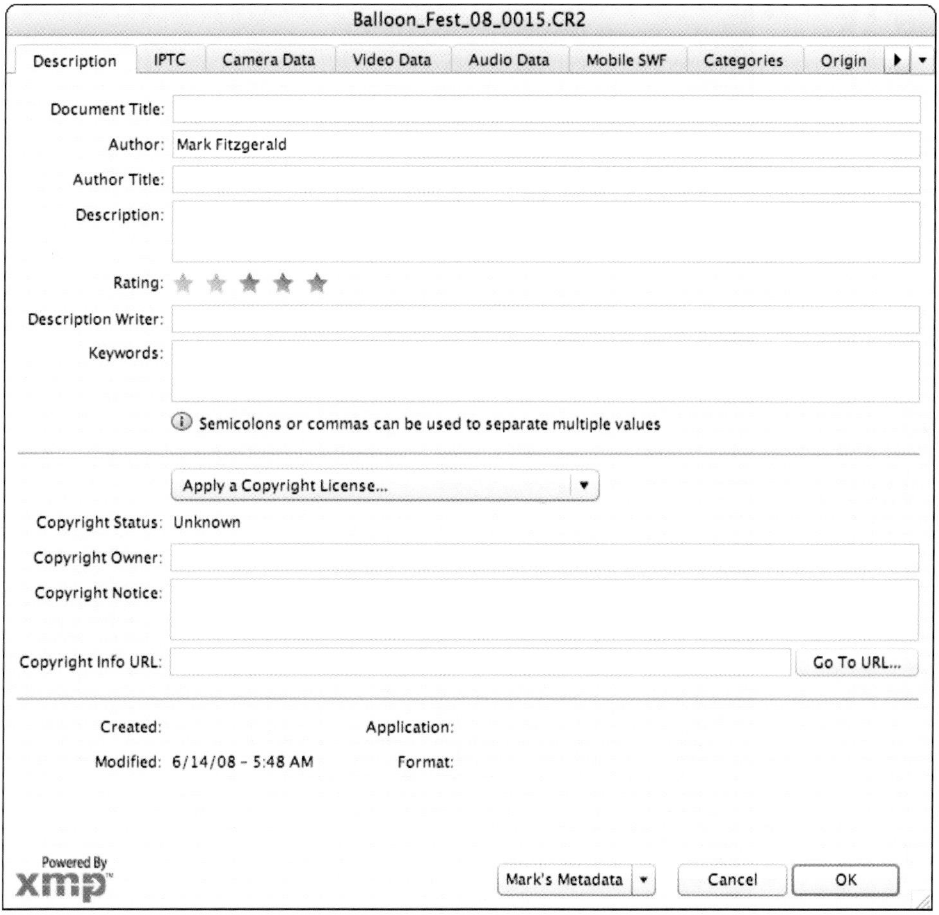

The File Info dialog box is an extremely useful way to view or edit metadata. You can use it or the Metadata panel to work with individual files, as well as groups of selected files. I just wish it had an easier keyboard shortcut! Some sections are useful for photographers and some — such as Video Data, Audio Data, and Mobile SWF — are not.

The following list contains details about the fields you are likely to use as a photographer:

- **Description.** This is a basic overview of the file's metadata. It includes descriptive information such as title, keywords, and copyright info. Most of this information can also be found in the IPTC section.

- **IPTC.** This section contains most of the same fields you saw in the IPTC section of the Create Metadata Template dialog box. However, they're laid out in a much more intuitive way.

- **Camera Data.** This section provides information about the camera settings when the exposure was made. Note that this section is not editable because there are no text boxes.

- **History.** The history section of a file's metadata allows you to record the complete editing history of a file. I've seen photographers use this to share the exact editing steps they used to accomplish a difficult task. This setting is also important in the forensic photography community because it's used to track the provenance and editing history of evidence photos. It's necessary to activate the History log in Photoshop's General preferences in order to begin recording history metadata. Choose Photoshop → Preferences → General (Edit → Preferences → General). Figure 3.16 gives you a preview of the History Log section.

You can save history steps as metadata, to a text file (which is useful if you want to share your steps with someone), or both. You can also use the Edit Log Item menu, shown in Figure 3.17, to choose the level of information you want to record; Sessions Only, Concise, or Detailed.

- **Sessions Only.** Makes a record of when a file is opened and closed.

- **Concise.** Records the session information and the text that appears in Photoshop's History panel.

- **Detailed.** Records all of the Concise information with much greater detail. This is the best way to track a file's complete editing history.

Figure 3.16

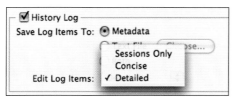

**Figure 3.17**

see also

In Chapter 5, you get a closer look at the General preferences in Photoshop.

Figure 3.18 shows a typical history log when Detailed is selected for Edit Log Items. Be advised that when history logging is turned on, it increases the size of files a bit because of the extra metadata.

**History**

2008-06-20T15:46:24-07:00    File sample.tif opened
Open  Macintosh HD:Photos:2006:10 things Sample Images:sample.tif

Levels
Levels Preset Kind: Custom
Adjustment: levels adjustment list
levels adjustment
Channel: composite channel
Input: 14, 247
Gamma: 1.04

Color Balance
Color Balance   Shadow Levels: 0, 0, 0
Midtone Levels: -5, 0, 6
Highlight Levels: 0, 0, 0
Without Preserve Luminosity

Hue/Saturation
Hue/Saturation Preset Kind: Custom
Without Colorize
Adjustment: hue/saturation adjustment list
hue/saturation adjustment
Hue: 0
Saturation: 11
Lightness: 0

2008-06-20T15:47:07-07:00    File sample_2.tif saved

**Figure 3.18**

# 4

# Introduction to Working with Raw Files

Today many serious photographers are shooting in the raw capture format. I'm convinced that even more photographers would be using this powerful capture format if they weren't intimidated by two things: the mystique of raw because it's an entirely different image file format, and the extra workflow that's necessary for converting raw files for use in Photoshop. In this chapter you learn everything you need to know about raw files and why they're important. Then you see just how easy it is to use the Adobe Camera Raw (ACR) converter to quickly and efficiently process large groups of files. If you're already shooting raw, hopefully this chapter will fill in some of the gaps in your understanding of the file format and the workflow surrounding it. If you aren't currently shooting raw, this chapter prepares you to make the switch when you're ready.

# What Is Raw?

In Chapter 1 I mentioned that there's a big difference between JPEG and raw capture file formats. Take a moment to review the main points of that discussion. When I point my dSLR at a scene and click the shutter, the camera's sensor captures a huge amount of information. If I have the camera set to capture JPEG files, the camera's onboard processor processes the captured information into a compressed JPEG file. It creates this file using the image settings I have dialed into my camera. This file contains only a fraction of the captured information. Any unused information is discarded.

The JPEG capture process seems easy because it allows the camera to make the file very quickly. However, it leaves something to be desired for photographers looking to maximize the quality of their images. The problem is that they don't get to look at all the information before most of it gets thrown away. What if you want to give the image a different interpretation and use some of the missing data after the photo was shot? Unfortunately, when you're using JPEG as your capture format, you have to live with the data the camera uses to create the JPEG files.

When you're shooting in the raw capture mode, nearly all of the information that the camera's sensor captured is saved in the file. This allows you to selectively choose which information becomes part of the file by manually converting the data from the raw file into a more common file type.

## note

Raw files can be created only by digital cameras. That's why they're often referred to as camera raw.

So back to my question: What is raw? A raw file is a grayscale image. This means that qualities such as color attributes and color space have not been assigned to the file. In fact, the only camera settings that are permanently part of a raw file are ISO, aperture, and shutter speed. Everything else is mostly up for grabs. Decisions about color space or white balance can be made after the fact, during the process of converting the raw file. This is why you often hear raw files described as being "digital negatives." They are open to a great deal of interpretation that can be done during conversion — just like the process a film photographer goes through to interpret a negative when printing in a darkroom.

Calling a raw file a digital negative makes sense because it shares another important trait of a film negative. Altering a raw file permanently in Photoshop is virtually impossible. The file can be interpreted in many ways, but none of the conversions alters the underlying file. Instead, a set of metadata instructions is written to describe the way the raw file is meant to look.

This means that no matter what you make a raw file look like when you convert it, you can always undo those settings on the original raw file and back up to what it looked like the day it was shot. (To do this in Bridge, choose Edit → Develop Settings → Camera Raw Defaults.) Any adjustments you make are simply written to a file that can be overwritten or deleted at any time. In fact, when you convert a raw file and open it in Photoshop, it has to become something different than a raw file — that's why it's called a conversion process. Photoshop can't work with raw files. All digital camera manufacturers have their own versions of raw. Nikon uses NEF and Olympus uses ORF. For example, my Canon shoots with the raw file format named CR2. However, when I save an open file in Photoshop, the Save As dialog box doesn't include an option for a format called CR2.

# note

If you see Photoshop Raw in the Save As dialog box, note that it's something completely different. It's used for transferring images between different computer platforms and applications.

I imagine that you're starting to see some advantages to shooting raw. I'd be remiss if I didn't take a moment to warn you about some of the disadvantages.

# Disadvantages of shooting raw

Raw files have to be converted into a more common format before they can be opened into Photoshop and most other editing or presentation software. This requires some time on the photographer's part because he has to do something that the camera automatically does when shooting JPEG. This extra time is worth it to serious photographers because they want to work with the best images their cameras are capable of producing.

Raw files are much larger in size than JPEG files. They can run two to four times larger because lots more information is being saved. This means that raw files consume media cards and hard drives much faster than their JPEG cousins. I've spoken to many wedding shooters who shoot their first raw wedding without being aware of this size issue. In a panic, halfway through the wedding, they had to switch the camera back to JPEG because they had already consumed most of their media cards with large raw files. This problem can be solved with a little preparation.

The biggest problem regarding the raw format is that there are many varieties of raw files. Each camera company creates its own "flavor" of the raw format. In fact, these companies can have several slightly different flavors that all have the same name. For example, my Canon camera shoots raw files with the extension of CR2. Other Canon dSLRs also share this file format, yet the files are different; different algorithms are used to convert the files. Adobe estimates that at least 200 different versions of the raw file format exist.

When a camera manufacturer comes out with a new camera, even though the raw file format still has the same name, Photoshop CS4's Raw converter (Adobe Camera Raw) can't open the files. Adobe must update the Raw converter and issue the update to Photoshop CS4 users. If you buy a new camera and you're having problems opening them, go to the Photoshop CS4 menus and choose Help → Updates to see if any updates to the Adobe Camera Raw converter are available — as well as updates to Photoshop and Bridge.

Some people envision a nightmare scenario when it comes to the expanding variety of raw file types. What would happen if one of the major camera manufacturers went out of business and no longer supported its raw format? At some point it could become difficult to convert those files because no one would have the software for them. Adobe is attempting to address this issue with the creation of a standardized raw format called DNG (digital negative). Its goal is to have the major camera manufacturers support this new format as new cameras are rolled out. Some are beginning to get on board, but the adoption rate is slow.

So yes, there are some downsides to shooting raw. The files take more time to deal with because they need to be converted and raw files consume more space in addition to the concerns over the long-term viability of various raw formats. But these are minor issues compared to the huge advantage of having access to the extra data contained in a raw file.

# Exposing a raw file correctly

One of the big things to understand about raw is that digital capture is linear in nature. Without getting too technical, this means that it devotes more bits to capturing highlights than it does to capturing shadows. This is the opposite of the way humans see things. We're really good at distinguishing detail in the shadows and not very good at seeing detail in the highlights.

A typical raw file captures 4,098 distinct tonal levels within a six-stop range, stretching from pure black to pure white. This range is graphically represented by a histogram. Because raw is a linear capture, a full 50 percent (2,048 levels) of the file's tonal information is devoted to the

brightest stop of information, which is represented by the right side of the histogram. Only 1.6 percent (64 levels) of the file's tonal information is devoted to capturing the shadow detail, which is represented by the left side of the histogram. When an image is underexposed by one stop, the histogram doesn't make use of the brightest stop that contains 50% of the tonal information, as shown in Figure 4.1, essentially wasting half of the capacity of the file on information that wasn't captured in the brightest stop.

# see also

Histograms are discussed in detail in Chapter 6.

**Figure 4.1**

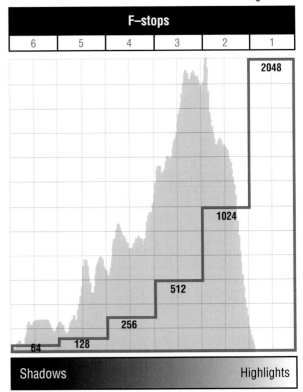

If the camera is adjusted to the correct exposure, the histogram moves to the right one stop, as shown in Figure 4.2. Now the brightest stop of information is used to describe the highlights in the image. Because so much information describes these highlights, detail that seems lost at first can be recaptured during the raw conversion process with Adobe Camera Raw. Another benefit to adjusting the exposure to the right is that now twice as much information is being used to describe the darkest shadows on the left side of the histogram, allowing you to have more information to work with when adjusting shadow tones with ACR.

I know this flies in the face of conventional wisdom for a JPEG shooter. When you shoot JPEG, a highlight that gets overexposed is gone forever. Many JPEG shooters intentionally underexpose all of their exposures in an effort to insure that they retain highlight detail. When you shoot raw, this isn't always the case. I shot the barn in Figure 4.3 when I was photographing at a local tulip field. When I shot this picture, I forgot that I had a +2-stop bias dialed into my camera's exposure setting. Later, when I reviewed the image, I realized that I had overexposed it by two stops, as shown in the first image in Figure 4.3. Fortunately, this was a raw file with 50 percent of its data-capturing bandwidth devoted to recording highlights. I was able to open the file in Photoshop's Adobe Camera Raw converter and recover all highlight detail, as shown in the second image of Figure 4.3. If this had been shot in JPEG, the file would have been useless because it would have been impossible to show the detail in the blown-out highlights.

**Figure 4.2**

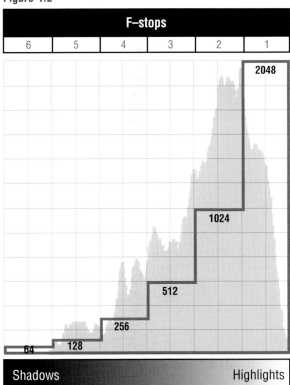

**Figure 4.3**

Something else about underexposure versus overexposure is that its better to darken a photo than it is to lighten it. That's because much of the noise in a digital photo is in the shadows. Noise refers to digital artifacts (unwanted leftovers) that often show up as specs that make an image look grainy. It's usually caused by shooting at high ISO speeds and by underexposure. When a photo is lightened, the tonal range of the shadows is expanded, revealing the noise. When a photo is darkened, these tonal ranges are compressed, helping to hide the noise.

So here's the thing to remember. If you're shooting raw, be sure to fully expose for the highlights. Naturally, nailing your exposures is always best. But if you're going to err on one side or the other of a perfect exposure, make sure that you err in the overexposed direction when shooting raw.

# Working with Metadata in Raw Files

One of the big advantages to shooting raw is that metadata is used to record any changes made to a file, preventing any editing changes from having a permanent effect on the image. Because there are so many versions of raw, it's difficult for Adobe to understand the inner workings of all of them. Especially when you consider that these formats are proprietary, meaning that the companies that create the formats don't openly share the code that's used inside them. Adobe decided a long time ago that they would not allow their products to write information to these files because they could not predict exactly how the file would be affected by a process as simple as writing some metadata to the file's header. Instead, Adobe came up with some other solutions for storing this metadata:

- **The Camera Raw database.** By default camera raw metadata is stored in Photoshop's Camera Raw Database. When adjustments are made to a raw file and it is reopened at a later date, the last settings stored in this database are referenced and used to display the image. This database is indexed by file content so the image retains all of its settings even if the file is relocated on the system or renamed.

- **XMP sidecar files.** Storing metadata in the Camera Raw database works fine for short-term uses, but it leaves something to be desired when files are moved off the system for sharing with another computer or for storage. For example, if I burn all of the raw files from the balloon fest photos I used for examples in Chapter 3 onto a DVD and place it in storage, I break the link between the files and their metadata. That's because the metadata stays behind in the Camera Raw Database.

This problem is solved by creating a special XMP sidecar file for each raw image. XMP stands for Extensible Metadata Platform. It is a labeling technology that allows you to embed information about a file into the file itself. Because that isn't an option with raw files, the XMP data is stored in a separate file that is placed next to the original raw file. It has the same root name as its parent raw file with an XMP file extension. Figure 4.4 shows some CR2 raw files and their XMP sidecar files. Notice how much smaller the XMP files are than their parent files.

When you use XMP sidecar files, it's easy to move files off the system without breaking the metadata connection. When you copy the original raw file, simply be sure to copy its associated XMP sidecar file. That way when the raw files are viewed in Bridge on another computer, all edits done to the raw file are visible.

## note

If a raw file's XMP sidecar file is deleted, the original file goes back to looking like it did when it was first downloaded from the camera.

Earlier I mentioned that in an effort to standardize the raw file format, Adobe created its own version of the raw format called DNG. But there's something really cool about DNG files that I didn't tell you. Because Adobe created this file type, they completely understand how it works under the hood. That means that XMP metadata can be written directly to the raw file without the need for sidecar files.

| Name ▲ | Size |
|---|---|
| Balloon_Fest_08_0001.CR2 | 7.2 MB |
| Balloon_Fest_08_0001.xmp | 8 KB |
| Balloon_Fest_08_0002.CR2 | 7.5 MB |
| Balloon_Fest_08_0002.xmp | 8 KB |
| Balloon_Fest_08_0004.CR2 | 6.9 MB |
| Balloon_Fest_08_0004.xmp | 8 KB |
| Balloon_Fest_08_0005.CR2 | 7 MB |
| Balloon_Fest_08_0005.xmp | 8 KB |
| Balloon_Fest_08_0006.CR2 | 6.9 MB |
| Balloon_Fest_08_0006.xmp | 8 KB |

Figure 4.4

So far only a few manufacturers are embracing DNG as a capture format, but that doesn't prevent you from using it. You can convert your raw files into DNG as they're downloaded by checking Convert to DNG when the Photo Downloader dialog box is in the advanced mode (see Figure 3.2). When Convert to DNG is selected, you click the Settings button next to it to configure the type of DNG files that are created during the conversion. Figure 4.5 shows the options that are presented to you. (You can also convert existing raw files using Save Options in ACR, which you see in a moment.)

Take a look at how these options are used:

- **Preview.** Some software isn't designed to work with raw files. Because of that, a JPEG preview is embedded into raw files to give this software something to display so you can view the image content with that software. This menu is used to control the type of preview that's embedded. The options are None, Medium Size, and Full Size. Remember that larger preview size equals larger file size.

- **Compression.** The Compressed (lossless) option uses lossless compression to make the DNG file smaller. This saves space, but files take longer to open because they need to be decompressed.

- **Image Conversion Method.** The Preserve Raw Image option keeps all of the data in its original structure. The Convert to Linear Image option changes the structure of the data so that other software programs can read it. I recommend against this because it permanently changes the fundamental data structure of the file in ways that can't be undone. Leave the Image Compression Method set to Preserve Raw Image.

- **Original Raw File.** The Embed Original Raw File option gives you the best of both worlds because you always have access to the original file if you need it. Naturally, this substantially increases the size of the DNG file.

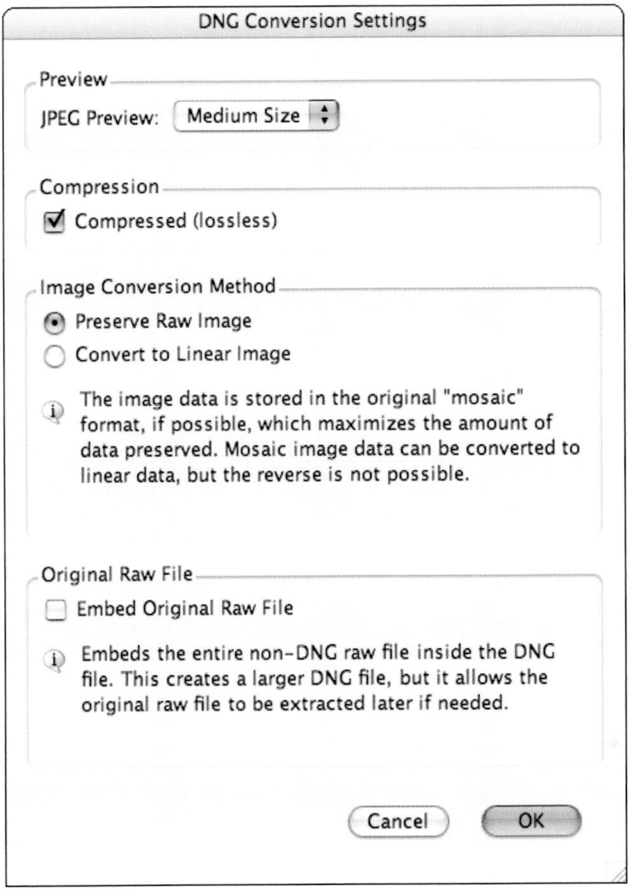

DNG Conversion Settings

Preview
JPEG Preview: [ Medium Size ▲▼ ]

Compression
☑ Compressed (lossless)

Image Conversion Method
⦿ Preserve Raw Image
◯ Convert to Linear Image

ⓘ The image data is stored in the original "mosaic" format, if possible, which maximizes the amount of data preserved. Mosaic image data can be converted to linear data, but the reverse is not possible.

Original Raw File
☐ Embed Original Raw File

ⓘ Embeds the entire non-DNG raw file inside the DNG file. This creates a larger DNG file, but it allows the original raw file to be extracted later if needed.

( Cancel )  ( OK )

**Figure 4.5**

# Setting Camera Raw Preferences

Adobe Camera Raw has its own set of preferences, allowing you to configure how raw files are handled and how their metadata is read and stored. To open the preferences, choose Bridge CS4 ➜ Camera Raw Preferences (Edit ➜ Camera Raw Preferences). These preferences, shown in Figure 4.6, are divided into five different areas.

Here's a quick look at each area:

- **General.** Use the Save image settings in drop-down menu to choose between XMP sidecar files and the Camera Raw database for storing the metadata for raw files. I recommend choosing XMP if you're not converting your files to DNG.

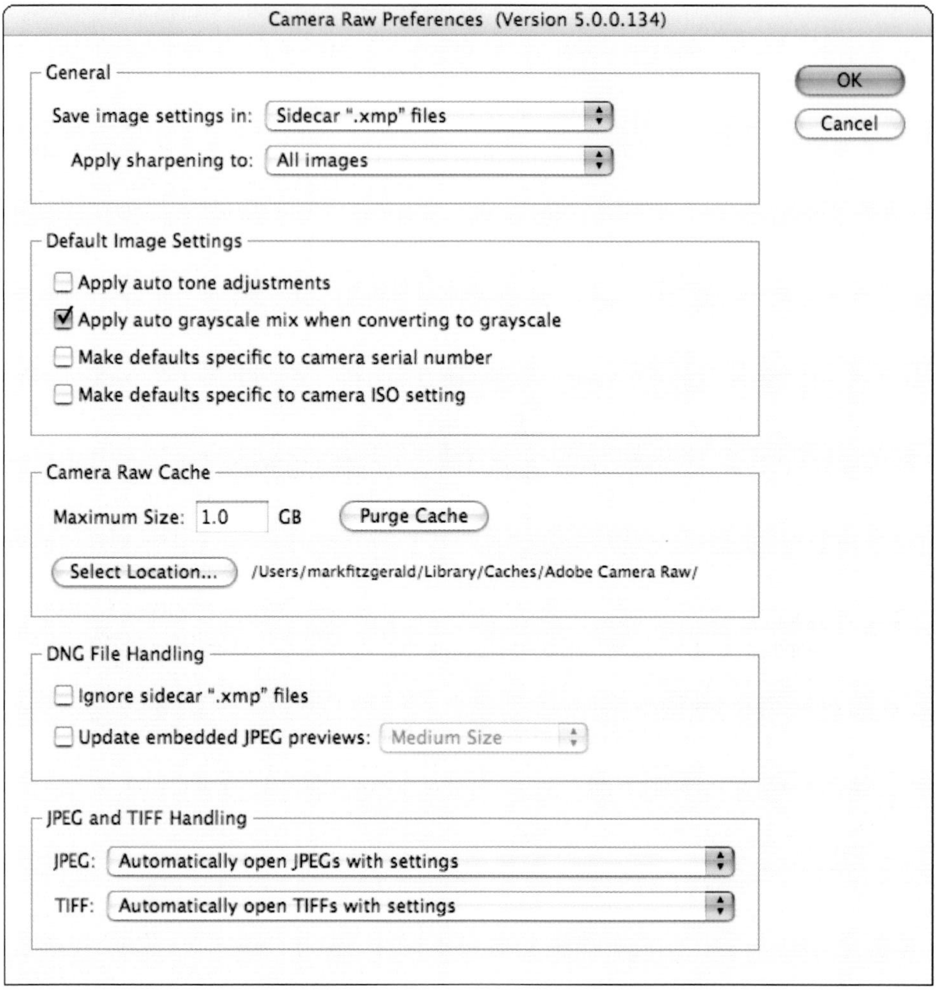

Camera Raw Preferences (Version 5.0.0.134)

General

Save image settings in: [ Sidecar ".xmp" files ▼ ]

Apply sharpening to: [ All images ▼ ]

( OK )
( Cancel )

Default Image Settings

☐ Apply auto tone adjustments

☑ Apply auto grayscale mix when converting to grayscale

☐ Make defaults specific to camera serial number

☐ Make defaults specific to camera ISO setting

Camera Raw Cache

Maximum Size: [1.0] GB ( Purge Cache )

( Select Location... ) /Users/markfitzgerald/Library/Caches/Adobe Camera Raw/

DNG File Handling

☐ Ignore sidecar ".xmp" files

☐ Update embedded JPEG previews: [ Medium Size ▼ ]

JPEG and TIFF Handling

JPEG: [ Automatically open JPEGs with settings ▼ ]

TIFF: [ Automatically open TIFFs with settings ▼ ]

**Figure 4.6**

There's a bit of debate over which selection to make in the Apply sharpening to drop-down menu. Go ahead and set it to All images for now, but don't change and default sharpening settings when using ACR to convert your files until you know more about applying sharpening this early in the workflow. Later on, when you know more about sharpening, you can make better-informed decisions.

# caution

If you use XMP sidecar files (or DNG files) and you need to open them from a CD or DVD, be sure to copy the files to your hard drive first because these discs are read-only (data cannot be written to them). When XMP sidecar files are used, they need to be written to the same place where the raw file is stored. When that can't happen, the data is automatically saved to the Camera Raw database.

# see also

Sharpening is discussed in detail in Chapter 12.

- **Default Image Settings.** This area is used to handle default adjustment settings. I recommend that you select Apply auto grayscale mix when converting to grayscale because ACR does a decent job of doing this. However, I strongly recommend against selecting Apply auto tone adjustments. That's because these automatic adjustments often do more harm than good. Leave the other two check boxes about defaults deselected too.

- **Camera Raw Cache.** This is similar to the Bridge cache you learned about in Chapter 2. The Camera Raw cache is used to store data for raw files that have been edited in ACR, allowing the photos to display more quickly in Bridge. I recommend leaving this set to its size and location defaults.

  If you suspect your cache is corrupted because files aren't displaying correctly in Bridge, you can use the Purge Cache button to delete the cache. When you do this, all thumbnail previews are deleted and then automatically regenerated by Bridge.

- **DNG File Handling.** Checking Ignore sidecar ".xmp" insures that all adjustments to the DNG files are stored inside the files themselves instead of in sidecar files. This prevents XMP sidecar files from being attached to DNG files, which is usually unnecessary.

  Checking Update embedded JPEG previews allows for embedded previews to be updated after DNG files are edited in ACR. This is a good idea if anyone will be viewing the files with software that isn't designed for working with DNG files.

- **JPEG and TIFF handling.** These menus are used to open JPEG and TIFF files into ACR. The main advantage to this is that ACR is designed to work with multiple files. If you have a bunch of JPEGs that all need the same tonal and color corrections, you can open all of them in ACR, adjust one, and then share those settings with all files.

  These menus have three choices: Disable support prevents these files from opening in ACR. Automatically open with settings, which means that JPEF or TIFF files with ACR metadata in them open in ACR. The third setting, Automatically open all supported, opens all JPEG and TIFF files in ACR.

# tip

You can also open JPEG and TIFF files by selecting them in Bridge and then choosing File → Open in Camera Raw (⌘+R/Ctrl+R).

# Converting Raw Files with Adobe Camera Raw

Now that you know all about raw files, it's time to see how the files are converted with ACR. In this section, I discuss ideas such as histograms and clipping, without completely defining them. That's because I cover them in detail as they relate to Photoshop in upcoming chapters. This section is intended as an overview of the process.

Those of you who aren't shooting raw may choose to skip this section. For those of you who are shooting raw, my aim is to give you a rudimentary understanding of the ACR workspace and how it's used to convert raw files so you're able to work with your own raw files as you explore upcoming chapters.

# Overview of the ACR workspace

To open a raw file in ACR, double-click it in Bridge. You can also open multiple files by selecting them in Bridge first, and then double-clicking one of them. Figure 4.7 shows the ACR workspace.

This workspace is packed with editing tools and lots of useful information. Here's a list of the main features:

- **Toolbar.** The toolbar at the top left contains tools for viewing the image, such as the Hand and Zoom tools, and other tools for editing the image, such as the Crop and Spot Removal tools. Oftentimes, the things you can do with the editing tools are best left for Photoshop, when you can make the adjustments after the file is converted.

However, when you're working with multiple photos, you can save time with some of these tools, such as the Crop tool, by using it on one photo and then sharing its settings with other, similar photos.

- **Main preview area.** Use the zoom presets at the bottom left of the screen to quickly change the preview magnification. Use the Hand tool to click and drag the image to reposition it.

- **Histogram.** A histogram is provided at the top right so that you can monitor its changes while adjusting tonality and color. The histogram has two small triangles above it. These triangles are used to indicate tonal clipping. (Clipping refers to the loss of highlight or shadow detail that occurs when data is pushed off the end of the histogram.) The triangle on the left is used to monitor shadow clipping and the triangle on the right is used to monitor

**Figure 4.7**

highlight clipping. In Figure 4.7, the shadow clipping indicator is active, indicating that shadow detail is being lost. (Histograms and clipping are explained in detail in Chapter 5.)

## tip

When clipping is occurring, you can see a preview overlay on the image by hovering over the clipping indicator on the Histogram. Highlight clipping is indicated as red and shadow clipping as blue. When you click on a clipping indicator you turn it on permanently so that clipping is always displayed on the image. You'll know the preview is turned on because it will have a white box around it. This is a great way to see exactly where tonal detail is being lost in the image, but it can be hard to see in images with lots of color, such as the shot of the balloons in Figure 4.7.

- **Adjustment panels.** Eight panels are stacked on the right side of the workspace. Select a panel's icon from the row to make it the active panel. The Basic panel is the active panel in Figure 4.7. It's used for 90 percent of the adjustments made to most raw files because it covers all of the basic tonal and color adjustments. The controls on it are arranged in the order they are typically used, starting from the top.

- **Workflow Options.** At the bottom of the workspace, in the center, is a hyperlink that allows you to create the kind of file you want to use in Photoshop. If you recall, attributes such as color space and resolution are not applied to a raw file when it's created in the camera. When you click this link, the Workflow Options dialog box opens, allowing you to choose the file attributes you want to apply before the photo is opened in Photoshop.

## note

The Size menu in the Workflow Options is used to resize the image during conversion, allowing you to create a file that's closer to the size you need. The size presets with a minus sign (-) to the right are smaller than the native pixel dimensions and the presets with a plus sign (+) are larger than the native size.

- **Action buttons.** After you make all your adjustments to an image, the action buttons at the bottom of the screen give you different choices as to how you proceed with the file. Open Image opens the file in Photoshop with all of the ACR settings applied. Cancel cancels the operation and closes ACR. Done applies any adjustments to the raw file without opening it into Photoshop.

- **Save Image button.** Use this dialog to save raw files to another file format without having to open them into Photoshop. For example, a folder of raw files can be converted to JPEGs for printing at a lab.

## note

Notice that there are no file types, such as TIFF or PSD, anywhere in the ACR dialog. That's because you choose this attribute later, when you save the file in Photoshop using the Save As command.

## Converting a raw file for editing in Photoshop

There are two basic ways to work with files in ACR. The first scenario is to open a single image in ACR, make some editing modifications to it, and then open the file into Photoshop for advanced editing. Here are the basic steps for converting a raw file for use in Photoshop. If you want to try this process out with one of my photos first, go to www.wiley.com/go/photoshopcs4ats and download the file named Balloon_Fest.CR2 and select it as the file you want to work on. This is the example used in the steps.

**1** In Bridge, select the raw file you want to convert for editing in Photoshop (your own or Balloon_Fest.CR2 from the Web site), and double-click it to open it in ACR. The ACR dialog box opens and looks similar to Figure 4.7. If you are walking through the steps with the file from the Web site, make sure you have it open now.

**2** Select the file in Bridge and double-click it to open the photo in ACR. When the ACR dialog opens, it should look similar to Figure 4.7.

**3** Click the White Balance dropdown menu to choose a different white balance preset to apply as an overall color correction. You can also use the Temperature and Tint sliders to make custom changes. The default shown is the white balance setting the camera was set on. The list in Figure 4.8 shows the presets available. These are the same presets usually found in a camera. The fact that you can change this file quality is an indication that the camera's white balance was not permanently assigned to the file when it was created. If none of the presets suits you, consider using the Temperature and Tint sliders to fine-tune the overall color balance. As soon as you move one of these sliders, Custom is displayed in the White Balance menu.

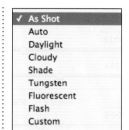

Figure 4.8

**4** If the clipping indicators above the histogram both display color, it means you are losing highlight and shadow detail. When turned on, highlight clipping shows up as a red overlay and shadow clipping is indicated by a blue overlay. You will definitely see this if you are using the Balloon_Fest.CR2 file.

**5** Drag the Exposure slider to the left while watching the highlight indicator on the right. The Exposure slider is used to control the brightest tones in the image. Stop dragging as soon as you see the color disappear from the indicator. For the Ballon_Fest.CR2 file, this should be somewhere around the value of –0.10.

**6** Move down to the Blacks slider and move it to the left while watching the Shadow Clipping indicator. The Blacks slider is used to control the darkest tones in the image. If you are using the Ballon_Fest.CR2 file, you will notice that it isn't possible to get the color to disappear from the clipping indicator, even with a Blacks value of 0. This means that some detail is still being lost in the darkest part of the image.

**7** **Adjust the overall brightness of the image by dragging the Brightness slider to the right to lighten the image.** I stopped at value of +75 in the Ballon_Fest.CR2 image. Red now shows in the Highlight clipping indicator because the brightest tones were affected by the Brightness adjustment. You could try readjusting the Exposure slider to compensate, but there's a better way.

**8** **Drag the Recovery slider to bring the brightest highlights into line and remove the color from the Highlight clipping indicator.** The Recovery slider is used to recover difficult highlight detail. For the Ballon_Fest.CR2 image, I used a value of 12.

**9** **Experiment with the Fill Light slider.** The Fill Light slider is used to lighten difficult shadows, much like a fill flash is used when shooting, but keep in mind that using it or the Recovery slider tends to reduce the contrast of the image and flatten the tonal range, which is why I skipped these originally — these sliders are only used when necessary.

# tip

The most important thing when preparing a file to open into Photoshop is to give yourself some editing headroom. That means being careful to leave space for adjusting highlights and shadows by not clipping them now.

**10** **Click on the Workflow Options hyperlink.** When the Workflow Options dialog box opens, fill it out with the values shown in Figure 4.9 and click OK.

**11** **Click the Open Image button from the ACR dialog box to open the file in Photoshop.** Feel free to explore some of the other editing panels before opening the file. The concepts behind them are discussed in future chapters as they relate to Photoshop. When you finish this book I recommend that you revisit these panels because you'll have a better understanding of how they're used.

# caution

Be careful about applying sharpening in the Detail panel at this point. Until you have a better understanding of sharpening, which is discussed in detail in Chapter 12, it's best to stay with the Camera Raw defaults.

**Figure 4.9**

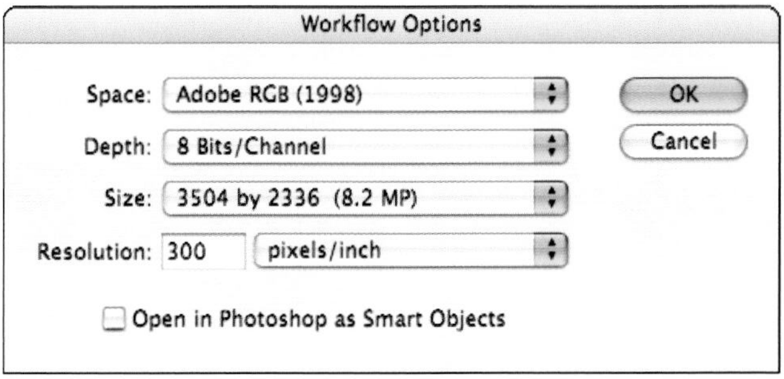

| Workflow Options | | |
|---|---|---|
| Space: | Adobe RGB (1998) | OK |
| Depth: | 8 Bits/Channel | Cancel |
| Size: | 3504 by 2336 (8.2 MP) | |
| Resolution: | 300  pixels/inch | |
| ☐ Open in Photoshop as Smart Objects | | |

# Working with multiple photos in ACR

Another way to use ACR is to open multiple files into ACR, edit them, and then click either the Done button or the Save Image button. This allows you to edit the tones and colors of the photos so that they look better. Then they can be used for slideshows or bulk conversion into another file format such as DNG without ever being opened in Photoshop.

Here are the steps for working with multiple files in ACR:

**1** **Select the files you want to work with in Bridge.** Double-click any one to open all of them into ACR. When the ACR dialog opens, all of the files you chose are displayed in a filmstrip running up and down the left side of the screen, as

shown in Figure 4.10. When you click one of these thumbnails, the image is displayed in the main viewing area. When multiple files are open in ACR, two new buttons appear above the thumbnails: Select All and Synchronize.

## note

The badge with the two horizontal lines and triangles that appears on the first thumbnail in Figure 4.10 indicates that ACR adjustments have been applied to the photo. These badges also appear in Bridge.

**2** **Select an image so that it's displayed in the main viewing area.** Use the Basic panel to adjust its tonality and color.

**Figure 4.10**

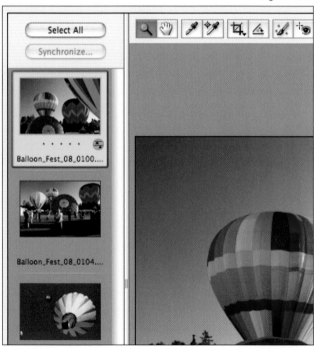

**3** Use the Workflow Options hyperlink to set up the type of file parameters you want to use with the file. These settings are sticky, meaning that they retain the values you give them. The settings are used for all ACR conversions until you change them to other values.

**4** When the first image looks good, move down to the next thumbnail and adjust it using the Basic adjustments panel. When it looks good, move to the next one, and so on.

**5** If you have similar images, you can quickly share settings by adjusting the first image and then selecting the other thumbnails with the Shift key or the ⌘/Ctrl key. If you want to select all of the thumbnails, click the Select All button above the thumbnails. Click the Synchronize button to open the Synchronize dialog shown in Figure 4.11. This button is only available when more than one thumbnail is in the filmstrip. Use the Synchronize dialog to selectively choose the information to be

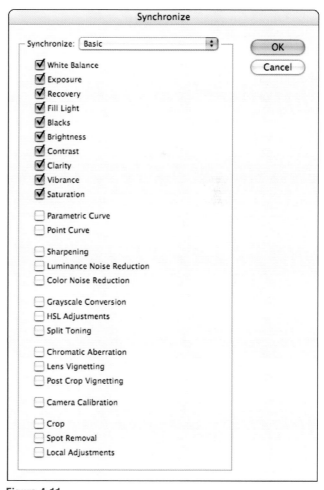

Figure 4.11

shared from the image in the main preview with the other selected photos. You can quickly isolate some of these common settings by choosing from the presets in the Synchronize menu at the top of the dialog. In Figure 4.11 I chose the Basic preset.

**6** **Click OK to apply the settings.**

# tip

When multiple thumbnails are selected, any changes made to the photo in the main preview are applied to all selected photos.

The ability to synchronize settings among similar photos is a real time saver. Even if they aren't exactly the same, it's a quick way to get them all into the ballpark. Then you can go back and quickly tweak each image to bring it into line. After all of the images are edited to your liking, you have a couple of options. The first is to click the Done button, which closes ACR and applies all of your changes to the raw file's metadata without opening them into Photoshop. Now when you create a Web gallery or a slideshow of them, they look just like you want them to look because when you reopen the photos into ACR, they open with the settings you last applied.

The second option is to click the Save Image button below the thumbnails in ACR. This opens the Save Options dialog box, shown in Figure 4.12. This dialog box allows you to create a second set of derivative files from your raw files that are a different file type.

**Figure 4.12**

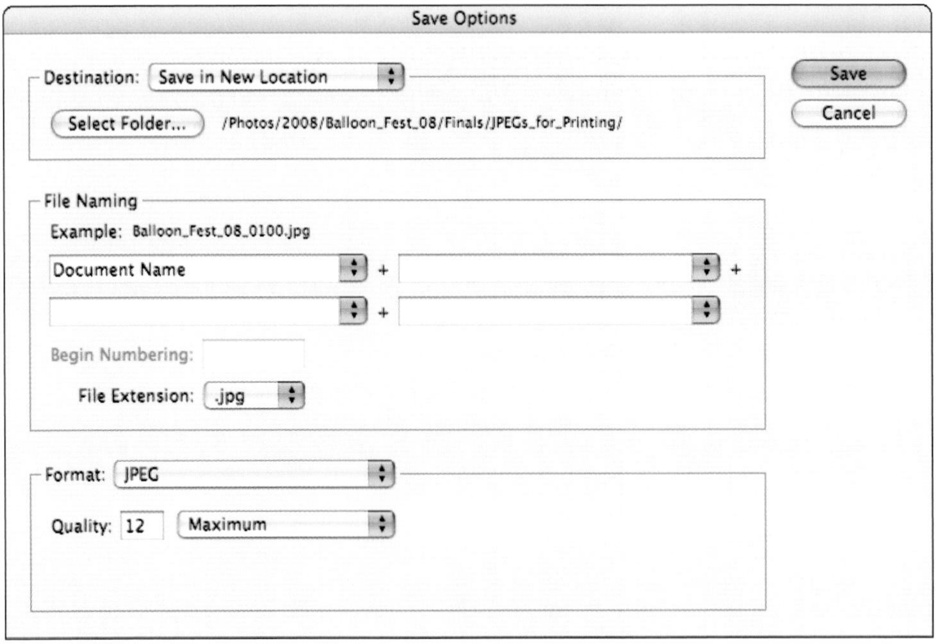

# tip

If your changes aren't showing in Bridge, it could be because the cache hasn't updated. Choose View→Refresh (F5) to allow Bridge to go back through the folder and update its cache.

Take a closer look at the options in the Save Options dialog:

- **Destination.** You can choose between saving the files in the same folder or selecting a different folder for them. For organizational purposes, it's best to use the Select Folder button to create a subfolder for the derivative files following the guidelines discussed in Chapter 1.

- **Fine Naming.** This field allows you to change the name of the derivative files. I generally recommend against this because it makes it more difficult to match the derivative file to its parent raw file.

  A second part of this area is the File Extension menu. Use this to determine the file format for the new files. The options are DNG, JPG, TIF, and PSD, all in upper- or lowercase. (On most modern computers, case doesn't make a difference. If you're in doubt, use lowercase.)

- **Format.** When you choose one of these file types, the Format area below it dynamically changes to offer options for that file format. Use it to create exactly the type of file you want.

The most common uses of the Save Options dialog are to convert large groups of raw photos into JPEGs for printing at a lab or for converting them into DNG files. For example, say that you need some JPEG files from 100 raw files for printing at a lab. One way to do that would be to open each photo in Photoshop and save it as a JPEG file. This would work, but it would take too long. A faster way would be to follow these steps:

1 **Select all of the photos for conversion in Bridge and double-click one of them to open in ACR.** You can now apply any editing that's necessary.

2 **Click the Select All button to select them when you are finished editing.**

3 **Click the Save Image button to open the Save Options dialog box.** Create a subfolder and choose JPEG from the File Extension menu and use the Format section to select the amount of compression you want. In this case, because you want to print the files, you should choose 12 for the highest quality.

4 **Click Save.** A set of JPEG files is created in the background without opening the files in Photoshop.

5 **Click Done.** ACR closes, revealing the Camera Raw Save Status dialog, shown in Figure 4.13, which allows you to monitor the progress of the saving.

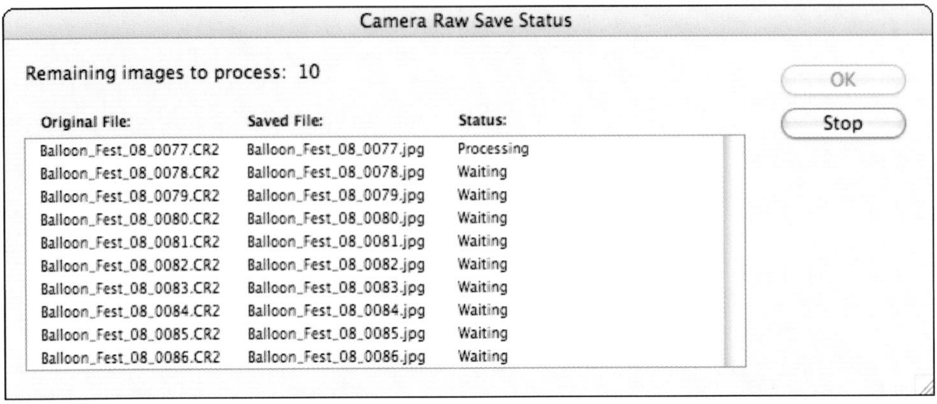

Camera Raw Save Status
Remaining images to process: 10
OK
Stop
Original File:
Saved File:
Status:
Balloon_Fest_08_0077.CR2 Balloon_Fest_08_0077.jpg Processing
Balloon_Fest_08_0078.CR2 Balloon_Fest_08_0078.jpg Waiting
Balloon_Fest_08_0079.CR2 Balloon_Fest_08_0079.jpg Waiting
Balloon_Fest_08_0080.CR2 Balloon_Fest_08_0080.jpg Waiting
Balloon_Fest_08_0081.CR2 Balloon_Fest_08_0081.jpg Waiting
Balloon_Fest_08_0082.CR2 Balloon_Fest_08_0082.jpg Waiting
Balloon_Fest_08_0083.CR2 Balloon_Fest_08_0083.jpg Waiting
Balloon_Fest_08_0084.CR2 Balloon_Fest_08_0084.jpg Waiting
Balloon_Fest_08_0085.CR2 Balloon_Fest_08_0085.jpg Waiting
Balloon_Fest_08_0086.CR2 Balloon_Fest_08_0086.jpg Waiting

**Figure 4.13**

# Comparing 8-bit and 16-bit files

Before you finish this chapter, there's one more issue that relates to raw that's good to know about. You may have noticed a field called Depth in the Workflow Options dialog box, shown in Figure 4.14. This setting allows you to leverage the huge amount of data contained in a raw file to create a 16-bit file instead of an 8-bit file. A 16-bit file uses 16 bits per color channel (red, green, and blue) to describe each pixel instead of the usual eight bits.

Though the number 16 is twice the number 8, the difference between 8-bit and 16-bit files is much larger. Consider this: an 8-bit file has 256 distinct tones and 16.7 million color definitions. A 16-bit file contains 65,000 different tones and 281 trillion colors. This may seem like overkill — and quite often it is. Humans can't even see 281 trillion individual colors. But if you're going to be making cumulative or massive adjustments in Photoshop, or if you're working with marginal original files, then having lots of extra editing headroom is good. That's because editing in Photoshop is destructive by its very nature. Data is even lost with simple tonal and color corrections. When you have a 16-bit file with lots of extra tones and colors, the data loss isn't as noticeable.

Workflow Options
Space:
8 Bits/Channel
Depth:
✓ 16 Bits/Channel
OK
Cancel
Size:
3504 by 2336 (8.2 MP)
Resolution:
300
pixels/inch
Open in Photoshop as Smart Objects

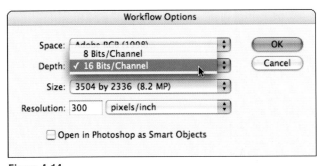

**Figure 4.14**

If you're not doing heavy editing to a file, the difference between 8-bit and 16-bit can be hard to see. For that reason it's best to work with 8-bit files when you can because 16-bit files are twice the size of 8-bit files, meaning they consume more hard drive space and other computer resources such as RAM.

# caution

Some commands in Photoshop don't work with 16-bit files. These commands are grayed out when a 16-bit file is open.

Another limitation to using 16-bit files is that not all file formats support 16-bit. For example, saving a 16-bit file in the JPEG file format is impossible. If you try to do it, you won't see a .jpg option under Format in the Save As dialog box. If you need a JPEG from a 16-bit file, you can convert the file to 8-bit by choosing Image → Mode → 8 Bits/Channel. Now you can save it as a .jpg, as well as all other common file formats.

# note

You can use the Image → Mode command to convert an 8-bit file to a 16-bit file, but in most cases this won't buy you much. It's like taking 30 kids out of a classroom and seating them throughout the school's auditorium. You still have the same 30 kids; they're just sitting further apart.

When you convert a raw file, you have the opportunity to do most of the tonal and color correction during the conversion process. This means that it won't be necessary to carry out these edits in Photoshop's destructive environment. Because of that, I recommend that you stick with 8-bit files for now. Just keep the 16-bit option in mind for those occasions that require heavy-lifting in Photoshop.

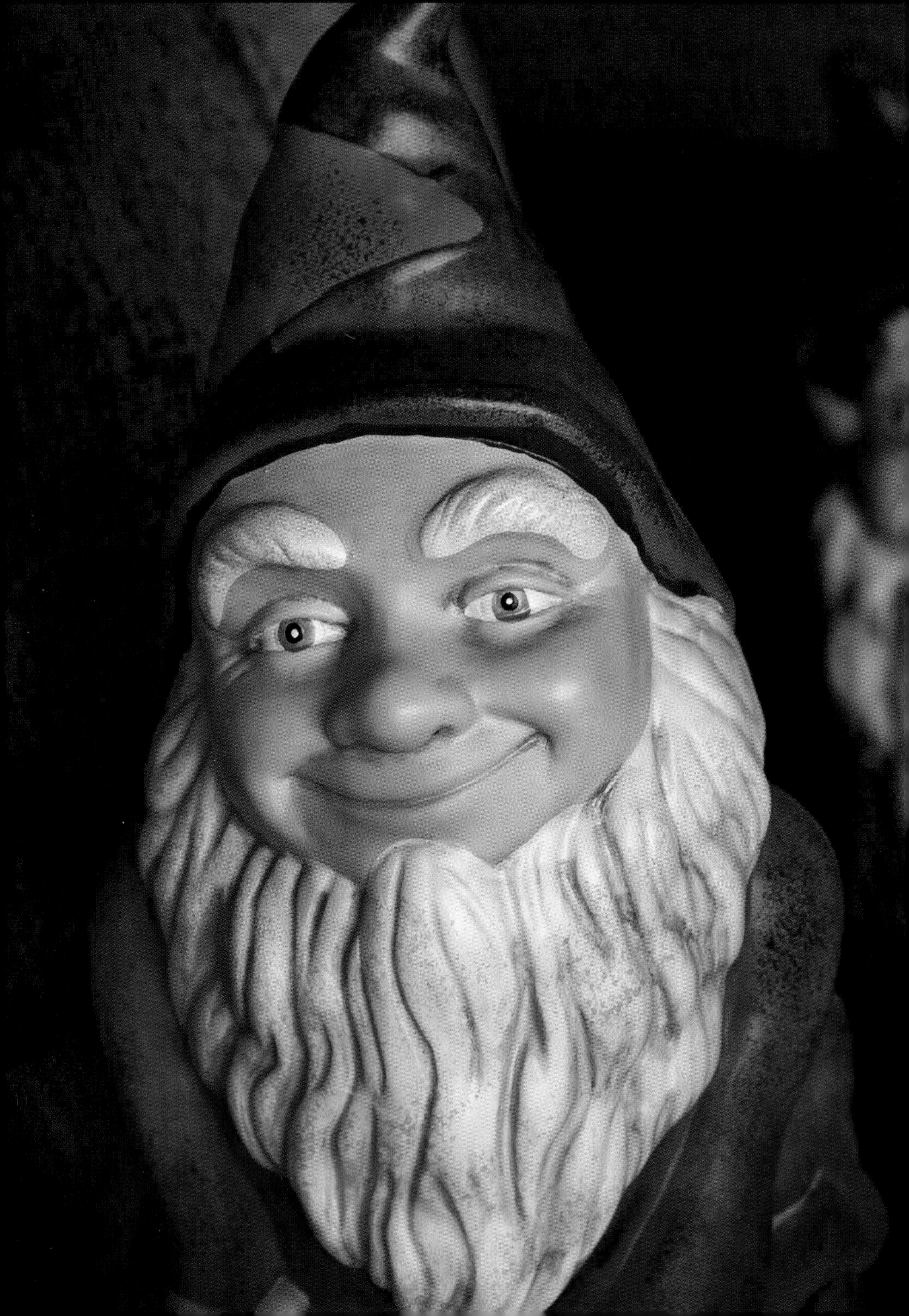

# 5

# Learning to Use the
# Photoshop Workspace

Photoshop is an amazing and powerful image editing application. It's the industry standard for just about anyone who works with digital images — in industries that range from architecture to medicine. Because Photoshop's workspace wasn't designed for a single workflow, it has a reputation for being non-intuitive and difficult to learn. The release of Photoshop Creative Suite 4 (CS4) signals a major effort on Adobe's part to minimize this problem, especially for photographers. Now the workspace is more intuitive than it's ever been, and important features are much easier to discover because Adobe has brought them to the surface. Because of these considerable efforts, this is the best time in years for a photographer to be learning to use Photoshop.

# Deconstructing the Workspace

In this chapter you learn everything you need to know about the workspace and how to customize it for your own needs. Then you see how Photoshop's preferences are used to control many aspects of Photoshop and its behavior. First, I'll begin deconstructing the workspace and breaking it down into its primary features, which cann all be seen in Figure 5.1.

- **Menu bar.** The menus across the top of the screen contain much of Photoshop's power. There are more than 400 commands buried in these menus so it's sometimes hard to remember where they are. Try to use the menu names as clues when you can. For example, if you're doing something with a layer, then you probably want the Layer menu. If you're working with a selection, then you want the Select menu.

## note

The Extended version of Photoshop CS4 has two menus that don't appear in the standard edition: Analysis and 3D. You don't need either of them to take advantage of what you learn in this book.

- **Application Frame.** This is new in Photoshop CS4 for Mac users. Traditionally Mac users are able to "see through" the application they're currently working in, allowing them to see other open programs or the desktop below the application. The Application Frame is a neutral gray background that fills the Photoshop workspace so that nothing below it can be seen. It's very similar to the standard Windows workspace. It can be expanded, minimized, or closed by clicking the

standard red, yellow, and green buttons. If images in the display area are undocked from the Application Frame, the frame can be minimized without hiding the images. This layout is similar to the way Photoshop looked on a Mac in previous versions. I like this new feature because it allows me to focus on the image at hand without being distracted by clutter in the background. If you don't like it, you can turn it off by choosing Window → Application Frame. (This option isn't available in the Window menu on a Windows system.)

- **Application bar.** The Application bar at the top of the workspace contains several application controls. On the left of the bar is the App icon. This icon is used to identify the application. On a Mac, it serves no further functionality. However, on a Windows system, it's used to access the standard system menu. In Windows, the Menu bar and the Application bar are combined into a single bar, whereas on a Mac, the menus are above the bar.

- **Options bar.** Directly below the Application bar is the Options bar. This section is used to modify the actions of the currently active tool. When a tool is selected from the Tools panel, the controls on the Options bar change to match that tool. (It's often called the Tool Options bar.)

- **Tools panel.** On the left side of the workspace is the Tools panel. This single column panel contains more than 60 tools. Several groups of similar tools are stacked together for organizational reasons. You can tell that a tool has other tools stacked below it by the small triangle icon that is at the lower right of the tool. Click and hold a tool to see the tools stacked below it.

**Figure 5.1**

To reposition the Tools panel, click and drag it by its title tab. To switch it to a double-column display, which is the way the Tools panel used to look before Photoshop CS3, click the double arrows on the panel's header. (Note that I will be referring to the single-column configuration throughout this book.)

- **Document window.** The central viewing area is where all of the work is done. Every time a photo is opened, it's displayed in this area. Information about the document appears at the top and bottom of its window. There are a number of viewing options that are used to change the way these images display. I discuss them in a moment.

- **Panels.** Panels allow you to make modifications to your photos as well as keep track of various aspects of them. Panels are quite powerful and flexible. They can be relocated, collapsed, or removed from the workspace. Some even have their own menus that allow you to access extra features and commands. Because you'll be working with panels extensively it's a good idea to take a closer look at how they function.

# Working with Panels

Photoshop's panels have been part of the program from the earliest days. They used to be called palettes because of their free-floating nature. Now the way they're managed and used has changed significantly, making the term panel more appropriate. Take a look at some of the main characteristics of working with panels.

## Panel groups

Panels are typically grouped together to save space. Figure 5.2 shows the Navigator, Histogram, and Info panel group. If this panel group isn't currently visible, you can add it to the workspace by selecting any of the panels in the group from the Window menu.

**Figure 5.2**

Clicking a panel's tab brings it to the front of the group. The order of the tabs is modified by clicking and dragging them to the desired location. An individual panel is removed from a group by clicking and dragging it out of the group. It then becomes a free-floating panel that can be located anywhere on the screen or closed by clicking the close button at the top.

## The panel dock

By default, panel groups are displayed in the panel dock. A dock is a collection of panels or panel groups that are displayed together in a vertical orientation. You can see the panel dock in Figure 5.1. You move a panel group out of the dock by clicking and dragging it by the right side of its gray header bar. When a panel group is removed from the dock, it becomes free-floating and can be placed anywhere on the screen. If you click and drag an individual panel's tab, that panel alone is removed from the dock.

Free-floating panel groups are added to the dock by dragging the group onto the dock. When the group is over the dock, a blue line indicates where the panel group is placed when the mouse button is released. Panels within the dock are rearranged using the same technique.

One of the nice things about the panel dock is that it can be collapsed when panels aren't needed, giving you more space for viewing images. Figure 5.3 shows the collapsed version and the expanded version of the same panels. The dock is collapsed by clicking the Expand/Collapse button (double-arrow icon) at the top right of the dock's header. Click the button again to expand a collapsed dock. When the dock is collapsed, you can click and drag it's left side to increase or decrease it's width. In the collapsed view in Figure 5.3, I expanded the dock so that you could still see the names of the panels. When the dock is fully collapsed, only the icons for the panels are shown.

**Figure 5.3**

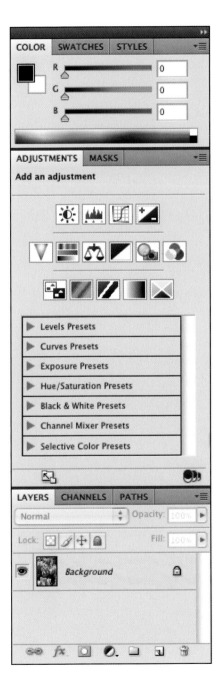

# note

When there are too many panels for the panel dock to display in a single column, the dock is expanded to a double-column dock. Each of these columns is individually collapsible.

A handy feature of the collapsed dock is the ability to quickly access a panel inside the dock by clicking its icon instead of expanding the dock. In Figure 5.4 you can see the Layers panel group opens when you click the Layers icon. This allows you to do something quickly with that panel and then collapse it back into the dock by clicking the icon again or clicking the Collapse button.

# tip

To temporarily hide all panels, press Tab. Press it again to unhide them. This is a great way to focus on your image by hiding all of the clutter.

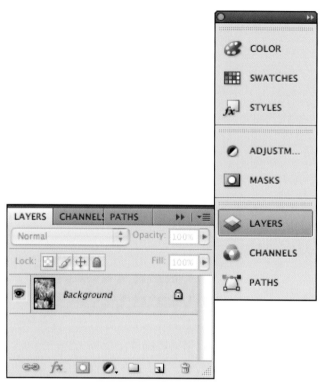

**Figure 5.4**

# The panel menu

Nearly every panel has its own menu that you access by clicking the Panel menu button at the top right of the panel. Because this menu is specific for the current panel, its contents vary from panel to panel. Sometimes, as in the case of the Layers panel, the panel menu's contents are extensive. Other times, as with the Histogram panel menu shown in Figure 5.5, the contents are somewhat basic.

The panel menu functions in two ways. First you use it to change properties of the panel. Secondly, and more importantly, it often contains shortcuts to common menu commands. This saves you time by not having to dig through menus to find the command you need. For example, when I need to flatten layers in an image, it's faster to access the Flatten command from the Layers panel menu instead of finding it at the bottom of the Layers menu.

**Figure 5.5**

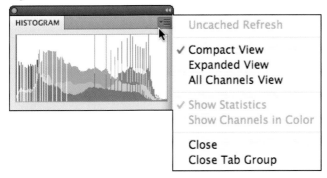

# Personalizing Photoshop

Photoshop can be used in so many ways that it's important for users to be able to customize its user interface to suit their particular needs. The two most important ways of personalizing Photoshop are creating a workspace that suits your particular needs and creating custom keyboard shortcuts and menus that allow you to work faster.

## Customizing the workspace

As you can see, there's quite a bit of flexibility in how the workspace can be laid out in Photoshop. Panels can be configured and located just about anywhere. You can even move them to a second monitor to free up more space for viewing documents. This allows you to create a workspace that suits the way you work. Like Bridge, Photoshop comes with several workspace presets. These presets are selected from the Workspace menu, shown in Figure 5.6, on the right side of the Application bar. (The can also be selected by choosing Window → Workspace.)

Like Bridge, Photoshop has a Workspace Switcher button on the Application bar. When you click on it you get a menu that's almost identical to the menu shown in Figure 5.6. The only missing item is the Keyboard Shortcuts & Menus option.

Each of the workspaces shown in the Workspace menu is designed to accommodate a particular workflow. For example, when the Video workspace is selected, the panels commonly used in video editing are opened, and panels not used for video editing are closed. I find that the Color and Tone workspace comes closest to the workspace I prefer, but it's missing the History panel, which is important to me. However, it's easy for me to create the workspace I want by selecting the History panel from the Window menu and then dragging it into the top panel group to add it. Then I save this workspace by choosing Window → Workspace → Save Workspace. My custom workspace is then added to the workspace presets in the Workspace menu and in the Workspace Switcher menu.

## tip

If you're using a workspace preset and you make changes to its layout, you can reset the layout by choosing the preset again.

**Figure 5.6**

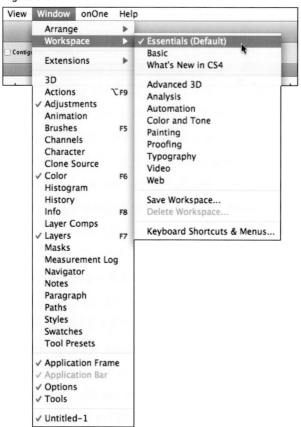

# Customizing menus

You can customize your menus to help you easily find important commands. This is quite helpful when dealing with menus that have lots of options, like the Layers menu. To check out this feature, choose Edit ➞ Menus. When the Keyboard Shortcuts and Menus dialog box opens, click the menu you want to work with from the list to expand it. Then find the specific command you're interested in and click None in the Color column. When the color menu opens, choose the color you want. In Figure 5.7 you can see that I assigned red to the File ➞ Open Recent command. When I click OK, that menu command

always has a color displayed around it until I change workspaces. If you make changes, be sure to save your workspace before switching.

Sometimes when you change workspaces you see the dialog box shown in Figure 5.8. This dialog appears when you make modifications to any of the menus or keyboard shortcuts. For example, when you switch to the What's New in CS4 workspace preset, every menu that has a feature that's been added or changed appears in blue. This is a great way for someone who upgrades from CS3 to hone in on new and improved features.

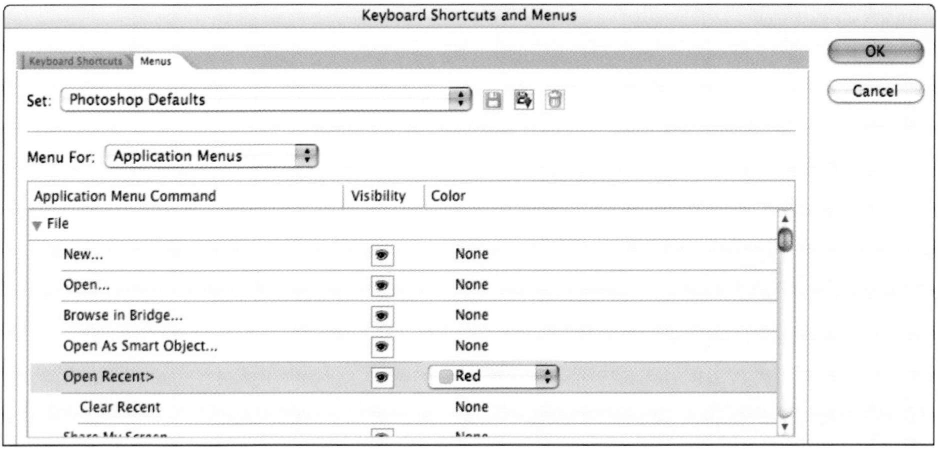

**Figure 5.7**

**Figure 5.8**

tip

You can also color code menu items in the panel menus by choosing Panel Menus from the Menu for pop-up menu in the Keyboard Shortcuts and Menus dialog box.

You can also customize keyboard shortcuts. To change any of them, use the Keyboard Shortcuts tab in the Keyboard Shortcuts and Menus dialog box. You can also access this dialog by choosing Edit ➔ Keyboard Shortcuts. I don't go into detail on that here because I want to encourage you to hold off on changing keyboard shortcuts for the time being. You'll want to learn the standard shortcut now to avoid confusion. Just be aware that you can customize them later after you're more comfortable with Photoshop's workspace.

# Different Ways of Viewing Images

When a photo is open in Photoshop, you have a number of options as to how you view that photo. In earlier versions of Photoshop, most of these options were buried in the menus. Now, in Photoshop CS4, they're in plain sight on the Application bar, which is shown in Figure 5.9. Take a look at these options and how you can use them to change your viewing environment.

## View Extras

You use the View Extras button, shown in Figure 5.10, to quickly hide or show guides or grid, in the display area. It's also used to add a ruler on the left side and the top of the document window.

- **Guide.** A guide is a horizontal or vertical line that's overlaid on a photo. It helps you align different image elements when you're moving layer content. To add a guide, choose View→New Guide. Then use the New Guide dialog to specify whether you want the guide to be vertical or horizontal, and how far you want it from the top or the left side of the image frame. If you need to reposition a guide, select the Move tool (V), the tool that's at the top of the Tools panel, and hover over the guide until a two-headed arrow appears. Then click and drag the guide. To remove a guide, click and drag it out of the frame. To remove all guides, choose View→Clear Guides.

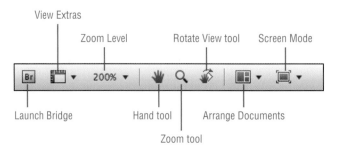

**Figure 5.9**

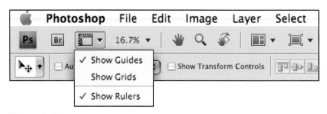

**Figure 5.10**

# tip

When you're using guides, they can sometimes be distracting. Instead of removing them by choosing View → Clear Guides, it's often better to use the View Extras button to temporarily hide them.

- **Grid.** A grid is just that: a grid overlay that you use to view image content. You add a grid to all open photos by choosing View → Extras → Show Grid. You change the properties of the grid (and guides as well), using Photoshop's preferences.

# note

Though guides and grids are visible in a photo when you open it in Photoshop, and in some other editing applications, they don't print when you print the file.

- **Ruler.** The Ruler is useful when you want to measure something or get an idea of how close your current zoom setting is to the actual size of the photo. Another very useful thing about the Ruler is that you can click and drag from the ruler into the image to add a guide. This is the method I always use to add a new guide because I can quickly place it exactly where I want it. To add a horizontal guide use the horizontal ruler, and to add a vertical guide use the vertical ruler. Just click and drag the guide to the desired position.

# see also

I discuss using the Ruler in more detail when I cover sharpening in Chapter 12.

## Zooming and panning

There are several methods for changing the magnification of the current photo. One way is to use one of the presets in the Zoom Level menu on the Application bar, just to the right of the View Extras button. However, these presets are limited to only four choices: 25%, 50%, 100%, and 200%. Sometimes one of these magnification presets is desirable, but not always. Because of that, it's best for you to know about a couple of other ways to change the magnification of your photo.

### The Zoom tool

You use the Zoom tool (Z) to change the magnification of an image. It looks like a magnifying glass. You can select it from the Application menu or from the Tools panel. Click on the photo to zoom in. Alt+click to zoom out. You can also select the magnifying glass icon with a minus sign (−) on it from the Options bar to switch the Zoom tool to zoom-out mode. If your system supports OpenGL (Open Graphics Library), you can hold the mouse button down to get continuous zooming. Release the button when the zoom is at the level you want. Additionally, OpenGL must be enabled in Photoshop's General preferences.

# tip

You can also use keyboard shortcuts to zoom the image. Use ⌘++/Ctrl++ to zoom in and ⌘+−/Ctrl+− to zoom out. These shortcuts zoom the image to standard presets that include: 16.7%, 25%, 33.3%, 50%, 66.7%, and 100%.

## What is OpenGL?

OpenGL, a type of video processing, was developed by Silicon Graphics in 1992 and is used in a wide range of applications such as flight simulators and computer aided design (CAD) software. It relies on a set of standard video functions that can be called upon by Photoshop when displaying an image. If your video card is unable to handle these functions, they won't be available to you. If you want them, you'll need to upgrade your video card to a more powerful card. Adobe has a list of approved video cards on its Web site.

When the Zoom tool is active, the Options bar, shown in Figure 5.11, is populated with choices for using this tool. When Resize Windows To Fit is checked, the size of the window area around the image resizes to fit the zoom level. Note that this only works when each open file is floating in its own window. You use Zoom All Windows to zoom all open documents at the same time.

The four buttons on the right of the Options bar are zoom presets that you can use to quickly change a document's magnification to a different set of standard size presets. The buttons are as follows:

- **Actual Pixels.** This button changes the magnification to 100 percent (also known as 1:1 magnification). This magnification preset is used to view the image on the pixel level, meaning that each pixel is discernable. You can also achieve this magnification using ⌘+1/Ctrl+1.

- **Fit Screen.** This magnification preset fits the image to the screen so that it fills as much of the screen as possible without hiding any of the image. If you use the Tab key to hide all panels, the image will fill even more of the screen.

# note

The current magnification amount is displayed on the photo's tab, or header section if it's not in Tab mode.

- **Fill Screen.** This setting is similar to Fit Screen except that the screen is filled to fit the photo's shortest dimension. For example, if the photo is horizontal, the screen is filled to fit the photo's height while hiding each end of the photo on the horizontal dimension.

- **Print Size.** This preset is used to display the image at the approximate size it will be when it's printed. This setting is affected by your system's display settings, as well as the photo's resolution. If you work with a high screen resolution, you'll find that the image displays smaller than actual size. A low resolution produces the opposite result.

# see also

Resolution and screen display are covered in detail in Chapter 12. In that chapter, you learn how to find the exact print size for your display.

**Figure 5.11**

## Bird's-eye view

A cool new zooming feature in Photoshop CS4 is called Bird's-eye view. This feature is used when you're zoomed in close to an image and you want to quickly pull back on the zoom and relocate a different area to zoom back in on. Here's how you do it:

**1** **Zoom in close on a photo so that you can only see a portion of it.** Try zooming to at least 100 percent.

**2** **Hold down the H key and click on the image, but don't release the mouse button.** When you do, the zoom backs out so that you can see the entire image and a box indicates the area you were previously zoomed in on.

**3** **Drag the box to the new area that you want to zoom in on and release the mouse button.** The magnification is now reset to the value you started with in step one.

The Bird's-eye zoom feature is a really fast way to reposition the zoom on the document. Experiment with it until you're comfortable using it. I guarantee it will become a staple in your workflow. This feature is dependent on the availability of OpenGL.

## The Hand tool

The Hand tool (H) is often used in conjunction with the Zoom tool. It's used to pan the image while it's zoomed in too much to see the entire image. To use the Hand tool, select it from the Application bar or from the Tools panel. It's located just above the Zoom tool on the Tools panel and is stacked with the Rotate View tool. When the Hand tool is selected, the Options bar has almost the same set of options as when the Zoom tool is selected.

Something new in Photoshop CS4 is the ability to flick the image by quickly clicking and dragging one side of it with the Hand tool and then releasing the mouse button. When you do this the image moves by itself until it slowly comes to a stop. You can stop the flick motion by pressing the Spacebar. Note that the ability to flick-pan is dependent on OpenGL.

# tip

A fast way to access the Hand tool without having to select it from the Tools panel or the Applications bar is to hold down the Spacebar. When you do, the tool becomes available until you release the Spacebar. This allows you to quickly access it without changing tools.

## Rotate View tool

The Rotate View tool is new in Photoshop CS4. It allows you to rotate the current view without actually rotating the image, which changes the image on a pixel level. This is extremely useful for people who do lots of painting and drawing on their images. It's similar to a painter rotating her canvas so that she can more easily apply difficult brush strokes in a natural manner. Before the Rotate View tool this wasn't possible in Photoshop without changing the image's pixels instead of just the way they're displayed.

To use the Rotate View tool, select it from the Applications bar or the Tools panel. Then click and drag the display area to rotate the image to the right or left. Click the Reset View button on the Options bar when you're ready to return the image to its original orientation. You can also press the Esc key to reset the original orientation.

# tip

You may have figured this out by now, but the Esc key is used to cancel almost any command or process in Photoshop.

Be advised that this tool is also tied to OpenGL. If your system isn't capable of processing OpenGL, you won't be able to use this tool. This cool new tool is a much better reason for upgrading your video card than flick-panning or Bird's-eye view, especially if you work with a graphics tablet.

## Arrange documents menu

When multiple photos are open in Photoshop, you can be arrange them inside the workspace several different ways. By default each image is opened in Tab mode, which means that the photos are stacked on top of one another with only the current image visible. Individual images are brought to the front of the stack by clicking their tabs. This is convenient when you want to focus on a specific image, but it makes it difficult when you want to compare images or transfer information between images. An individual image can be completely removed from the tab by clicking and dragging it by its header bar. If you want view all files at once, use the Arrange Documents menu, shown in Figure 5.12. This menu is accessed using the Arrange Documents button on the Applications bar.

The Arrange Documents menu lists several buttons that represent different configurations. These configurations are called n-up, with n representing the number of images to be displayed. 2-up refers to two images and 5-up refers to five images. Only buttons that correspond to the number of open images are available. For example, if three images are open, all configurations higher than 3-up are grayed

out. Open a few images and try experimenting with the various configurations so you can see how they work.

Another feature of this menu is the list of display options shown at the bottom of the menu. You're already familiar with a couple of these commands; here's a look at the others.

*   **Float All in Windows.** When this option is chosen, each photo is placed into its own window and the windows are tiled on top of one another. This is similar to the default arrangement Photoshop has used for many years. An individual photo is brought to the front by clicking it, making it the active photo — the photo that is affected by any commands or editing steps.

**Figure 5.12**

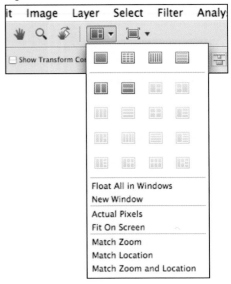

# caution

If images are free-floating and the application frame is minimized, when the frame is un-minimized it will open on top of the free-floating image, hiding them. To solve this, click the Consolidate All button, the first button in the Arrange Documents menu. Then click Float All in Windows to float them again.

- **New Window.** This opens the currently active photo as a new document. The second document is a live copy of the original photo. Any changes made to either version are applied to the other. It's tabbed next to its corresponding original. This is useful when you want a second version of the current photo; for example, when you want to compare two different zoom levels. You can work zoomed in close on one document, while checking the affects on the entire image in the second window.

- **Match Zoom, Match Location, and Match Zoom and Location.** These options are used to match the zoom and/or location of all photos to the currently active photo.

## Screen Mode menu

You use the Screen Mode menu on the Application bar, shown in Figure 5.13, to change the way the area surrounding a photo is displayed. There are two options in addition to the Standard Screen Mode, which is the default.

## Figure 5.13

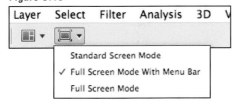

- **Full Screen Mode With Menu Bar.** This option brings the selected image to the front and hides any other images behind it. This is different from the Tabbed mode because none of the other photos are directly available while in this mode.

# tip

You can always access any open document using the Window menu. Simply choose from the list of open files displayed at the bottom of the menu.

- **Full Screen Mode.** This option is similar to Full Screen Mode With Menu Bar except that it also hides the Menu bar, the Applications bar, and all panels. Panels are accessed by mousing over the side of the screen where they're hidden, or by pressing the Tab key. Photoshop reminds you of this when you select this mode by displaying the dialog box shown in Figure 5.14.

Another thing that's different about Full Screen Mode is that the image is surrounded with a black field instead of a gray one. I find this useful when I want to isolate a photo to get a better look at it.

# tip

You can cycle through these three modes using the F key. Every time you press the F key, the mode advances to the next one on the list.

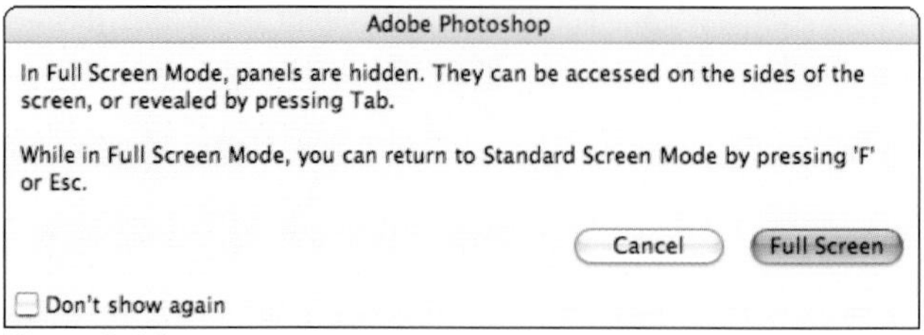

Adobe Photoshop

In Full Screen Mode, panels are hidden. They can be accessed on the sides of the screen, or revealed by pressing Tab.

While in Full Screen Mode, you can return to Standard Screen Mode by pressing 'F' or Esc.

Cancel    Full Screen

☐ Don't show again

**Figure 5.14**

# Setting Up Preferences

Before you begin using Photoshop, it's a good idea to insure that the preferences are correctly set up for the way you want to work. To open Photoshop's preferences choose Photoshop → Preferences (Edit → Preferences) and then choose a preference set from the menu. Photoshop is loaded with preferences, but some are more important than others. I focus on those important preferences here, starting with the General preferences.

## General preferences

In Chapter 3 you got a quick look at the History Log section of Photoshop's General preferences. Now is a good time to look at the rest of the options in the General preferences, shown in Figure 5.15. All the selected preferences are selected by default. If your system doesn't support OpenGL, Animated Zoom and Enable Flick Panning are grayed-out.

# note

If you make a change to a specific preference, but you don't see any change in Photoshop's behavior, close and reopen Photoshop to update the preferences.

# tip

Select other preferences sets by choosing from the menu on the left or by using the Prev or Next buttons on the right.

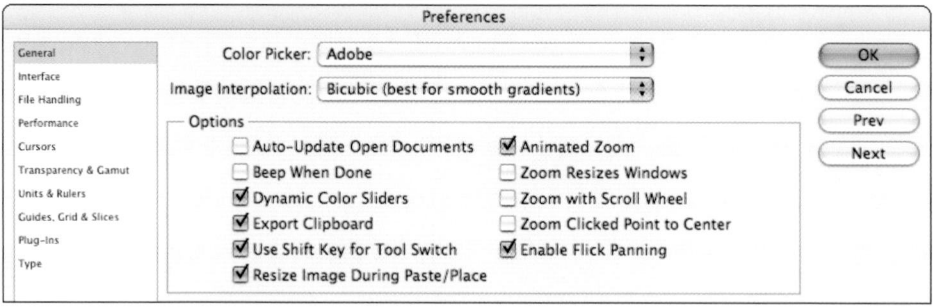

Preferences

| General | Color Picker: | Adobe | | OK |
| Interface | Image Interpolation: | Bicubic (best for smooth gradients) | | Cancel |
| File Handling | | | | Prev |
| Performance | Options | | | Next |
| Cursors | ☐ Auto-Update Open Documents | ☑ Animated Zoom | |
| Transparency & Gamut | ☐ Beep When Done | ☐ Zoom Resizes Windows | |
| Units & Rulers | ☑ Dynamic Color Sliders | ☐ Zoom with Scroll Wheel | |
| Guides, Grid & Slices | ☑ Export Clipboard | ☐ Zoom Clicked Point to Center | |
| Plug-Ins | ☑ Use Shift Key for Tool Switch | ☑ Enable Flick Panning | |
| Type | ☑ Resize Image During Paste/Place | | |

**Figure 5.15**

Selecting Zoom Resizes Windows insures that the size of the window surrounding the open photo resizes to match the size of the photo when its magnification is changed. This is most convenient when zooming out. Another option to consider here is Zoom with Scroll Wheel. This changes the function of your mouse's scroll wheel from panning up and down to zooming it in and out. It's the fastest way to change the magnification of a photo. It also allows you to zoom to a wide range of zoom settings, unlike the standard zoom presets.

## Interface preferences

The Interface preferences, shown in Figure 5.16, allow you to change the look and feel of Photoshop's preferences. The options here are greatly expanded from previous versions of Photoshop. The upper area in the General section allows you to control the background color in all three screen modes.

The Panels & Documents section is used to control how panels and documents are displayed. Some people, especially some Mac users, don't like working with tabbed documents. If you're one of those people, this is where you can turn off that display behavior permanently so that you don't have to change the document arrangement every time you open Photoshop. This option isn't available with the Windows version.

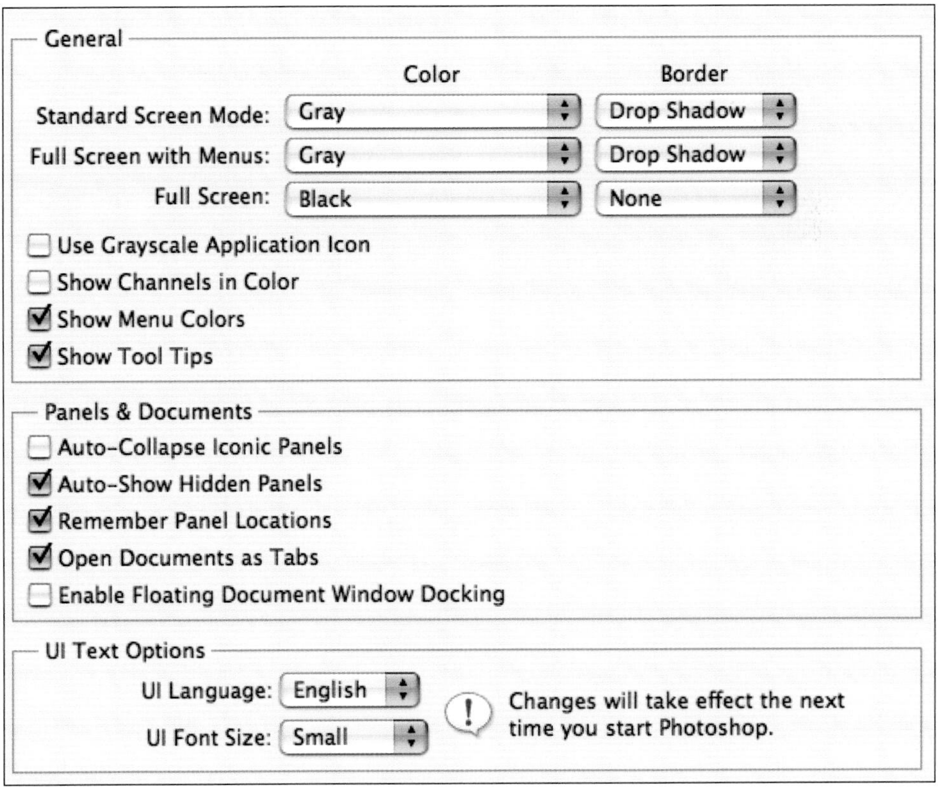

Figure 5.16

| | Color | Border |
|---|---|---|
| Standard Screen Mode: | Gray | Drop Shadow |
| Full Screen with Menus: | Gray | Drop Shadow |
| Full Screen: | Black | None |

General
- ☐ Use Grayscale Application Icon
- ☐ Show Channels in Color
- ☑ Show Menu Colors
- ☑ Show Tool Tips

Panels & Documents
- ☐ Auto–Collapse Iconic Panels
- ☑ Auto–Show Hidden Panels
- ☑ Remember Panel Locations
- ☑ Open Documents as Tabs
- ☐ Enable Floating Document Window Docking

UI Text Options
- UI Language: English
- UI Font Size: Small

(!) Changes will take effect the next time you start Photoshop.

Figure 5.16

Another option that's only in the Mac version is Enable Floating Document Window Docking. When this is selected, floating document windows can be docked as tabs in another document window by dragging it by its title bar and dropping it onto the second document. This option is on by default when using the Windows version of Photoshop and cannot be changed. The reason it was added to the Mac version is to accommodate the way Mac users are accustomed to working with document windows.

# File Handling preferences

The File Handling preferences are used to manage some idiosyncrasies of how some files are opened and saved. The File Compatibility section, shown in Figure 5.17, is the most important section here. You use the Camera Raw Preferences button to access the Camera Raw preferences you learned about in Chapter 2. There are two other settings to be aware of in this section.

- **Ask Before Saving Layered TIFF Files.** When you edit images in Photoshop it makes sense to save layered files as Photoshop PSD files, rather than TIFFs. If this is always your practice, you'll probably never need to save a layered TIFF file. Because of that, it's a good idea to be

reminded when saving a TIFF file with layers so that you don't accidentally create a layer TIFF. The reason this is a good idea is that if you send a layered TIFF file to someone who is using other software to view the image, that person may not be able to see all layers. I have seen this lead to confusion more than once.

**Maximize PSD and PSB File Compatibility.** When this option is selected, a composite of all the layers in a PSD (as well as PSB) file are flattened into a composite that's embedded into the photo file. This composite is viewable by software that isn't capable of displaying all of the layers in a Photoshop PSD file. It helps when you use an older version of Photoshop or Photoshop Lightroom to view a layered PSD file. I set this to Always instead of Ask so I don't have to take an extra step every time I save a PSD file.

# note

PSB is Photoshop's Large Document Format. It's designed for documents as large as 300,000 pixels in any dimension. These files can be as large as 500GB! PSB files can only be opened in Photoshop CS or later.

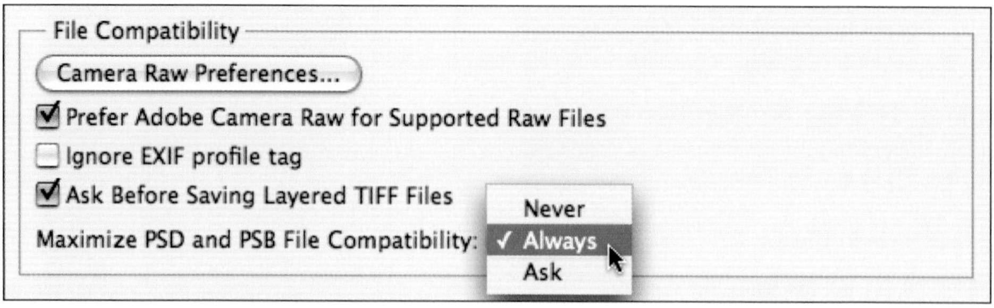

Figure 5.17

## Performance preferences

Figure 5.18 shows the Performance preferences. This preference set is used to enhance Photoshop's performance on your system. Here's a look at how each section is used.

- **Memory Usage.** I recommend that you leave Memory Usage set to its default setting. If this is set too high, it negatively affects overall performance because Photoshop will take needed resources away from the rest of your system. Adding more RAM, which has gotten very cheap, is always a better way of giving Photoshop more memory to work with.

- **History & Cache.** Increasing the number of history states is a good idea. This allows you to look further back into the past when you want to undo a series of editing steps on an open file. The default setting is 20. I like to increase it to at least 40. Be aware that higher values make greater demands on system memory because all of those states must be held in memory.

- **Scratch Disks.** When Photoshop uses all available memory (RAM), it creates what's called virtual memory. It does this by using some of the free space on one of your hard drives to perform the same function as the system's RAM. This is one of the best ways to improve Photoshop's performance when a system is short on RAM. You just need an extra hard drive with lots of empty space.

In Figure 5.8 you can see that there are three hard drives on this system. I chose an internal drive named Storage as the scratch disk because it's only used to store photos and is seldom in use when Photoshop needs it. I didn't choose the Free Agent drive because it's an external USB drive. The USB data pipeline is too slow for the kind of data transfer Photoshop needs for this purpose.

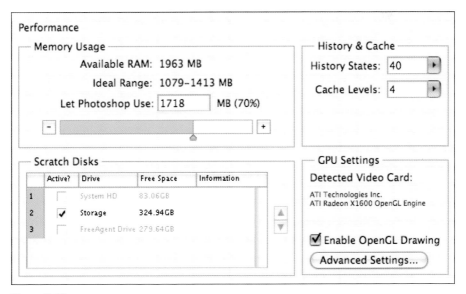

**Figure 5.18**

# caution

If your operating system (OS) is using its own virtual memory, be sure to select a different drive for Photoshop's scratch disk. Otherwise your OS and Photoshop may end up fighting over the drive, severely affecting your overall performance.

- **GPU Settings.** These settings are used to detect your graphics processing unit (graphics card) and allow you to enable OpenGL if the graphics card supports it. If your systems graphics card doesn't support OpenGL, this area is grayed-out.

## Cursor preferences

The last set of Photoshop preferences you'll look at here is the Cursors preferences, shown in Figure 5.19. There are two sets of cursors you can control here:

- **Painting Cursors.** This section allows you to control the way cursors are displayed for painting tools. The Standard setting displays the cursor with an icon representing the currently active tool. If you think about it, this isn't especially useful. It's easy enough to see the active tool by looking at the Tools panel. Beyond that, using a tool icon as a cursor makes it harder to use the tool with precision because it's difficult to determine which part of the cursor is affecting the image.

When cursors are set to Precise, a small crosshair is displayed instead of the tool's icon. This allows you to use the tool with precision, but you won't have any idea of how large the brush is. The Normal Brush Tip, the default setting, displays the cursor in the size of the brush. This gives you a much better idea of the size of the area affected by the brush. If you want to see a cross hair, select Show Crosshair in Brush Tip.

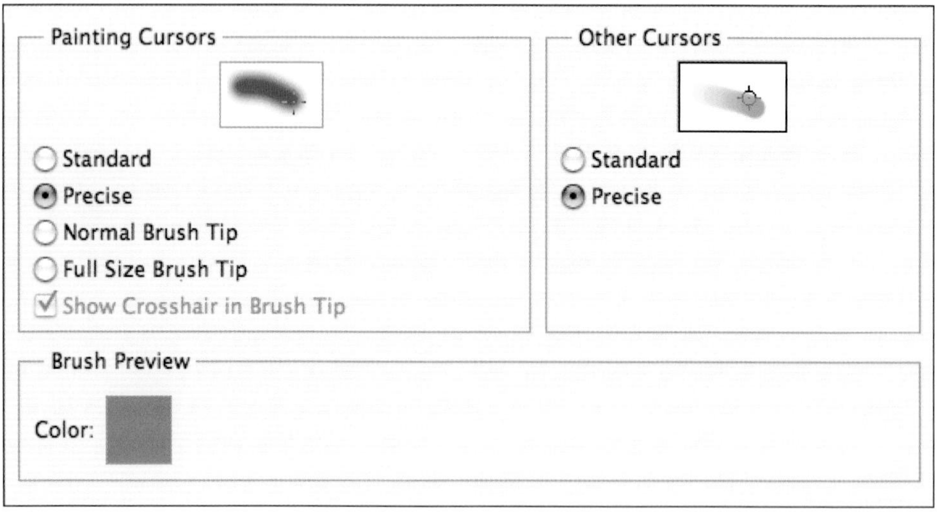

Figure 5.19

- **Other Cursors.** Use this section to designate which style you want to use for all other cursors. Standard displays an icon of the tool, and Precise displays a crosshair, which is what I prefer.

For now, the rest of the preferences are best left at their default settings until you learn more about the things they control later in this book. Here's a list of what each is used for so that you'll know for future reference:

- **Transparency & Gamut.** This is where you can change the way Transparency and Gamut warnings are displayed.

- **Units & Rulers.** These settings allow you to control some of the common units of measure and how they're displayed.

- **Guides, Grids, & Slices.** I mentioned this section earlier when discussing guides. Use these settings to change the way guides and grids, as well as slices display.

- **Plug-ins.** Plug-ins are third-party software packages that work in unison with Photoshop. If you have some plug-ins in a special folder, you can select that folder here so that Photoshop will know where to look for them.

- **Type.** These settings allow you to control some of options that are used when working with type.

# tip

Sometimes Photoshop starts acting up and not working the way it's supposed to. When you notice this behavior, it's often an indication that the file that stores preferences has been corrupted. To fix this you need to restore all preferences to their default settings. This is done by launching Photoshop while holding down the Alt+⌘/Ctrl+Shift. You will then be prompted to delete the current settings.

This completes your orientation to Photoshop's workspace and how it's laid out and controlled. Before you move on to the next chapter, I encourage you to take a moment to explore the rest of the preference sets I haven't covered here. They don't come into play for what you're doing in this book, but it's nice to be aware of them.

# 6

# Adjusting Brightness and Contrast

The foundation of a photograph begins with its tonal qualities — the brightness and contrast range of the image. If these are not adjusted correctly, the rest of the process suffers. These tonal qualities are best addressed when the image is originally captured. However, even a well-exposed image photo often needs tonal adjustment. Fortunately, Photoshop is well equipped to help you analyze the tones in an image and modify them when necessary.

In this chapter, you learn to use three of Photoshop CS4's primary tonal adjustment tools: Levels, Curves, and the Shadows/Highlights commands. You also learn to make non-destructive tonal adjustments using adjustment layers. However, before you begin modifying tones, you need to know something about how Photoshop interprets the tonal range of a digital photo.

# Understanding Histograms

The primary tool that's used to evaluate the tones in a digital image is the histogram. A histogram is a graphical representation of the distribution of the tones in an image. It consists of a graph that ranges from pure black on the left to pure white on the right. The graph is formed by 256 side-by-side columns, one for each of the individual tonal values that a histogram represents. The columns start with black (0) on the left and end with white (255) on the right. In between there are 254 other columns representing all the shades of gray between pure black and pure white. Together these 256 levels equal the sum total of the tones in an image. Figure 6.1 shows a histogram and the photo that it was generated from.

**note**

Pure black is black with no detail. This could be a deep shadow that's underexposed. Pure white is white with no detail, such as a white shirt that's overexposed so you can't see anything but white.

The height of a tonal column is governed by the number of pixels in the image having that particular tone. If the image includes lots of midtones, then the columns around the middle of the histogram are taller. Because these columns are standing right next to each other, they form a graph when viewed as a group.

## How exposure affects the histogram

The histogram in Figure 6.1 covers a broad range from almost black to almost white. This tells you that most of the midtones are represented. There's a tall area on the left, representing the darkest areas in the stems and greenery on the lower left. However, the darkest and the brightest tones fall short of pure black and pure white so you know that the image is holding detail in the shadows and the highlights — which is usually the goal in photography.

When a photo is underexposed, the entire histogram shifts to the left. The emphasis is on the darker tones and fewer highlights are represented. Figure 6.2 shows an underexposed

**Figure 6.1**

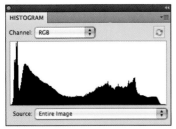

**Figure 6.2**

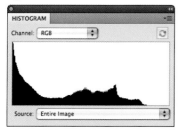

version of the daffodils. Notice that everything is darker and that it's difficult to discern detail in the deepest shadows of the greenery. This tonal shift is confirmed by looking at the histogram. The darkest tones on the left, which were fully represented in the histogram of Figure 6.1, are now being pushed off the end of the graph. When this happens, all those tones that used to describe the darkest shadows are forced to black (0). This tonal loss is called clipping because the tones are essentially clipped off the end of the tonal scale.

Figure 6.3 shows what happens when highlights are clipped by overexposure. The histogram is pushed to the right and the tones that used to describe bright highlights that still held detail in them are forced to pure white (255). This highlight data loss is easy to see in the photo where the lightest parts of the sky are clearly being blown out. There's still a tall section on the left of the histogram representing the darker areas in the stems of the flowers, but it's moved to the right indicating that the darkest areas are much lighter now.

**Figure 6.3**

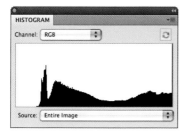

The shape of the histogram's middle region is going to vary a lot depending on the photo's subject matter. Quite often you don't have much control over that shape. The parts of a histogram that are important, and that you do have control over when you're shooting, are the left and right edges because they are controlled by your camera's exposure settings.

Most dSLR cameras have a feature that you can turn on to display a histogram every time you take a photo. Some of the newer cameras with live view function allow you to see the histogram before you shoot. This is a great way to evaluate an exposure as soon as you shoot it. You don't even need to see the image preview to know whether your exposure is good. If you see clipping in the shadows, increase your exposure. If you see clipping in the highlights, decrease your exposure.

# note

Sometimes clipping is unavoidable in a well-exposed image. For example, when a bright light reflects off the chrome on a bumper. In a case like this it isn't possible to record detail in that reflection without adversely affecting the image by reducing the overall exposure.

## How subject matter affects the histogram

Something else to consider when evaluating a histogram is the tonal key of the image. When an image is a bright scene (high-key) or a dark scene (low-key), the histogram can fool you. Figures 6.4 and 6.5 show photos and their accompanying histograms. At first glance, the

**Figure 6.4**

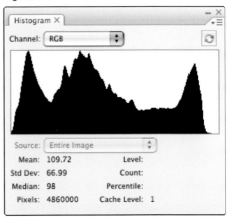

©Denyce Weiler

**Figure 6.5**

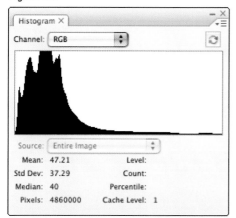

©Denyce Weiler

histogram in 6.4 appears normal and the histogram for 6.5, which is the darker image, appears to indicate underexposure. The first clue to indicate underexposure isn't the case is that there isn't any shadow clipping in the histogram in the second histogram.

In fact, both of these images were made with exactly the same exposure. The differences in the histograms come from the differences in subject matter. Figure 6.5 contains more dark tones while Figure 6.4 contains more medium tones and bright tones.

I can prove they were exposed the same by drawing a selection around similar areas of both faces. When I do that, the histogram displays information only about the tones inside the selections. Figures 6.6 and 6.7 show close-ups of the selections and their resulting histograms. Now you can be sure that these two images have the same exposure. All the dark tones were throwing off the histogram.

# see also

You get a close look at selections in Chapter 8.

Always remember to factor in the tonal range of the subject matter when evaluating a histogram. Allow low-key images to have a histogram that's weighted to the darker regions (the left side) and allow higher-key images to have histograms that lean toward the lighter end of the scale (the right side). The main thing to watch for is shadow or highlight clipping.

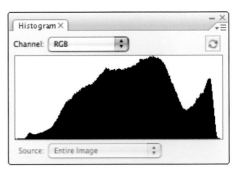

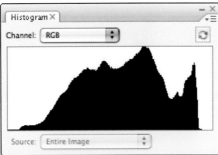

Figure 6.6

Figure 6.7

# Working with the Histogram panel

The histograms I've shown you so far in this chapter are all from the Histogram panel in Photoshop CS4. You may be noticing that your histograms look different than these — that yours are in color and these are all black. That's because I chose to keep things simple up to this point by changing the way the Histogram panel displayed data for these examples. Let's look how this panel works and some of the things you can do to change the way it displays your information.

To see the Histogram panel, choose Window → Histogram. Drag the panel from its group by its header to make it free-floating for the moment so you can see it better. There are several ways to display tonal data in a histogram. Figure 6.8 shows the default view, which displays data for each of the three color channels in their particular colors (red, green, and blue). Overlapping colors are displayed as the combination of those colors. For example, where the red and green channels overlap, the overlapping area is shown in yellow. When the red, green, and blue channels overlap, they're displayed in gray.

# see also

Color channels and color theory is discussed in detail in Chapter 7.

Click the panel menu button to open the Histogram panel's menu. This menu allows you to change some of the ways tonal data is displayed.

Select from the options to change the display:

- **Expanded View.** Increases the overall size of the panel.

- **All Channels View.** Adds three additional histograms that display data for each channel.

- **Show Channels in Color.** Shows each channel in the All Channels view in its color.

- **Show Statistics.** Adds a second window with interesting, though mostly useless information for our purposes.

You can also display individual channels one at a time in the main histogram window by choosing them from the Channel pop-up menu. The default setting is Colors. (I used the RGB — red, green, blue — preset for the histograms I showed earlier in this chapter because I wanted to show a black histogram.)

# tip

You evaluate an individual layer by choosing Selected layer from the Source menu at the bottom of the Histogram panel. Otherwise, the histogram displays information for the entire image.

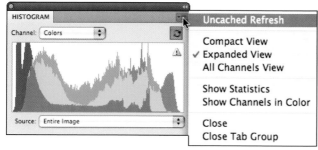

Figure 6.8

You may have noticed a small, triangle-shaped exclamation icon in the Histogram panel. It indicates that the currently displayed histogram is being created with cached information — not the very latest info. This happens when you make an edit to an image. The histogram changes, but it isn't a precise representation of the changes. To update the histogram so it's using the most current information, click the exclamation icon or the Refresh button directly above it. (You can also select the Uncached Refresh option in the panel menu to update the cache.)

One of the cool things about the Histogram panel is that it updates in real time as you edit a photo, allowing you to monitor how your changes are affecting it. I recommend that you leave it visible in your workspace so that you can use it to help you get a feel for how tonal and color adjustments affect the histogram.

Even with the best exposure, the scene may not contain the darkest and brightest tones you would like to see. In these cases it becomes necessary to adjust the tonality of the image, which in turn affects the histogram. You can do this in a couple of ways: using the Levels command and using the Curves command, which are discussed in the next few sections.

# Adjusting Brightness and Contrast with Levels

The Levels command is one of the primary tools for tonal adjustment in Photoshop. It allows you to pinpoint the darkest and lightest tones in an image so that you know whether you're loosing detail in the highlights or the shadows through clipping as you adjust tonality. You can also preview exactly where any clipping is happening in the image. Here's how you use the Levels command to adjust the brightness and contrast of a practice image together.

**1** **Open the Two_Geese.tif practice file from the downloadable practice files from the Web site (www.wiley.com/go/photoshopcs4ats).** Zoom to the Fit Screen view so that you can see the entire image. Also be sure you can see your Histogram panel. Notice that the image seems to look flat tonally, indicating that it lacks contrast.

# note

When I use the words "brightness" and "contrast" I am referring to qualities of an image. I am not referring to Photoshop's Brightness and Contrast command. Though that command is improved in Photoshop CS4, it's still considered a fairly blunt instrument because it doesn't give you the kind of control you get from the Levels command.

2 Open the Levels command by choosing Image → Adjustments → Levels (⌘+L/ Ctrl+L). Notice that the Levels dialog box, shown in Figure 6.9, uses a histogram to display information about the image. In this example the data doesn't cover the entire range from black (0) to white (255) in the histogram. This confirms the lack of contrast in the image.

The small triangles below the histogram at each end allow you to control where the ends of the histogram stop. These triangles are called Input sliders. When you click and drag them inward, you modify the histogram by changing its endpoints. The numbers below the sliders tell you exactly which tones are being affected. The slider on the left is the black Input slider, and the slider on the right is the white Input slider. This means that whatever values these sliders are set on becomes the new black (the black-point) and the new white (the white-point) when you click OK.

# caution

The Levels dialog box includes another set of sliders at the bottom. These sliders are called Output sliders because they're used to limit the tones in an image for specific printing (output) scenarios. It's best not to use them for image adjustment at this stage.

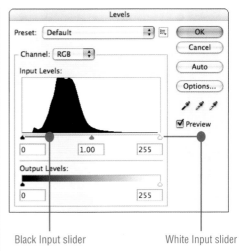

Black Input slider            White Input slider

**Figure 6.9**

3 Click and drag the black Input slider to the right until you get to a value of 40 and the white Input slider to a value of 150, and then click OK. Now the old value of 40 becomes the new 0 (black) because values 1–39 are being clipped from the end of the histogram. The original value of 150 becomes the new 255 (white), clipping over 100 tonal levels from the highlights. You can verify this by checking the Histogram panel, shown in Figure 6.10. The histogram data that originally occupied the range between 40 and 150 is now expanded to cover the range of 0 to 255. This expansion causes gaps to appear between tonal levels because there isn't enough data to cover the entire range. (More about these gaps in a moment.)

This tonal loss is reflected in the image as well. The darkest and lightest tones are compressed, losing most of their detail. This causes the image to become more contrasty because the range from black to white has been shortened considerably.

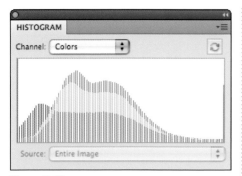

**Figure 6.10**

**4** **Choose Edit → Undo Levels (⌘+Z/ Ctrl+Z) to undo your Levels modification and return the practice image to its opening state.** This photo needs some added contrast, but the amount applied in Step 3 was too much because detail was removed from the darkest and lightest areas from clipping. You can try adjusting the sliders to more conservative amounts, while monitoring the Histogram panel, but you still won't know for sure if you're losing detail in important areas. Fortunately, there's an easy way to monitor the effects of these two sliders.

**5** **Open the Levels dialog again (⌘+L/ Ctrl+L).** Position the dialog box to one side so you can see the entire image behind it.

**6** **Click and drag the black Input slider to the right while holding the Alt key.** Notice that the screen goes white until you get to a value of about 20. That's when some detail begins to show against the white background. This preview indicates that shadow details are beginning to clip. Figure 6.11 shows what this clipping preview looks like with a value of 40. Slowly move the slider back to the left until any details disappear from the white clipping preview and then release the mouse button and the Alt key. Now you know that you have maximized the shadow detail without compromising any dark tones.

**7** **Repeat Step 6 with the white Input slider.** Notice that the clipping preview is black this time. Drag the slider until you see some detail appear in the preview, and then slowly back off until it just disappears — around the value of 235. Use the Preview check box on the Levels dialog to hide the Levels adjustment so that you can see what the image looks like without it. Notice that the contrast looks better than the original and that the blacks and whites aren't being overly compressed.

## tip

If you learn only one keyboard shortcut, it should be ⌘+Z/Ctrl+Z. This shortcut, which is common to a wide range of software, is used to go back in time one step. However, unlike most other programs, when the shortcut is used a second time in Photoshop, it moves forward in time again to replace the action that was undone. This ability allows you to repeatedly undo and redo an editing step to quickly compare before and after versions.

**Figure 6.11**

Our brains get used to what's in front of them pretty fast. The Preview option in most Photoshop dialog boxes helps you to "remember" what an image looked like before any changes were made. This is a great way to see whether you're on the right track with your adjustments before clicking OK.

**8** **Adjust the overall brightness of the image using the gray Input slider that's in between the white and black Input sliders.** When you move this slider to the left, it lightens the midtones and when you move it to the right, it darkens them. However, it has little effect on the darkest and lightest tones. Note that the Alt key doesn't provide a preview when using this slider.

**9** **Click OK to apply the Levels changes.** The brightness and contrast adjustments of this image are complete.

Something to keep in mind about histograms and clipping is that the clipping preview is intended as a guideline. You don't always have to follow it. Let go of the Alt key once in a while when moving the black or white point sliders to see what the actual image looks like. For example, sometimes I allow shadow detail to clip if it's not part of the main subject because it provides deeper blacks. If I'm adjusting a portrait of someone in front of a dark forest, I may allow some shadows in the forest to go completely black if I think it makes the image look better. I just make sure that none of the shadow detail on the subject is clipped.

When it comes to highlight clipping, I'm much more conservative. I rarely allow a highlight to clip whether it's part of the main subject or not. That's because a clipped highlight is pure white with no detail. When it's printed, it's the color of the paper the image the printed on. A highlight like this often distracts from the overall image.

## note

The Levels dialog box has an Auto button. Like most automatic things in Photoshop, its results are hit-and-miss. I recommend that you learn the technique I just showed you so that you know exactly what's going on with the tones in your image instead of experimenting with uneven results.

So here's the lowdown on Levels. When adjusting an image with Levels, always start with either the black Input slider or the white Input slider. Do both ends first to get the black-point and the white-point set before adjusting the image's brightness with the gray Input slider in the middle. If you begin with the gray Input slider before working with the ends, you'll most likely have to readjust it before clicking OK.

# Advanced Tonal Adjustment with Curves

Curves works along the same lines as Levels. You set the black point and the white point and then adjust midtone values. The main difference with Curves is that you have much greater control when adjusting midtone values because you can target specific tonal ranges for adjustment.

The interface can be intimidating, but after you understand basics, it begins to make sense. Give it a try with these steps:

1  **Open the Two_Geese.tif practice file again.** If it's still open from the last example, click the image thumbnail at the of top the History panel to return it to its opening state.

## note

The History panel allows you to go back in time while you're editing a file. To back up to a previous history state, you simply click on it. This allows you to undo several steps at one time. Be aware, though, that history states are volatile. They disappear when you close the file and they're no longer available when you reopen it.

2  **Choose Image → Adjustments → Curves (⌘+M/Ctrl+M) to open the Curves command.**

3  **Click the button next to Curve Display Options to show the options.** Make sure that Light (0-255) is checked under Show Amount of in the Curve Display Options. That way, the Curves dialog box will be oriented the way I have it in Figure 6.12.

4  **Click and drag the black Input slider, below the graph on the left, horizontally toward the middle.** Notice that the blacks get blacker just like the black slider in Levels.

5  **Grab the white Input slider, below the graph on the right, and slide it horizontally toward the middle.** The whites get whiter just like the white slider in Levels.

6  **Select the Show Clipping option to turn on the clipping preview, and then slide the black and white sliders inward until you almost see clipping in the preview.** Remember that it can be okay to clip shadows a bit to get richer blacks, but you never want to clip highlights if you can help it.

**7** After you have both sliders set deselect the Show Clipping option to return the image to its normal appearance. Figure 6.12 shows my adjustment. I ended up with a black Input value of 20 and a white Input value of 235. The image looks very similar to what it looked like after adjusting the Levels black and white Input sliders in the previous example because the Input values are the same. Notice how much steeper the diagonal line is now that you moved the endpoints inward. Something to be aware of with the Curves command is that the steeper the diagonal line is, the more contrast the image has.

## tip

Use the histogram overlay in the Curves dialog box to get an idea of where the predominant tones in the image are located. For example, in Figure 6.10 most of the data is weighted to the darker tones on the left.

Now that the overall contrast of the image has been established with the Input sliders, it's time to unleash the real power of the Curves command. Notice that the Curves dialog box doesn't have a gray Input slider like the Levels dialog box. You adjust midtones a bit differently with Curves. Instead of using a slider below the graph, you create adjustment points by clicking the diagonal line. After an adjustment point is in

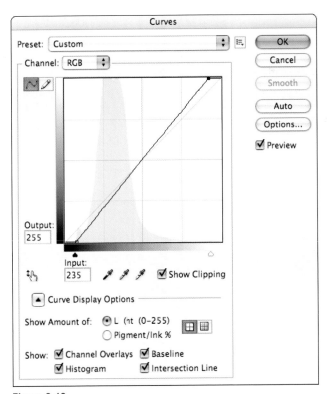

Figure 6.12

place, you modify the tones around it by dragging the point up or down. The higher up on the line you place the adjustment point, the lighter the tones that are affected by it. To lighten the tones around the point, drag the point upward. To darken that region, drag the point downward.

# tip

Though you can place up to 14 adjustment points on the Curves line, I strongly recommend that you use no more than two until you get the hang of Curves.

These adjustment points are like the gray Input slider in the Levels command because they modify the input values of the image's midtones. The big difference, however, is in the effect that adjustments have as compared to the Levels command. When you move the gray Input slider in the Levels command, the effect on the tones around it is linear — it affects all adjacent tones equally. With the Curves command, the effect of the adjustment is stronger on tones that are close to the adjustment point and weaker on tones that are further away. That's why the command is called Curves: the adjustment slopes away.

# tip

If you want to nudge a setting a small amount, click the point you want to move to make it active; then use the up and down arrows on the keyboard to change it one value at a time. This works with almost any slider in Photoshop, including the Levels command's Input sliders.

Because the points represent tonal regions in the image, you want to be informed about the tones they represent before placing them. One way to see how the tones of your image correspond to the points on the curve is to click the image while the Curves dialog box is open. When you do so, small circles temporarily appear on the

diagonal Curves line to indicate where the tones you're clicking are located on the line. To place one of these preview points on the line, ⌘+click/Ctrl+click the corresponding tone in the image. To remove a point from the diagonal line, click and drag it out of the Curves window, or click it and press the Delete key.

An even cooler way to make an informed adjustment is to use the Curves command's new Targeted Adjustment tool. It looks like a hand with an extended index finger. Click this tool to make it active, and then click the tones in the image you want to change. While holding the mouse button down, drag the mouse upward to place an adjustment point on the diagonal line and lighten the selected tonal range. Drag the mouse downward to darken the tones and modify the diagonal line accordingly.

Go ahead and finish adjusting the geese photo by clicking the diagonal line in the middle region of the histogram overlay, as shown in the Curves dialog box detail in Figure 6.13. Drag this line up or down to lighten or darken the image to your liking. (Or use the Targeted Adjustment tool.) Then click OK to complete the Curves adjustment.

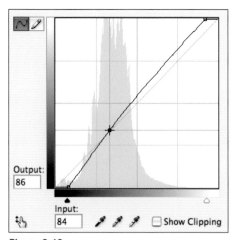

**Figure 6.13**

When you're first starting out with Photoshop, you should master the Levels command before going too deep into the Curves command. When you're ready to transition to the Curves command, remember that it's a powerful tool. In the hands of a skilled Photoshop user, its precision is like a scalpel for making finely tuned tonal adjustments. But remember that a scalpel in the hands of someone who doesn't know how to use it can lead to a real mess. The same is true for Curves. If you aren't careful, you can do more harm than good with the Curves command. So take it easy with Curves by making small adjustments until you become more comfortable and confident with this powerful tonal adjustment tool.

# Gaining Control with Adjustment Layers

Earlier you saw an example of the kind of data loss that happens when you execute a simple Levels adjustment. This data loss manifested itself as gaps in the histogram. These gaps are called combing because they make the histogram look like a comb. Another sign of data loss is called spiking because it looks like tall, narrow spikes that stick up from the histogram. Spiking occurs when tonal ranges are compressed during an adjustment. The histogram in Figure 6.14 shows combing and spiking after three separate Levels adjustments to the geese practice file.

Some data loss is inevitable when working with Photoshop. The problem is that when cumulative tonal adjustments are made, this loss is also cumulative. If you make a Levels adjustment, then come back later and make another Levels adjustment to fine-tune the first adjustment, you wind up with two separate instances of data loss. If this kind of loss continues, it eventually affects the image because necessary tones are eliminated. For example, imagine you have a photo with a nice graduation in the sky from light blue to dark blue. When tonal loss is excessive, the graduated sky begins to show banding. Banding is when you see bands of color instead of gradual shifts in tone. This happens because there are no tones to describe the intermediate tones in the sky. It's similar to the banding you saw in Figure 1.3 when data loss was caused by repetitively opening and saving a JPEG file.

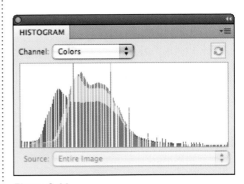

**Figure 6.14**

The best way to minimize the destructive nature of Photoshop is to only make tonal and color adjustments one time. In theory this sounds nice, but in practice it can be difficult to accomplish. When working on an important image, especially when you're first learning

Photoshop, it's quite common to make cumulative adjustments as you explore the image, or as your knowledge and skills increase and you revisit previously edited images. Fortunately Photoshop solves this problem by allowing you to isolate tonal adjustments to individual layers. Those layers are called adjustment layers.

# What are Photoshop layers?

Think about music for a moment. When a band is in a recording studio putting together a song, a sound engineer records each singer and instrument individually on separate sound tracks. In fact, vocals and instruments often are recorded at different times with different musicians in attendance. No one really knows what the song sounds like until all the pieces are blended together on a mixing board and played back as a single musical piece.

All these separate tracks give the producer a tremendous amount of creative control. If she doesn't like the way a particular instrument sounds, she can modify it — or even toss it out and recreate it — without affecting all the other pieces. If she had to work with a single track of all vocals and instruments recorded at the same time, massaging the sound would be very difficult. This is very similar to the concept of layers in Photoshop.

Photoshop has used layers since version 3.0. They allow you to isolate various elements of an image so one element can be managed separately from other elements. Just like the sound engineer in a recording studio, you control all the separate elements of an image by stacking image content in layers. If you don't like the way all these pieces fit together, you can modify some of them or throw them away without compromising the whole image. This ability creates a huge amount of flexibility when editing an image.

# Working with the Adjustments panel

The Adjustments panel is a new feature in Photoshop CS4. It's designed to take the guesswork out of creating and modifying adjustment layers. Figure 6.15 shows the Adjustments panel default view. The upper portion of the panel is populated with buttons that are used to create specific types of adjustment layers. When you click one of these buttons, a new adjustment layer is created and the panel changes to display the controls for that layer.

- **The first row contains the common tonal adjustment tools.** From left to right they are: Brightness and Contrast, Levels, Curves, and Exposure.

- **The second row contains the most common color adjustment tools.** They are Vibrance, Hue/Saturation, Color Balance, Black & White, Photo Filter, and Channel Mixer.

- **The third row has the more esoteric adjustment tools.** They are Invert, Posterize, Threshold, Gradient Map, and Selective Color.

# note

All the adjustment layer tools are standard adjustment tools found in the Image → Adjustments menu. That's where they get the name adjustment layers.

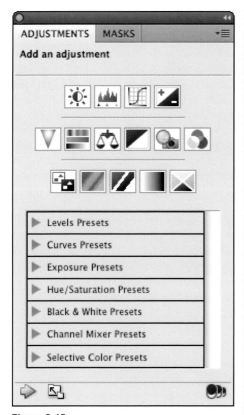

**Figure 6.15**

The lower half of the panel contains groups of common presets for many types of adjustment layers. Click the twirly next to a heading to see the presets for that adjustment. Specific presets are also available when a particular adjustment layer is in use. You select them from the menu at the top of the Adjustments panel when an adjustment layer is active.

# Creating an adjustment layer

Now revisit the previous project with the Geese photo. This time adjust its tonality with a Curves adjustment layer instead of the Curves command.

**1** Be sure that the Adjustments panel is visible. If you don't see it, choose Window → Adjustments.

**2** Open the Two_Geese.tif practice file one more time. If it's still open from the last example, click the image thumbnail at the top the History panel to return it to its opening state.

**3** Click the Create a new Curves adjustment layer button on the top row of buttons in the Adjustments panel. (It's the one with the small Curves icon.) When you do, the panel changes to display a version of the Curves dialog, shown in Figure 6.16. This smaller version has most of the important features of the Curves dialog box, including the Targeted adjustment tool. The only obvious exception is the Show Clipping option. That's okay because you can use the Alt key while dragging the black and white Input sliders just as you did when working with Levels.

**4** Go ahead and make adjustments that are similar to those you made with the Curves command in the previous exercise. Notice that you don't have to click an OK button when you're through with your Curves adjustments. That's because this adjustment remains open allowing you to revisit it later.

Now look at the Layers panel, shown in Figure 6.17. A new layer named Curves 1 is above the Background layer, which is the original image layer. Click the eyeball icon next to the Curves 1 layer to hide the layer. Now the image looks the way it did without the adjustment. Turn the layer's visibility back on by clicking the eyeball again.

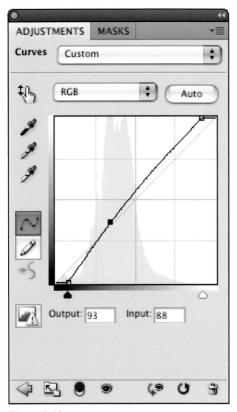

**Figure 6.16**

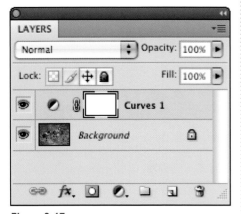

**Figure 6.17**

You can readjust the layer any time you want to by clicking it in the Layers panel to make the layer active and then adjusting the settings in the Adjustments panel. (If you click the Create a new Curves adjustment layer button again, a second Curves layer is created.) The only time the image suffers data loss is when the layers are flattened (Layer ➔ Flatten) and the adjustments become a permanent part of the image. Ideally, this happens at the end of the workflow so any data loss only happens once, no matter how many times you modify the adjustment layer.

When a specific adjustment tool is in use, a set of buttons appears along the bottom of the Adjustments panel. These buttons, shown in Figure 6.18, allow you to manage the layer and your adjustments to it. Here's a quick description of what each button is used for:

- **Return to adjustment list.** Use this to go back to the display shown in Figure 6.16. It allows you to add an additional adjustment layer, such as a Color Balance layer.

- **Switch panel to expanded view.** Use this to make the panel larger, more like the Curves dialog box.

- **Clip to layer.** Sometimes you want an adjustment layer to only affect the layer directly below it. Say, for example, that I have a project where I need to cut someone's head from one image and add it to another. If the tone or color on the head layer is different than the rest of the image, I can add an adjustment layer and click the clip to layer button to make the adjustment layer affect only the layer directly below it.

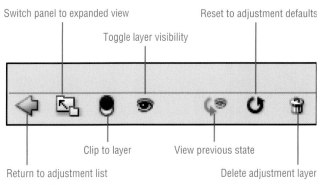

Switch panel to expanded view          Reset to adjustment defaults

Toggle layer visibility

Clip to layer          View previous state

Return to adjustment list          Delete adjustment layer

**Figure 6.18**

# tip

You can test this by making cumulative adjustments to the Curves 1 layer while monitoring the Histogram panel. Notice that data loss in the histogram stays about the same every time you make a new adjustment because the adjustments aren't applied until the layers are flattened.

- **Toggle layer visibility.** This is the same as clicking the eyeball icon in the Layers panel. It simply turns the adjustment layer's visibility off and on.

- **View previous state.** Use this when you want to undo some changes you just made. You back up one step every time you click it. You can also use the \ key to step backward to a previous adjustment state.

- **Reset to adjustment defaults.** Use this to reset the adjustment layer to its default settings.

- **Delete adjustment layer.** Click this to delete the currently active layer.

If I'm working quickly with an image, spending only a few minutes or even seconds with it, I don't use adjustment layers. In those cases, I don't need the flexibility of an adjustment layer because I'm not making cumulative adjustments. However, when I spend lots of time editing an image or if I know I'll be editing it again later, I'm sure to use adjustment layers to do all tonal and color adjustment.

There's one more thing about adjustment layers you should know before you move on: You can have more than one of a particular type. It's quite common to have one Levels adjustment layer for overall image adjustment and another Levels adjustment layer that's used only for a particular printer. This way the second Levels layer is used to compensate for any variations with that printer. It's only made visible when you're ready to print. This is a very common use of Levels, Curves, and Color Balance adjustment layers.

This flexibility you learned about here is only the beginning of what you can do with adjustment layers.

# see also

You revisit adjustment layers in Chapter 9 when you learn about masking.

# Balancing Contrast with the Shadows/ Highlights Command

Sometimes you make a perfect exposure but the dynamic range of the scene being photographed is too wide for you to get an exposure that looks good in the shadows and highlights. Dynamic range refers to the distance between the brightest tones and the lightest tones. It's similar to the contrast of the image. You often run into this scenario when you photograph a scene with bright backlighting where the main subject is in a shadow. Usually, the best way to solve this problem is to use a fill flash on your camera when you shoot the original scene so that you fill in the shadows with some light to balance the highlights. Sometimes, though, a flash isn't an option, and you have to deal with what you have.

When editing a file that suffers from this problem, making the image look its best with Levels or Curves can be hard. That's why Adobe introduced a new command a few years ago in Photoshop CS. The command is called Shadows/Highlights (Image → Adjustments → Shadows/Highlights) and it's used to balance discrepancies between extreme shadows and highlights. Figure 6.19 shows the Shadows/Highlights dialog box with the Show More Options option selected.

## note

The Shadows/Highlights command is one of the few tools found in the Image → Adjustments menu that isn't available as an adjustment layer.

The first thing you should notice in Figure 6.19 is that the Shadows/Highlights command allows you to work on the shadows and highlights independently via the two areas marked Shadows and Highlights. Each area is controlled by three sliders: Amount, Tonal Width, and Radius.

Here is what these sliders do:

- **Amount.** Controls the amount of adjustment. Higher values in Shadows lighten the shadows more. Higher values in Highlights darken the highlights more.

- **Tonal Width.** Controls the range of tones that are affected by changes in amount. Lower values confine the adjustment to the darker regions when adjusting shadows, and lighter regions when adjusting the highlights. Higher values expand the range of tones being affected. When adjusting the shadows this extends affected tones from the shadows into the midtones. When highlights are being adjusted the range extends from the lightest highlights into the midtones. A Tonal Width value of 100 in the Highlights affects the highlights the most. The midtones are partially affected and the darkest shadows are unaffected.

- **Radius.** When the Shadows/Highlights command looks at an image, it detemines whether a pixel is a shadow or a highlight by evaluating its surrounding pixels. The Radius slider allows you to fine-tune how the command decides by determining how many surrounding pixels are evaluated. Lower values restrict the area that's evaluated, and higher settings expand that range. The optimal value varies with image content, so it's best to experiment with this value.

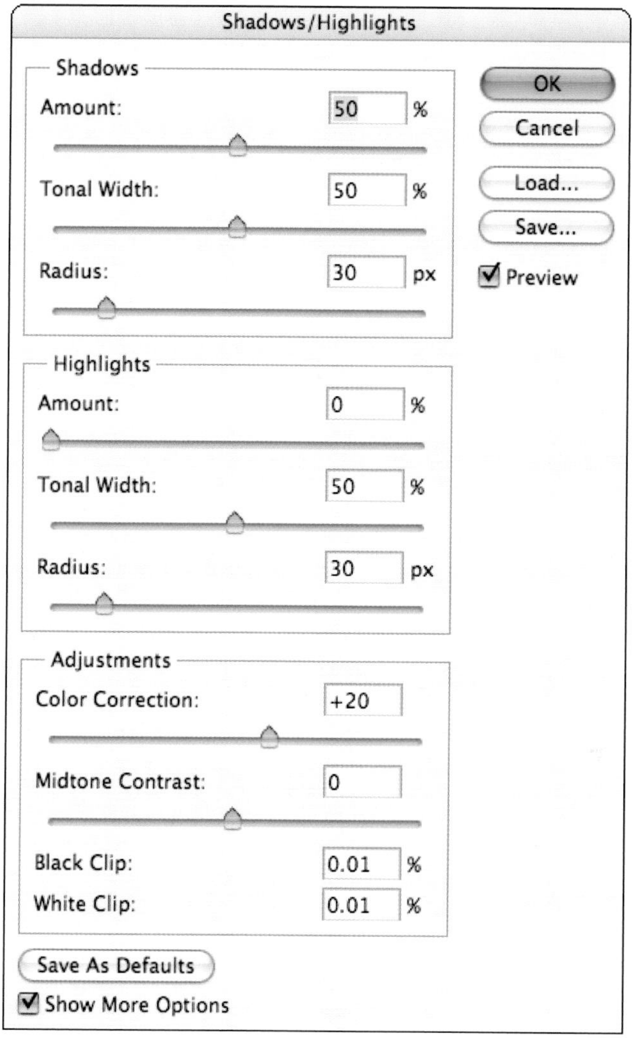

**Figure 6.19**

tip

If you start seeing halos around dark or light edges, you need to lower the Tonal Width setting for the respective halos — Shadows for dark tone halos and Highlights for light tone halos.

In addition to the Shadows and Highlights areas on the Shadows/Highlights command, there is an area labeled Adjustments. These additional sliders are used to help undo any unwanted shifts that might occur when the shadows and highlights are adjusted.

- **Color Correction.** When tonal values are changed, colors often shift. For example, when shadows are lightened, a color that was dark before becomes lighter. The Color Correction slider allows you to control color saturation — the intensity of the color. Increasing the value of the Color Correction slider tends to increase saturation, and lowering it tends to decrease saturation. This command is available only when working on color images.

  Keep in mind that the Color Correction affects only portions of the image affected by the Shadows and Highlights sliders. When those adjustments are more extreme, the range of adjustment to Color Correction is greater.

- **Midtone Contrast.** Slider movement to the right increases midtone contrast, and movements to the left reduce it. In most cases, I'd rather change this with a Curves adjustment. However, if you're working quickly with the Shadows/Highlights command on some images, it may be faster to take care of it here.

Take a look at how all this works:

1. **Open the practice file titled Bike_ Racing.tif, from the downloadable practice files.** As you can see in Figure 6.20 this exposure isn't bad, but it could be better. I want to lighten the faces of the riders and darken the track in the background.

2. **Choose Image → Adjustments → Shadows/Highlights.** When the dialog box opens, it most likely will have the default settings shown back in Figure 6.19. These tend to be way over the top so you'll notice that the adjustment in the shadows is too strong. Also, the track in the background is still too light.

**tip**

The default settings on the Shadows/Highlights command tend to be too strong in the shadows and too weak in the highlights. After you've used the command a couple of times, you'll get a feel for the kinds of settings you like. When you do, open the command and dial in the settings you want. Then click the Save As Defaults button on the lower left of the dialog box. The next time you open the Shadows/Highlights command, you can begin with more normal settings as a starting point.

3. **Adjust the Shadows first by moving the Radius to the right until you see the shadows begin to look more realistic.** Moving it to the right limits the range of tones being affected. I moved it to 190px.

4. **Adjust the Amount in Shadows.** I moved it down to 35% to back it off a bit.

5. **Try experimenting with Tonal Width to see the effect this slider has on the image.** I left it at 50%. Now that the shadows are looking pretty good, you'll address the highlights.

6. **In the Highlights area, move the Amount slider to the right until the track darkens.** I stopped at 60%. If you notice any haloing around the riders, try adjusting the Radius slider in the Highlights area. If you decrease the Radius to 0px, the haloing goes away, but the image takes on a flat, fake look. Instead, try raising the Radius. I turned it up to 95px. There is still a slight haloing effect, but I like the way it looks.

7. **Again, try experimenting with Tonal Width here.** I left it at 50%.

**Figure 6.20**

**8** Select and deselect the Preview check box a couple of times to toggle back and forth between before and after. If you want to fine-tune your adjustments, do so now. Now take a look at the Color Correction slider.

**9** Try moving the Color Correction slider to the left. As you do so, pay attention to the colors on the rider's jerseys. When you get close to a value of 0, the colors on the chests of riders 1 and 3 are desaturated — the colors lose some of their richness. Values of much less than 0 have little more effect. If you move the slider to the right, the colors on riders 1 and 3 chests get more saturated. Notice that the effect of saturating and desaturating with the Color Correction slider affects only the areas that were affected by adjustments in the Shadows portion of the Shadows/Highlights command.

**10** When you like what you see, click OK. Now the image should look more like Figure 6.21. The dynamic range of the photo is now much better with brighter shadows and darker highlights.

Be sure to look for two side effects when using the Shadows/Highlights command. The first is that your image can become flat in contrast if you overdo it. If this happens, try making a Levels or Curves adjustment to compensate for the loss in contrast. In fact, if you think you need to make a tonal adjustment with the Levels or Curves commands, do it after using the Shadows/Highlights command when possible, or use an adjustment layer so you can modify it after adjusting shadows and highlights.

**Figure 6.21**

# caution

The Black Clip and White Clip boxes are used to clip shadow and highlight tones. Increasing these settings causes the image to become more contrasty as shadow and highlight tones are clipped. Generally, I prefer to use the Levels or Curves commands to better control clipping.

The second side effect is that when you lighten shadows with any tonal adjustment tool, you reveal noise because noise tends to hide in the shadows. If you watch for this as you adjust the Shadows sliders, you know when to take it easy on areas of extreme noise.

# 7

# Working with Color

**W**hen photographers were primarily shooting film, they had few choices about how the colors in a scene were represented in the final print. Rudimentary global adjustments were possible during printing, but they affected all the colors in the image equally. Now that digital files are replacing film, photographers are realizing that they not only have precise control over the color of the image, but they also have precise control over each individual color in it. It's just a matter of learning about color and how to use a handful of Photoshop's color correction tools to modify it. In this chapter, I explain color theory as it relates to photography and digital files. Then I tell you how to set up color management in Photoshop CS4, and I give you the primary tools you need to measure and modify color in your photos.

# Calibrating Your Monitor

Think about this for a moment: You've seen banks of televisions in electronics stores where every TV is displaying the same channel in different colors. When you buy a TV, you don't really worry about those differences. You simply want a TV that has a good picture when you get it home. No one will be comparing your TV's picture to his and wondering why they don't look the same.

The same phenomenon exists when dealing with digital images: Not all computer monitors display tonal information and color the same. Unlike TV sets, this can be problematic. What's the use of tweaking an image in Photoshop if the color is going to look different as soon as it's viewed somewhere else or printed?

Digital files are viewed on a wide range of equipment. If appropriate measures aren't taken, predicting what an image looks like when someone else sees it in her particular viewing environment can be difficult — if not impossible. That's why monitor calibration is the first step to managing the color of your photos.

The idea behind monitor calibration is to establish a set of standards and get everyone to use them. These standards refer to the color temperature, brightness, and contrast the monitor displays. A hardware calibration device is used to measure these qualities in your monitor, and then allow you to adjust your monitor to bring them into alignment with the standards. This is called monitor calibration. After you calibrate your monitor, the calibration device allows you to create a custom color profile that describes the way the monitor displays color. Color profiles allow all the devices in a digital workflow to interpret and understand color so that they all speaking the same language. Cameras, monitors, and printers all have color profiles.

A number of monitor calibration devices are available on the market. I have experience with the ColorVision Spyder2 Pro and the Greytag Macbeth Eye-One Display 2, as shown in Figure 7.1. Each of these devices currently retails for about $250 and both do a great job of helping you bring your system into alignment.

## The Difference between CRT and LCD Monitors

There are some differences in CRT (Cathode Ray Tube) and LCD (Liquid Crystal Display) monitors that affect the way they're calibrated. CRT monitors create color by using three electron guns that project color for each color channel, (red, green, and blue). When calibrating a CRT the settings on these guns are adjusted to change their individual intensities. An LCD monitor doesn't use electron guns so color can't be adjusted in the same way. Even if the monitor has buttons for changing color, they do not work on the monitor itself. It's best to leave them at their default settings and allow your calibration device to calibrate the monitor by making changes to the video card.

**Figure 7.1**

These calibration devices work a little differently from one another, but for the most part you use them in the following manner:

**1** Install the software that comes with the calibration device.

**2** Plug the device into a USB port on your system — preferably a port on the back of your machine, not a USB hub.

**3** Launch the software, and tell it to calibrate and profile your system. The software takes you through some preliminaries and asks you a couple of questions. Pay special attention to the questions about color space and gamma. Choose 6500k for color temperature and 2.2 for gamma (midtone contrast) as your starting points to be consistent with most of the rest of the world.

# tip

If you're planning to move from a CRT to an LCD and you have an older calibration device, think about upgrading to the newer generation of devices. When I moved from CRT to LCD, my older device didn't do a very good job on the LCD. When I bought a newer model, all my systems came into balance. caution

# caution

Some Mac users believe they're supposed to choose 1.8 as their gamma because 1.8 is known as a Mac setting. In the very early days, 1.8 was the gamma setting for Macs so that those monitors would match the limitations of early Apple dot-matrix printers. Today, 2.2 is the standard gamma setting for computer displays. The 1.8 setting is no longer necessary and can cause problems if used.

**4** When the calibration software is finished, it prompts you to save the newly created profile and automatically make it your default.

**5** The profiling software reminds you to recalibrate at certain intervals so that your viewing environment stays consistent. This is a good idea because monitors tend to drift, especially CRTs. I recommend that you recalibrate at least once a month.

You can reach a point of diminishing returns when striving for perfect color — especially when you're dealing with outside printing sources. Make an effort to get calibrated, but don't worry if you aren't getting a perfect match to your prints.

# see also

A lot of variables can affect printing. I discuss some of them in Chapter 14.

# Understanding Color Theory

One of the first things to understand about color is that it's personal. Everyone has his or her own preferences. When I worked in a professional photo lab, we had a lab standard for skin-tone colors. However, there were certain customers who wanted the skin tones in their prints to have a particular tint. Even though we didn't like the color the customer liked, we did everything in our power to make them happy.

Some of this bias relates to personal taste, and some of it has more to do with individual color perception. Not everyone sees color the same. In fact, your own color perception can shift as blood sugar levels go up and down. Some people are deficient in seeing color on a red-green axis; others are deficient on a blue-yellow axis. However, few people are completely colorblind.

# note

Here's an interesting fact — more men are affected by color blindness than women.

Even though our experience of color can be highly subjective, the physics behind color theory is rock solid. The main distinction to make about color is whether it's *subtractive color* or *additive color.*

## Subtractive color

Subtractive color describes the way pigments, such as paints, dyes, inks, and natural colorants reflect light. When white light strikes a pigment, the pigment absorbs some wavelengths of light and reflects the unabsorbed wavelengths. The wavelengths that are reflected are the colors we see and what give the pigment its color. That means that a subtractive color system begins with white light made up of colored wavelengths. The color we see is the reflected light with some wavelengths subtracted from it — or absorbed by the pigment.

Here's an easy way to remember how subtractive color works. If you add equal amounts of red, green, and blue paint together, you get a muddy gray. It's impossible to mix any of these three colors together in a way that they create white. In order to get white, all paint needs to be removed from the white canvas

## Additive color

Additive color describes the way light waves combine to create color. This is the way humans see things, and it's the system used for most color management and adjustment in Photoshop. This system is called additive because it begins with black (no light). A light source adds wavelengths of that have a specific color. With additive color, white is created by adding together equal amounts of red, green, and blue. This can seem counterintuitive to people who are used to working with pigments and subtractive color. Technically, six colors are used when working with additive color. The primary colors, red, green, and blue, and their opposites (or complimentary colors), cyan, magenta, and yellow. Figure 7.2 shows the primary colors and their compliments. When you have equal amounts of two complimentary colors, you end up with neutral gray — in other words, the colors cancel each other out.

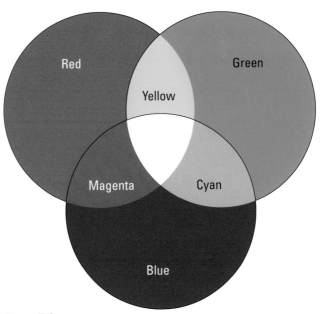

**Figure 7.2**

The relationship among these six colors gets even more interesting because each is composed of two component colors — and those component colors are always going to be two of the six colors. Here's how the colors break down into components:

- Red is composed of magenta and yellow.
- Green is composed of cyan and yellow.
- Blue is composed of cyan and magenta.
- Cyan is composed of green and blue.
- Magenta is composed of red and blue.
- Yellow is composed of red and green.

This may seem confusing at first, like an endless shell game — especially if you're used to thinking about the way pigments such as paint combine. But Figure 7.3 shows an easy way to remember these relationships: The primary colors — red, green, and blue — are directly above their complimentary colors (the ones that cancel them out) — cyan, magenta, and yellow. Here's the trick to understanding this: The two component colors of any color are the two colors that are not directly across from it. For example, red is composed of magenta and yellow. Cyan can't be a component of red because it's the opposite of red, (it's complimentary color).

When I learned this system many years ago, it completely changed the way I thought about colors and their components. All I have to do now is visualize this simple chart, and I know how all the colors relate to one another — which colors are compliments and which are components.

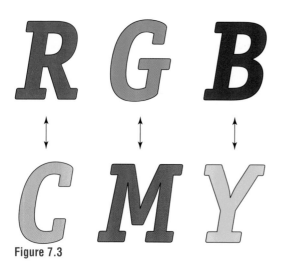

**Figure 7.3**

# Managing Color in Photoshop

Photoshop CS4 gives you a great deal of control over color. This control begins as soon as you open a photo file. To understand how that takes place, you first need to understand the method Photoshop uses for describing color.

## Comparing color spaces

The primary colors discussed here (red, green, and blue) are the colors of a color model called RGB. A color model is an abstract way of mathematically describing colors and their relationships to one another. This common vocabulary is important when discussing specific colors within that RGB model. Otherwise, when I say "red," how do I know you're picturing the same color that I'm picturing?

Colors are further classified into color spaces. A color space, among other things, defines the gamut, or range of colors that a device is capable of capturing or reproducing. For example, my monitor is capable of displaying only a certain gamut of colors. Many of the colors I can see out in nature can't be displayed on my monitor. However, my monitor can display colors that can't be printed on my inkjet printer. The monitor's gamut isn't as large as the spectrum that a human eye can see, but in some cases it's larger than the gamut of the printer. These kinds of color spaces — monitor and printer — are called device-dependent color spaces. A device-dependent color space describes the range of colors that a particular device can see and/or reproduce.

## note

Devices can be subcategorized into input and output devices. A digital camera is an input device, and a printer is an output device.

The second type of color space is device-independent color space. A device-independent color space is not limited by the gamut of any particular device. These color spaces are used to describe the range of colors in color editing spaces. An editing space describes the total palette, or gamut, of colors available when editing a photo in Photoshop. The two most common editing spaces in Photoshop are Adobe RGB (1998) and sRGB:

- **Adobe RGB (1998).** This is a large color space that is more applicable to high-end printing and reproduction.

- **sRGB.** This is a limited color space that is intended to be common to a wide range of devices.

The main difference between these two editing spaces is that the gamut of Adobe RGB (1998) is larger than sRGB. It has a much wider range of colors than sRGB.

Think about it this way: Imagine that I have two boxes of crayons. One box has 24 different colors, and the other box has 120 colors. Suppose you and I both want to do a drawing of the same scene outside. If I give you the 120-count box and keep the 24-count box, the results of our drawings would be quite different. The greens and browns in my trees would be more limited than yours because I don't have the same range of greens and browns to work with as you do.

This is sort of the way it works in Photoshop. When you edit digital files, you need to standardize the way color is managed in your Photoshop workflow. You can choose to work in a smaller color space like sRGB, or you can work in a larger color space like Adobe RGB (1998).

The graph in Figure 7.4, created with ColorThink software, a product of Chromix in Seattle, Washington (www.chromix.com), compares the color gamuts of Adobe RGB (1998) (the wireframed shape) and sRGB (the solid shape). Notice that the Adobe RGB (1998) gamut is much larger in some areas, especially the yellows and greens.

## Choosing a color space

At first it seems like a no-brainer to choose to work in a larger color space so that you're working with more colors, but that's not always

the case. When you consider working spaces, you also must think about device color spaces — devices such as printers. Even though a working space may be device-independent, the color of a print is limited to the printing device's gamut. Usually that printer's limited gamut is much smaller than the Photoshop working space. This means that some of the colors in the file are not printable, leading to disappointments at printing time.

The real key to deciding which color space to use as your main Photoshop working space is how you plan to output your files. If you're using a commercial photo lab, ask what color space

**Figure 7.4**

s RGB

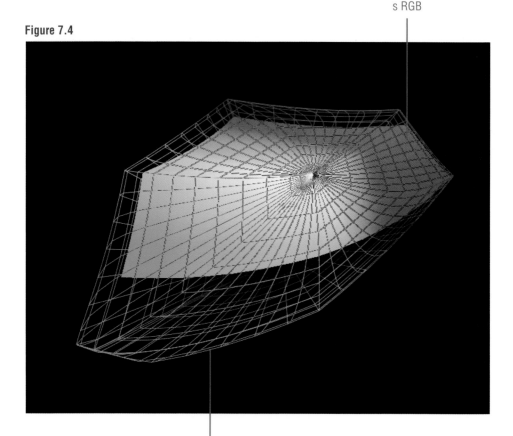

Adobe RGB

the lab prefers. Most will tell you that their equipment works in the sRGB color space. If you plan to do most of your printing at this lab, use sRGB as your working space. Some labs do work in the Adobe RGB (1998) color space. If your lab is one of them, take advantage of the larger color space.

This is even more important when preparing photos for the Web. The sRGB color space is ideal for the Web. In fact, it was created with the Internet in mind. Back in the mid-90s, Microsoft and Hewlett-Packard proposed a new standard color space that was best suited to the limited gamuts of cameras, printer, and monitors. With a common color space, users could have more confidence that when they placed photos on the Web, people who viewed the images would see them the way they were intended to be seen. (Naturally, individual monitor calibration comes into play here, as well as the Web browser that's being used.)

Many people use inkjet printers for outputting prints. Most inkjet printers work with a limited gamut of color. However, this can be misleading because the gamut isn't limited in every color of the spectrum. Figure 7.5 shows the color profile of an inkjet printer (the solid shape) compared to the sRGB and Adobe RGB (1998) color spaces (the wireframe shapes).

# see also

Some labs provide a profile that describes their particular printer. Having one of these allows you to preview your image onscreen with the colors that the lab's printer is capable of reproducing and make any necessary final adjustments. I show you how to do this in Chapter 13.

In the top image of Figure 7.5, you can see that the printer is capable of printing yellows that are well outside the limits of sRGB. In the bottom image, you can see that Adobe RGB (1998) contains most of the yellows that the printer can print, although it's capable of printing some extreme yellows that are outside the gamut of Adobe RGB (1998). If I were photographing a yellow Corvette and planning to print it on this printer, I would edit it in the larger Adobe RGB (1998) space. In fact, because the larger gamut is a closer match to the printer, I always recommend that anyone printing on an inkjet printer use the Adobe RGB (1998) working space in Photoshop.

You must think about these sorts of things as you consider which working space to use in Photoshop because your working space choice really does depend on how you plan to output the files. With that in mind, here's the bottom line:

- Use sRGB when you know that all your workflow is oriented to producing images for the Web or for photo labs with printing equipment that is using sRGB. Doing this helps you to better predict what your color looks like when it's time to view images online or in print.

- Use Adobe RGB (1998) when you're dealing with a lab that uses the larger color space, when outputting to an inkjet printer, or when you just aren't sure what you're going to do and you want to keep your options open.

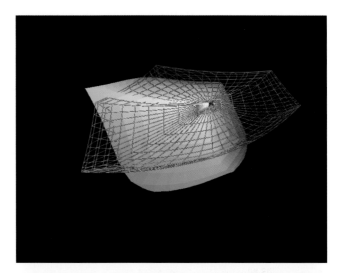

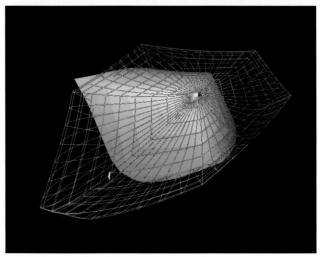

**Figure 7.5**

# note

A third editing space is gaining popularity in the photography world. It's called ProPhoto RGB. Its color gamut is even larger than Adobe (1998). Currently, few output devices support such a large gamut, but that will change as technology moves forward. In the meantime, it's better to stay away from ProPhoto as a working space because converting images for output on some devices results in unpredictable color shifts.

## Setting up Photoshop's working space

Now that you know about color spaces, you need to tell Photoshop how you want color handled when you open a photo file — which color space to use as a working space and what to do when the color space (color profile) of the photo doesn't match the working color space. Do that by following these steps:

**1** Choose Edit → Color Settings to open the Color Settings dialog box.

**2** Click the pull-down menu in the Settings box, and select North America Prepress 2. This configures the color settings with the best starting points, as shown in Figure 7.6.

**3** Click OK if you plan to use Adobe RGB (1998) as your working space as you're finished. If you plan to use sRGB, then click the RGB drop-down menu under Working Spaces. Select sRGB IEC61966-2.1, and click OK.

For the purposes of this book you're not concerned with the other working spaces in this dialog box (CMYK, Gray, and Spot), so leave them as they are.

The reason I encourage people to configure the Color Settings dialog box by initially selecting North American Prepress 2 is because this setting checks all the boxes under Profile Mismatches and Missing Profiles. When these boxes are checked and Photoshop finds a discrepancy between the color space you're using and the color space of a file you're opening, which is called a profile mismatch, it refers to the Color Management Policies boxes to resolve the conflict.

## note

The warning notice in the upper left corner of the Color Settings dialog box, shown in Figure 7.6, only appears when Photoshop CS4 is used with other Adobe Creative Suite products, such as Illustrator CS4 and InDesign CS4. It's used to insure that colors look the same in these color-managed applications. To Synchronize the color for all of these applications, go to Bridge and choose Edit → Creative Suite Color Settings. When the dialog opens, choose a color setting from the list and click Apply.

**Figure 7.6**

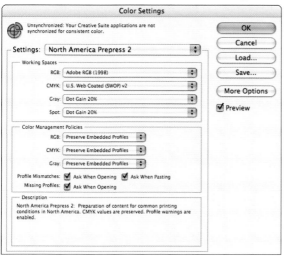

When you tell Photoshop to warn you and you open a file with a color space that doesn't match your working space, Photoshop prompts you to make a decision about how you'd like to handle the profile mismatch by opening the dialog box shown in Figure 7.7. These are your choices:

- **Use the embedded profile.** Opens the photo in its own color space using the photo's embedded profile.

- **Convert document's colors to the working space.** Moves the file into your working space by mapping its colors to the appropriate equivalents in your color space.

- **Discard the embedded profile.** Strips the image of any color information by ignoring its profile. This usually isn't a good idea — though I have used it when experimenting.

Choosing one of these settings allows you to manage your color space choices on the fly when opening a file. Don't bother trying to convert a file that's in the smaller sRGB color space into the larger working space of Adobe RGB (1998). When you begin with a small gamut, you pretty much have to live with it. The range of the original colors doesn't expand and change when the image is converted to a larger color space.

## tip

If you're using a dSLR camera, you can set your preferences to tell your camera which color space to use for capturing images. I recommend that you set this preference on Adobe RGB (1998). This way, you can decide to work on photos in a smaller space or leave them their larger native color space when you open them in Photoshop.

However, if you're opening a file with Adobe RGB (1998) into a working space of sRGB and you know that you need a smaller color space for output, converting an Adobe RGB (1998) file to sRGB before editing it is a good plan; that way, you'll see only colors that are reproducible.

After you get a handle on what's happening with profile mismatches and you get tired of being asked the same question every time you open a file, you can uncheck the question box in the Color Settings dialog box. I generally recommend against this, but I know that you may have reasons to make this choice.

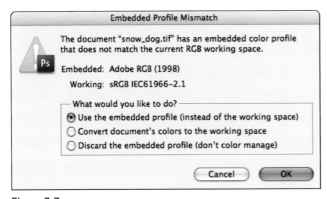

Figure 7.7

# Understanding Color Channels

Because you're working with an RGB color model, your images are composed of three separate color channels. One channel represents the red/cyan content of the image, another channel represents the green/magenta content of the image, and yet another channel represents the blue/yellow content of the image. Here's the weird part: Each of these channels is composed of grayscale data — all the tones are gray.

The best way to understand what's going on here is to look at the channels in a specific image. Follow these steps:

**1** Open the Spring_Flowers.tif practice file from the downloadable practice files on the Web site (www.wiley.com/go/photoshopcs4ats).

**2** **Find the Channels panel on your desktop; it's usually grouped with the Layers and Paths panels.** If you don't see the Channels panel, choose Window → Channels to open it.

**3** **Click the red channel icon.** This hides the other two channels so that you see only the red data in your image preview, as shown in Figure 7.8. Notice that everything that is red in the photo looks really light.

**4** **Click the green channel icon.** This hides the red channel and shows the green channel. Now the greens are lighter, and the deep reds at the top are quite dark.

**Figure 7.8**

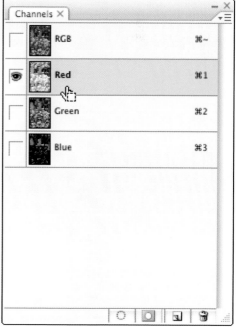

**5** **Click the blue channel icon to see only the blue channel.** Now just about all the flowers are dark except for a few pinkish flowers at the top. Notice that in all three channels the tonality of the fence stays about the same. That's because its color is mostly neutral — a shade of gray where red, green, and blue values are about the same.

**6** **To get back to full color, click the composite channel, labeled RGB, at the top of the stack.** Notice that all three channels become visible again because the little eye icons next to them are turned on.

**7** **Even though each of these channels is a grayscale image, when combined, they create color.** To see how it happens, start with only one channel visible. Then turn on the visibility of another channel by clicking the eyeball next to it. Notice how these two grayscales combine to create a limited amount of color. When the third channel is added, all the colors appear.

The main thing to get from this experiment is that when you're working in an RGB color model, every digital image is composed of three individual channels; one for each primary color: red green, and blue.

# Using the Info Panel and the Color Sampler Tool

Photoshop provides two useful tools for evaluating color in your digital photos: One is the Info panel, and the other is the Color Sampler tool. In combination, these two items allow you to monitor and measure each color channel as you make adjustments to your image. Take a look at the Info panel first. Follow these steps:

**1** **Open the Spring_Flowers.tif practice file.** If you still have it open from the preceding exercise, return it to its opening state by clicking the image icon at the top of the History panel.

**2** **Click the Info panel; it's usually nested with the Navigator and Histogram panels.** If you don't see the Info panel, go to Window → Info.

**3** **Move your cursor over the white horizontal fence section between the two vertical slats on the left.** Look at the RGB readout on the Info panel while doing this. The three channels are very

close in value — in the low 220s, as shown in Figure 7.9. That means the color of the fence in that spot is a very light shade of gray.

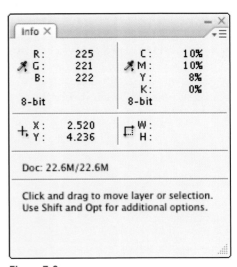

**Figure 7.9**

**4** **Now move the cursor over some of the flowers.** Notice that the red flowers at the top have high values in the red channel and low values in the green and blue channels. The yellow flowers in the foreground have readings that are high in the red and green channels and low in the blue channel.

**5** **Move the cursor over the middle vertical slat.** Notice that it has a high red value and a low blue value. That's because it's reflecting the red and yellow flowers in the foreground.

# tip

Here's another way to put theory into action and see how various color channels combine to create the color you see in an image: Practice looking at a color and guessing its RGB values.

Having the ability to measure color is cool, but you can make this feature even cooler by adding the Color Sampler tool to the mix. The Color Sampler tool is stacked with the Eyedropper tool and some other measurement tools, as shown in Figure 7.10. (The Count tool is only available in Photoshop CS4 Extended.)

With the Color Sampler tool, you can place up to four sample points anywhere in an image. Each is labeled with a number ranging from 1 to 4. An RGB (red, green, and blue) readout for each of these points is added to the bottom of the Info panel. When you make changes to tone or color a second readout is added to the right of the original sample readout on the info panel. This new readout displays the updated RGB values for the sample points, reflecting the changes your edits are having on the RGB values for those points.

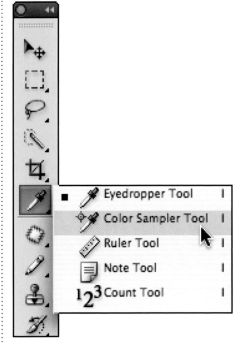

**Figure 7.10**

**1** **Select the Color Sampler tool from the Tools panel.**

**2** **Go to the Options bar at the top of the screen and change the setting from point sample to at least 5 by 5 Average, as shown in Figure 7.11.** This tells the tool to sample a grid of pixels that is 5 by 5 and average them instead of sampling a single point. This assures that some renegade pixel isn't accidentally sampled alone. This setting also affects the Eyedropper tool, which is okay because it shouldn't be set to sample single pixels for the same reason.

**3** **Return to the Spring_Flowers.tif practice file.**

**Figure 7.11**

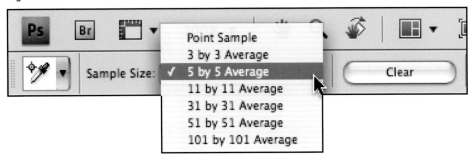

**4** Find a spot that looks white, but where the three channels are not quite the same by monitoring the Info panel readout. Click in the area to add a sample point. A sample point is placed on the image with the number 1 beside it. Numbers that correspond to the RGB values at the sample point are added to the bottom of the Info panel with #1 beside them.

**5** Add another sample point to the same area you measured on the middle slat in Step 5 from the preceding exercise. Its values also are added to the Info panel with #2 beside them.

**6** Choose Image → Adjustments → Levels (⌘+L/Ctrl+L) to open the Levels command.

**7** Move the middle gray Input slider to the left while watching the Info panel. Notice that a second row of numbers appears next to the sample values. These new numbers change as you move the gray Input slider, indicating what the new values are.

**8** Click OK. The second set of numbers disappears, but their values become the new sample points.

**9** You use this image again in just a moment so click ⌘+Z/Ctrl+Z to undo the Levels adjustment you just did.

## tip

After you place a sample point, you can move it somewhere else by clicking and dragging it. To delete it, click it and drag it out of the image frame. To clear all sample points, click the Clear button on the Tool Options bar. If you leave the sample points in the image, they won't show when you print it.

The ability to sample a particular area of the image and measure any changes can be very useful. This is especially the case when you're adjusting an image with something in it that should have a neutral color balance: All three color channels have the same value.

# Adjusting a Photo's Color

There are a number of ways to adjust color in Photoshop. In this section, you learn about the main color correction tools in Photoshop and some methodologies for using them. I'll begin with the least likely — the Levels command.

## Removing a color cast with Levels

When using the Levels command in Chapter 6, you may have noticed that its dialog box, shown in Figure 7.12, has its own set of three eyedroppers, located below the Options button. They are, from left to right:

- **Black Point Eyedropper.** This eyedropper is used to assign a black point to the darkest part of the image. If you know where the darkest area of the image is, click it with this tool to set the black point and convert that spot to 0 red, 0 green, and 0 blue. Any tones that are darker than the tone you click on are clipped.

- **Gray Point Eyedropper.** This eyedropper is used for creating a neutral gray; the RGB values become the same anywhere you click.

- **White Point Eyedropper.** This eyedropper works just like the Black Point Eyedropper except that it's used to set the white point in the image. When you click the lightest part of the image, this tool sets it as the white point and converts that tone to 255 red, 255 green, and 255 blue (the default settings). Any tones that are lighter than the tone you click on are clipped.

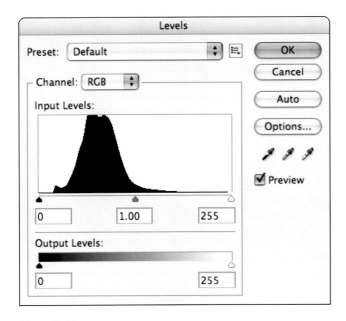

Figure 7.12

The tonal values that the Black Point Eyedropper and the White Point Eyedropper use for clipping points can be modified so that they don't clip to pure black (0) and pure white (255). For example, you can set them to clip at 15 and 240, meaning that the black point is 15 instead of 0, and the white point is 240 instead of 255. This allows you to leave some room for printing processes that don't handle extreme shadows and highlights very well, such as newspaper. You can modify them by double-clicking the eyedroppers and setting the RGB values to the value you want to call pure white or black.

Although this sounds useful, I have never found much use for the Black Point Eyedropper and White Point Eyedropper tools. The biggest problem with them is that you need to know where the lightest and darkest areas in an image are. I would rather handle clipping manually with clipping preview in Levels or Curves where I have more control. So I won't spend more time on the Black Point Eyedropper and White Point Eyedropper tools. Instead, I focus on the middle tool here: the Gray Point Eyedropper.

# note

The Gray Point Eyedropper is designed for color correcting; therefore, it is available only when editing color images.

The Gray Point Eyedropper is designed to neutralize the color and remove all color casts wherever you click with it. It does this by setting the values to the red, green, and blue channels to the same value. This new value is an average of the three original values unless a huge correction is being applied. You can use it anytime you know that a certain area of an image should be neutral in color.

Follow these steps to get a feel for how this tool works:

**1** **Go back to the flowers photo you were using in the preceding exercise.** If that image is not open, open it and repeat Steps 1 through 4 from the previous exercise.

**2** **Choose Image → Adjustments → Levels (⌘+L/Ctrl+L) to open the Levels command.** When you use the Gray Point Eyedropper, it affects any other Levels adjustments from that Levels session. Because of this, you should start a Levels adjustment with the Gray Point Eyedropper if you plan to use it. Then do other Levels adjustments to finish fine-tuning the tones in the image.

**3** **Click the Gray Point Eyedropper to activate it.** Now, anywhere you click in the image becomes neutral.

**4** **Click sample point number 1 in the image.** Notice that the readout in the Info panel shows that the numbers have been nudged into alignment. If they aren't exactly the same, it's probably because you didn't click in exactly the same spot as where the sample is placed. Not a problem — they don't have to be absolutely perfect. Remember, however, that every time you click the image, the gray point is reset.

**5** **Click sample point 2.** Notice that the whole image gets cooler. This is because that part of the white fence was reflecting all the red flowers. When you force the color to white, it removes the color being cast by the reflection, but adjusts the rest of the colors correspondingly, which is unacceptable. The lesson to be learned here is that not all neutrals are created the same. When you use this tool, you must be sure that the color you're clicking is actually supposed to have neutral color values.

**6** **Click sample point 1 to get the color back into alignment.** Now the image is ready for Levels adjustments using the Input sliders, covered in Chapter 6.

**7** **Click OK when you're finished.**

# tip

Curves has this same set of eyedroppers, which you use the same way to set black point, white point, and neutral gray.

Sometimes, the image may not have anything that is supposed to be a neutral gray. Or maybe you use the Gray Point Eyedropper, but you still want to do some further adjustment to get the colors to look the way you like them. When that's the case, you're ready to move on to Photoshop's main color adjustment tools.

## Learning color correction with the Variations command

Correcting color is a skill that takes time to develop. The real trick to color-correction is this: Identify the color that you don't like, and add its opposite until you don't see the offending color anymore. In order to pull this off, you must be able to see and identify the colors in an image. As you've seen, color is a science, but the perception of it is very personal.

I learned color theory when I began working in professional labs several years ago. Over the years, I color-corrected thousands of prints at those labs, so color correction became second nature to me. I sometimes have to remind myself just how difficult it was to learn in the beginning. With that in mind, I want to show you one of the best color-correction learning tools: the Variations command.

I encourage people who are new to color adjustment to begin with the Variations command because it can be a great tool for learning the differences among the six colors used. After you're able to identify these colors in a photo without the Variations ring-around, you'll find it much easier to use Photoshop's more powerful color correction tools.

Follow these steps to do some color-correcting with the Variations command:

**1** **Open the Garden_Gnome.tif practice file from the downloadable practice files on the Web site (www.wiley.com/go/photoshopcs4ats).** This photo looks a little cool in color, though it's hard to know exactly what the color of a gnome's skin tone should be.

**2** **Choose Image → Adjustments → Variations to open the Variations dialog box.** When the dialog box opens, you're presented with what's called a color ring-around. The uncorrected image is in the center, and it's ringed by equal amounts of the individual six colors, as shown in Figure 7.13.

**3** **To warm up this image, you need to add some red and possibly some yellow.** Click the thumbnail just above where it says More Red. Notice that the current pick at the top of the screen has changed to reflect the addition of red. Also notice that the whole ring-around has also been updated. The addition of red warmed up the photo, but it may have been too much. You need better control of this tool so you can be more discriminating with your color adjustment.

**Figure 7.13**

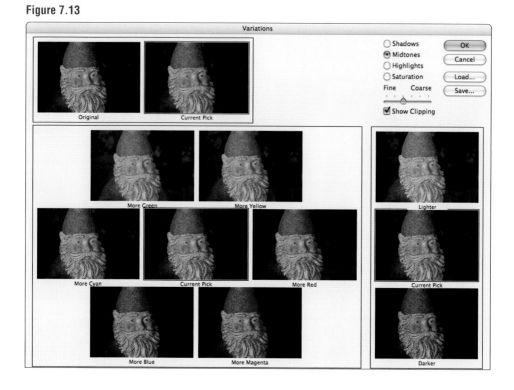

4 **Click the Original thumbnail at the top left to reset the Current Pick thumbnail to its original setting.**

5 **Go to the Fine/Coarse slider and move it to the left so that it lines up with the first vertical mark on the left of the scale.** Notice that the color value difference in the ring-around is much lower now. Lowering the amount of color correction makes the Variations tool usable for color correction. Now you can make minor adjustments and build them up until you have added the appropriate amount of color.

6 **Click the More Red thumbnail again.** A small amount of red is added to the Current Pick preview. Continue to click the red thumbnail until you feel that you've added enough red. To back up

and remove some red, click the More Cyan thumbnail — the opposite of red. If you want to add some yellow, do it now.

## tip

You can adjust the shadows, midtones, and highlights in variations by clicking the appropriate buttons at the top right of the dialog box. If you're having trouble with a color cast that's only in the shadows, for example, you can try to address it without shifting the highlights as much.

7 **When you're happy with the new color, click OK.** This is the moment of truth. It can be hard to see your adjustments in the Variations window because everything is small. After you click OK,

you really get a look at it. If you're not satisfied with what you see, press ⌘+Z/Ctrl+Z to undo the color adjustment. Go back to Variations and try again with a slightly different adjustment.

# note

The Variations command is the only command covered in this section that isn't available in the Adjustments panel as an Adjustment layer.

## Adjusting color with the Color Balance command

The Color Balance command has most of the adjustments the Variations command has, but it has some differences too. One of the main differences in the dialog box, shown in Figure 7.14, is that you don't get thumbnails in a ring-around for visual comparison, though you do get a better preview because you see real-time adjustments in the image itself as you move the sliders.

Another big difference is that you can make color adjustments one color unit at a time by moving these sliders. With Variations, you don't really know how many units of color you're adding when you adjust the Fine/Coarse slider.

The Color Balance tool gives you incredible control over the overall color balance of your images. When you understand color theory, you'll realize that it's the perfect tool for making global color adjustments to an image, especially when you want to use an adjustment layer. I use the Color Balance command on just about everything that needs an overall color adjustment.

Try adjusting a file with the Color Balance command:

1 **Open the Garden_Gnome.tif practice file again.** If it's already open, use the History panel to reset it to its opening state.

2 **Choose Image → Adjustments → Color Balance (⌘+B/Ctrl+B) to open the Color Balance dialog box.**

3 **Make sure the Preserve Luminosity box is checked.** This prevents any color adjustment from shifting the tonal values in the image, causing the image to get lighter or darker.

4 **Move the Red/Cyan slider to the red side and stop short of making a full correction.** As you do, notice that your image responds by getting redder.

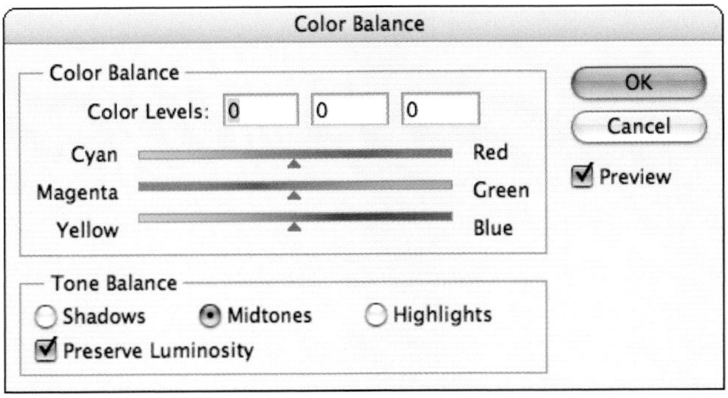

Figure 7.14

**5** Click the Highlights button to switch to highlight correction, and add more red to finish off your correction. I use this technique of splitting my correction between midtones and highlights often, especially in portraits. I add about 75 percent of the color I want to the midtones and the remaining 25 percent to the highlights.

**6** Add some yellow to the midtones and highlights.

**7** When you like the color, click the Preview button in the Color Balance dialog box to turn off the preview function. This shows you what the image looks like without the correction. Turn Preview on and off a few times to evaluate your correction.

**8** When you like what you've got, click OK. I used +39 red and –8 blue in the midtones and +14 red and –2 blue in the highlights. Figure 7.15 shows the image before and after color correcting with the Color Balance command. The left side is uncorrected and the right is adjusted with the Color Balance command.

# Fine-tuning color with the Hue/Saturation command

Even though the Color Balance command is my faithful companion, my favorite color adjustment tool is the Hue/Saturation command. With this amazing tool, you can work with color in a variety of ways that aren't possible with the Color Balance command.

# note

You may have noticed earlier that the Variations command has a saturation control. There's a reason I didn't point it out during that discussion. It's because the control is quite crude when compared to the real thing.

**Figure 7.15**

To open the Hue/Saturation dialog box, shown in Figure 7.16, choose Image→ Adjustments→ Hue/Saturation. The sliders in this dialog box allow you to modify three different aspects of a color:

- **Hue.** This is the color of a color — the difference in the red of an apple and the yellow of a banana is the hue. Use this slider to change the base color of a color.

- **Saturation.** This is the purity of a color — the difference between a black and white print and a color print. Use this slider to increase the saturation of a color with positive values or lower it with negative values.

- **Lightness.** This is just what it sounds like — it's the lightness of a color. Positive values add white to the color, and negative values add black to the color.

With these three sliders, you're able to have amazing control over the colors in an image. Take a look at some of the standard uses of the Hue/Saturation tool with these steps:

**1** Open the Hot_Air.tif practice file from the downloadable practice files on the Web site (www.wiley.com/go/photoshopcs4ats).

**2** Choose Image→ Adjustments→ Hue/Saturation (⌘+U/Ctrl+U). The Hue/Saturation dialog box opens.

**3** Move the Hue slider to right and stop when you get to a value of +120. Notice that as you drag the slider, the color bar on the bottom of the dialog box shifts to the left. This color bar, shown at the bottom of the dialog in Figure 7.17, gives you a preview of how the relationships in the color spectrum are changing as you adjust. For example, find the blue color on the upper color bar and look directly below it. Notice that the color below it is red, which is the same color as the sky. The color below yellow is cyan, which is the color of the yellow panels in the hot air balloon.

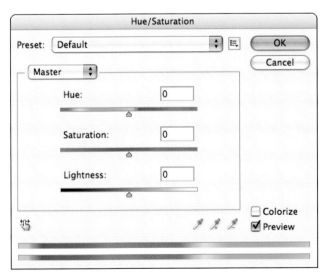

**Figure 7.16**

**Figure 7.17**

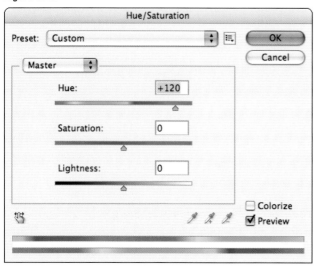

# note

The Colorize box is used to colorize an image with an overall color cast.

**4** Reset the Hue slider to 0.

**5** **Drag the Saturation slider all the way to the left.** When you do this, all color is removed from the image and it takes on a black and white appearance. This change is reflected in the color bars. Adjust the slider all the way to the right, and notice how all the colors become too saturated — almost florescent.

# note

If you're wondering why I haven't talked about the Lightness slider, it is because it's more useful when specific colors are being targeted for adjustment, which is discussed next.

**6** **Take a moment to experiment with the Hue and Saturation sliders to see the different kinds of effects they have when used in combination.**

The reason the Hue/Saturation command is my favorite color correction tool is that it can be used on specifically targeted colors. This is where this amazing tool really shines. Follow these steps to learn how to adjust specific color ranges within the image:

**1** **Open the Hot_Air.tif file again.** If it's still open from the last exercise and you didn't click OK, hold down the Alt key and click Reset to reset the dialog box values to their defaults.

# tip

Anytime you press the Alt key when a dialog box is open, the dialog's Cancel button turns into a Reset button. This is a much faster way to start over than canceling and re-launching the command.

**2** Choose Reds from the six colors shown in the channel pop-up menu, shown in Figure 7.18.

**3** Click and drag the Hue slider to the right and left. Notice that only colors that have red in them are affected. The same thing happens when you move the Saturation and Lightness sliders. That's because this adjustment is only taking place on the red channel.

**4** Reset all values to 0.

**5** Use the Targeted Adjustment tool icon on the lower left of the dialog box to directly select and adjust the saturation of a color by clicking and dragging on the image instead of choosing adjustments from the pop-up menu. After the color is selected, you can use the other sliders to make additional modifications. Go ahead and experiment with it for a moment and then reset all values to 0.

**6** Choose any color from the pop-up menu to activate the Eyedropper tools in the Hue/Saturation dialog box. These eyedroppers allow you to take targeted adjustment to a much higher level. When the Hue/Saturation dialog first opens, they're grayed out because you need to select a specific color from the pop-up menu to make them active.

**7** Click on the first Eyedropper tool on the left, and then click on the darker green color in the photo, near the top of the balloon, to sample it. Click in a few different spots in the green region of the baloon and notice that the preview color bar at the bottom of the dialog shifts to reflect the exact color range of the green you click. Also notice that the color in the channel menu shows Greens when you click the colors on the right side, and Cyans when you click those on the left. Clearly, all greens in this photo were not created equal.

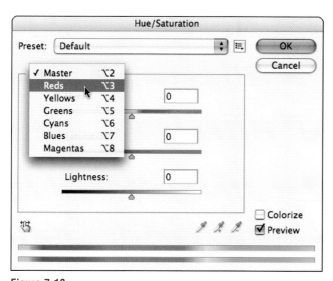

Figure 7.18

**8** Click on one of the darker green panels near the center of the green panels on the balloon. Adjust the Hue slider to –120. Notice that some of the greens are affected, but not all of them. That's because the variety of the color green in the green panels.

# caution

Be aware that when you target specific colors with the eyedropper tools, all similar tones anywhere in the image are affected.

**9** Click on the eyedropper with a plus sign (+) next to it. This is called the Add To Sample Eyedropper tool because it's used to add other similar colors to the originally selected color, expanding the range that will be affected. Click one of the green panels on the left that wasn't affected by the last step. When you click, the color is added to the colors being affected by the Hue adjustment and the colors are modified. Continue clicking the green panels until all of them are affected. Use the Preview button to compare before and after.

**10** If you notice that any of the yellow panels on the balloon are being unintentionally affected, use the eyedropper with the minus sign (–) beside it, the Subtract From Sample Eyedropper tool, to click on the colors you don't want to affect and remove them from the selected colors. Keep working with the Add To and Subtract From tools until only the two rows of green panels are being affected by the Hue adjustment.

**11** Drag the Lightness slider all the way to the left to –100. This adds black to the selected color range, changing the panels to gray and black. Figure 7.19 shows a detail of the before and after colors on the balloon. Positive values with the Lightness slider add white to the color, which lightens it.

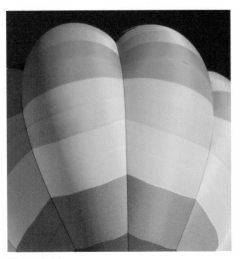

**Figure 7.19**

In this exercise the goal was to experiment with the techniques for adjusting specific color ranges with the Hue/Saturation command. This kind of color correction control allows you to do things like: change the hue and saturation of the blues in a sky, change the color of the greens in the grass or foliage, or change the color of someone's shirt, to mention a few examples. Just be aware that when using Hue/Saturation to target a specific color range that all colors within that range are affected. For example, if you change the blues in the sky, it will most likely affect the color of the blue jeans someone in the image is wearing.

## Using the new Vibrance command

The latest addition to the color correction lineup in Photoshop is the Vibrance command. Its dialog box, shown in Figure 7.20, has two sliders: Vibrance and Saturation. These two sliders combine to refine, and ultimately replace, the Saturation slider in the Hue/Saturation dialog box when adjusting overall saturation.

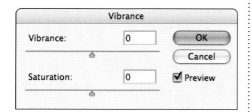

**Figure 7.20**

Here's how they work:

- **Vibrance.** This slider affects the image in a similar way to the Saturation slider in the Hue/Saturation dialog box, but there are some significant differences. One of the problems with using the Saturation slider in

the Hue/Saturation dialog box is that some colors that are already saturated become oversaturated. The Vibrance dialog box tries to minimize oversaturation as full saturation of a color is approached. It does so by affecting colors with lower saturation more than colors that have higher saturation. (It also tends to apply less saturation to skin tones.)

- **Saturation.** The effect of this slider is similar to the Saturation slider in the Hue/Saturation dialog box. However, the same values in each command can have different effects. That's because the Saturation slider's effect is combined with the Vibrance slider effect in the Vibrance dialog box.

# tip

The only downside to Vibrance is that there is no shortcut key for it. That's okay because you can create your own in the Keyboard Shortcuts menu (Edit → Keyboard Shortcuts).

Here's a cool experiment to show the difference between the effects of the Vibrance and Saturation sliders:

**1** Open the Hot_Air.tif file again one last time or return it to its opening state if it's still open.

**2** Choose Image → Adjustments → Vibrance. The Vibrance dialog box opens.

**3** Increase the Vibrance value to its maximum: +100. Notice that the colors in the image barely change. (Use the preview button to compare.) That's because the colors in this photo are already very saturated, especially the blue. The Vibrance slider prevents them from becoming oversaturated. Return the Vibrance value to 0.

**4** **Increase the value of the Saturation slider to its maximum of +100.** Notice that the colors nearly glow as they all become oversaturated.

The comparison in Figure 7.21 shows the difference between the effects of the two sliders in the Vibrance command (though they'll be even more extreme on your monitor than here in this book). Notice that the extreme clipping in the reds is beginning to obscure detail.

When using the Vibrance dialog box, it's best to focus your efforts on the Vibrance slider. Use the Saturation slider when you're more interested in lowering the intensity of colors.

This new smart color correction method replaces the old way of making straight saturation adjustments in the Hue/Saturation dialog box because it protects already saturated colors. Use it when you need to increase the overall saturation of an image. The only time you need the Saturation slider in the Hue/Saturation dialog box is when you need to change the saturation of a specific color range using the Targeted Adjustment tool or the Eyedropper tools — which are very handy when you need them.

**Figure 7.21**

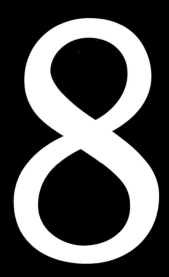

# Using Selections to Control
# Your Adjustments

Selections have been part of Photoshop since the earliest days. It's one of the concepts that seems to be most familiar to new users. By that I mean that most people have seen the "marching ants" (the moving, dashed line that surrounds a selected area), and they understand that selections are usually created around objects in an image. These selections are used to isolate content from the rest of the image so that it can be independently modified or repositioned. Some of Photoshop's selection tools require you to make precise drawings, while other "smart" selection tools help you with the process. In this chapter you learn about both types of tools and how to combine them to quickly create perfect selections.

# Using Photoshop's Main Selection Tools

The primary tools used to create selections are located on the Tools panel, and are called the the Marquee tools, the Lasso tools, the Magic Wand tool, and the Quick Selection tool. As I discuss these tools, notice how each is best suited to creating a particular type of selection.

## The Marquee tools

The Marquee tools are the second toolset from the top on the single-column Tools panel. This toolset, shown in Figure 8.1, consists of four tools that are stacked together:

- **Rectangular Marquee tool.** Use for making rectangular selections.

- **Elliptical Marquee tool.** Use for making elliptical selections.

- **Single Row Marquee tool.** Use for selecting a row that's only one pixel high.

- **Single Column Marquee tool.** Use for selecting a column that's only one pixel wide.

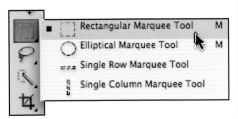

**Figure 8.1**

I don't think I've ever used the Single Row Marquee or Single Column Marquee tools. However, I use the Rectangular Marquee and Elliptical Marquee tools quite a bit. They both work in pretty much the same way; here's an example of how you would use the Rectangular marquee tool:

**1** Choose File → New to create a new file, and give it the following properties:
- Width = 6 inches
- Height = 4 inches
- Resolution = 300
- Color Mode = RGB Color / 8-bit
- Background = White

**2** Choose the Rectangular Marquee tool (M) from the Tools panel. Go to the top-left area of the new file. Click and drag downward to the lower right. As you do, you see a rectangular shape outlined by the marching ants and anchored at the spot where you first clicked. When you let go of the mouse button, the selection floats on the image.

**3** Remove the selection by going to the Select menu and choosing Deselect (⌘+D/Ctrl+D). It's cool you're able to draw a rectangle, but what if you really need a square?

## tip

You also can deselect by clicking outside the selected area with any of the other Marquee tools.

**4** Draw a square by holding down the Shift key while you draw the selection. This time you get a square because the Shift key locks the aspect ratio to a square ratio.

## tip

When used with the Elliptical Marquee tool, the Shift key modifier lets you create a perfect circle.

**5** Remove the selection by going to the Select menu and choosing Deselect (⌘+D/Ctrl+D).

**6** Select the Brush tool (B) from the Tools panel (it's eighth from the top on the single-column Tools panel). Use the Brush menu on the Options bar to set the Master Diameter to 400 px and the Hardness value to 0 percent. Be sure the Opacity value is 100 percent.

## see also

Brushes are discussed in detail in Chapter 9.

**7** Look at on the color swatches at the bottom of the Tools panel and click the swatch to open Photoshop's color picker, shown in Figure 8.2. The large swatch on the left, Set foreground color, controls the color of the paint that's applied with the paintbrush.

**8** Use the vertical color bar to select a hue and click a bright color in the preview window to choose a variation of it, and click OK. Notice that the red, green, and blue values of the color appear, along with other ways of describing the color. (The smaller swatches on the Tools panel, above the main swatches, are used to return the color swatches to their default colors of black and white.)

Figure 8.2

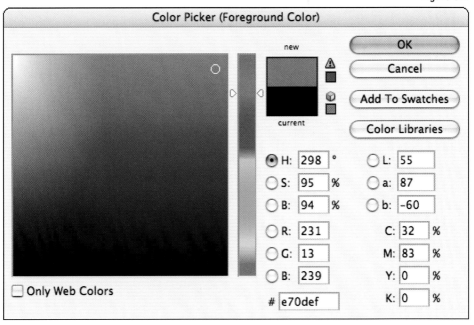

**9** Use the paintbrush to draw a stroke across the entire image that begins and ends outside the boundaries of the selection. Notice that the stroke appears only within the selection, as shown in Figure 8.3. This is what a selection is all about. When a selection is active, any action taken affects only pixels within the boundaries of the selection. All the pixels outside the selection are protected from any changes.

**10** Undo the paint stroke you just made (⌘+Z/Ctrl+Z), and then choose Select → Inverse (Shift+⌘+I/Shift+Ctrl+I). This inverts, or flips, the selection so that pixels outside the original box are now selected and the pixels inside the box are protected (unselected). The only change you'll notice is that the marching ants begin to march around the perimeter of the image. (If you can't see the edges of your image, zoom out.)

**11** Draw another stroke across the image. This time the paint gets applied only outside the box, as shown in Figure 8.4. The ability to invert any selection is very useful. It allows you to make a difficult selection by selecting something easier and then inverting it.

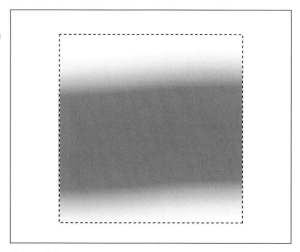

Figure 8.3

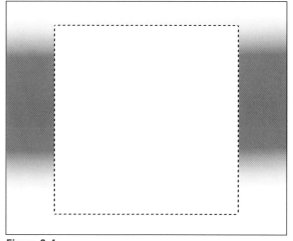

Figure 8.4

In the previous exercise, you visited the Select menu twice. That's because the Select menu is the main place to go to modify the properties of a selection after it's been created. Another way to access some of the commands in the Select menu is to right-click when a selection is active and a selection tool is chosen. Give it a try by right-clicking now with the Marquee tool. Notice that the context-sensitive menu has some options that aren't in the Select menu. They normally appear in other menus, but they're often used with selections.

# note

Be aware that if you right-click with a selection when no selection is active, you get a different context-sensitive menu.

## The Lasso tools

Quite often you need to make selections that are more organic, freeform shapes. Lasso tools are perfect for those kinds of selections. I've always liked the name "Lasso" for the set of tools discussed here. It implies that the tool is used to throw a selection around something to gain control of it. In this case, instead of a rope, you throw a line of marching ants. The Lasso toolset is the third icon from the top on the single-column Tools panel. The three Lasso tools shown in Figure 8.5 are stacked together.

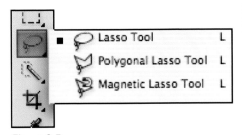

**Figure 8.5**

- **Lasso.** This is a true freeform tool. You can create a selection with just about any type of organic shape. This tool is not very well suited to creating selections with hard lines, such as when selecting the side of a building, especially when you're drawing with a mouse.

- **Polygonal Lasso.** This special tool is used to create selections with straight lines. Every time you click with this tool, a straight line is drawn between your current click and the most pervious click. It works quite well for selecting areas with straight edges.

- **Magnetic Lasso.** This tool is a "smart" selection tool. It's designed to see the lines that divide regions of differing tonal contrast — the boundary between the edge of a building and a bright sky, for example.

The Polygonal Lasso tool is useful when straight lines are needed, but I rarely use it. Most of the time, I need a selection that follows the contours unique to a specific situation in a specific image rather than a straight line. For that reason, I focus here on the two other tools: the Lasso and Magnetic Lasso.

These exercises help you compare and contrast the two tools:

1. **Open the Snow_Dog.tif practice file from the downloadable practice files on the Web site (www.wiley.com/go/ photoshopcs4ats.com).** Before you continue, make a quick Levels adjustment (⌘+L/Ctrl+L) to bring the overall brightness and contrast into line. I used 23, 1.08, 226. In this exercise, your goal is to enhance Ruby's colors — as neutral as they are — so that they're richer against the neutrality of the snow.

2. **Use the Fit on Screen viewing mode (⌘+0/Ctrl+0) to quickly zoom out until all of the dog is visible.** You need to see the entire dog for this exercise to be effective.

**3** Select the Lasso tool (L), and draw a selection around the dog so you can isolate her from the snow — you don't want to intensify the tint of the snow. Try to stay as close to the edges of the dog as you can. Go all the way around until you get back to the place where you started drawing. When you connect the beginning and end points, the selection is complete. As you can see, making an accurate selection like this is difficult with the Lasso tool. This selection tool does have good uses. It's great for creating freeform selections that are loose and don't have to follow an exact line. It just isn't the right selection tool for this job.

**4** Remove the selection you just created by choosing Select → Deselect (⌘+D/ Ctrl+D), or just click somewhere outside the selection with the Lasso tool.

**5** Select the Magnetic Lasso tool, stacked with the other Lasso tools.

**6** Set the options on the Options bar to the following settings, which are explained in a moment:

- Feather = 0px
- Anti-alias = checked
- Width = 5px
- Contrast = 40
- Frequency = 40

**7** Click near the tip of one of the ears to get the tool started and then release the mouse button. Begin outlining the dog again without clicking. Stay as close to her edges as possible. Notice how much easier it is to follow the edge of the contrast between the dog's dark fur and the snow with the Magnetic Lasso.

As you trace, notice that fastening points are being laid down by the Magnetic Lasso. These points anchor the selection to the edge between areas of contrast. If the tool won't place a point where you want one — maybe near the tip of Ruby's white tail or paw or along her back, click to manually insert a fastening point. If a point is placed in a spot where you don't want one, either by you or the Magnetic Lasso tool, use the Delete key to remove it as soon as it's placed. Successive points are removed every time you press the Delete key, so you can back up and remove several points if you need to. If you want to bail and start all over, press the Esc key.

## tip

If you have your cursor preferences set to Standard under Preferences → Cursors → Other Cursors, your cursor looks like the icon of the Magnetic Lasso tool. If you want to see the actual width of the tool, press the Caps Lock key. Just remember to press the key again when you're finished, because it modifies the way many cursors look. An easier way to accomplish this is to change your cursor from Standard to Precise in the Cursor preferences, which allows you to always see the brush size (unless the Caps Lock key is active).

**8** Continue tracing the entire outline around Ruby until you get back to where you started. When you return to the starting point, a small circle appears next to the cursor. This indicates that a click connects the beginning point with the end point, completing the selection. If you have problems closing the selection, try a gentle double-click. Your selection should now look something like Figure 8.6. Don't knock yourself out making a perfect selection at this point. In fact, notice that the selection in Figure 8.6 isn't perfect. I missed the tip of one of her ears, as well as the edge of her fur in a couple of places. You learn to fine-tune selections in a moment.

Figure 8.6

9 **Choose Image → Adjustments → Vibrance and, change the Vibrance value to +100, and click OK.** (Don't use an adjustment layer.) Notice that the dog's colors intensify, especially her blue eyes. The white fur begins to look more yellow, which is accurate to true life.

10 **Choose Select → Inverse to invert the selection. Now the snow is selected, which allows you to remove some of the cool tints and make it look whiter.** The marching ants begin moving around the outside perimeter of the image.

**11** Choose Image → Adjustments → Hue/Saturation.

**12** Select Cyans in the Edit pop-up menu, and use the eyedropper to sample the snow colors in the top-right corner of the image.

**13** Lower the Saturation value to −100, and click OK. The change is very subtle, but I like snow more without the cyan cast. If you made this adjustment to the entire image — without any selections — Ruby's eyes would lose their blue color.

# caution

Anytime you're adjusting an image and unpredictable things are happening, check to see if you have something selected. Even if you don't think you have, choose Select → Deselect to be sure. Sometimes, you select something without realizing it.

**14** Choose Filter → Blur → Gaussian Blur. The Gaussian Blur dialog box appears.

**15** Enter a value of 5, and click OK. This blurs the snow around the dog a bit, making her pop out of the background a bit more. Using a selection to isolate areas for selective blurring or sharpening is a very common technique.

As you can see, the Magnetic Lasso tool is powerful, especially in a scenario with edges between regions of contrasting tones like this one. When edges aren't so well defined, it becomes necessary to modify the Magnetic Lasso tool's properties in the Options bar, shown in Figure 8.7, so that it accurately follows the edge.

# note

All the settings on the Tool Options bar — except Refine Edge — are applied before the tool is used.

Look at some of these settings:

- **Feather.** Used to blur the edge of the selection, creating softer selections. I tend to leave Feather set to 0 because feathering can be applied after a selection is in place, keeping more options on the table.

- **Anti-alias.** Used to smooth jagged edge transitions. This should be turned on and left on. It's available for the Lasso tools, the Elliptical Marquee, and the Magic Wand.

- **Width.** Specifies the size of the area where edge detection occurs. It specifies the maximum distance from the pointer where an edge will be seen by the Magnetic Lasso tool.

- **Contrast.** Used to modify the Lasso's sensitivity to edge contrast. Higher settings cause the tool to see edges with higher contrast only.

- **Frequency.** Specifies the rate at which fastening points are attached to the edge. Higher settings tend to anchor the selection more quickly, adding a higher frequency of fastening points.

- **Use tablet pressure to change pen width.** Appears as an icon; used to quickly turn the pen pressure setting on and off when working with a graphics tablet.

- **Refine Edge.** Allows you to do a number of modifications to a selection after it's been created.

Figure 8.7

# see also

Graphics tablets are discussed in Chapter 9.

Experiment with different Width, Contrast, and Frequency values on the Snow_Dog.tif file. Get a feel for how each affects the Magnetic Lasso's selection process. However, keep in mind that it isn't necessary to tweak this tool to perform perfectly. When used properly, it creates a selection that's 90 percent complete in just a few moments. You can quickly add areas that you miss to the selection with more appropriate selection tools.

## The Magic Wand tool

The Magic Wand tool — as I'm sure you can tell by its name — is another smart selection tool. It's best suited for selecting colors that are similar to one another. In fact, in the right scenario, few selection tools can match its speed.

When you select the Magic Wand tool, the Options bar has these options available:

- **Tolerance.** Affects the range of similar colors that the tool selects. Low settings restrict the selection to colors that are quite similar to one another. High values allow the tool to select a broader range of colors that are less similar. Settings range on a scale of 0 to 255.

- **Contiguous.** When checked, only similar pixels that are touching are selected. This is a great way to control the Magnetic Lasso's power. When you want to select every similar color in the image, uncheck Contiguous. When you only want to select similar colors that are touching one another, check it. Using Contiguous allows you to do things like select a single flower out of a field of similarly colored flowers, as long as their borders aren't touching one another.

- **Sample All Layers.** This allows you to sample similar tones from all layers instead of the currently active layer.

- **Refine Edge.** Used to modify the edge of a selection.

Here, you play with the Magic Wand a bit to get a feel for it:

**1** **Open the Seagull1.tif practice file.** The goal here is to select the bird as quickly as possible. You could probably select it with the Magnetic Lasso in under a minute, but I want to show you a method that's even faster.

**2** **Select the Magic Wand tool (W) from the Tools panel.** It's fourth from the top on the single column Tools panel. It's stacked with the Quick Selection tool.

**3** **Set the tool options in the Options bar to the following values:**

- **Tolerance = 30**
- **Anti-alias = on**
- **Contiguous = on**
- **Sample All Layers = off**

**4** **Click the sky.** When you do, everything but the bird is selected.

**5** **Choose Select → Inverse to invert the selection, and the job's done.** The bird was selected with two clicks.

It's pretty rare for an automated tool to work this flawlessly. If the background behind the bird were full of detail, such as lots of clouds with large tonal and/or color variations, the previous method wouldn't work very well. You would have to select the bird instead. Look at how you'd do this using the Magic Wand tool with multiple selections:

**1** **Go back to the Seagull1.tif file.** If any selections are active, deselect them.

**2** **Select the Magic Wand (W) tool, and click on the bird to select it using the same tool options that you used in the previous set of steps.**

**3** **Click in a couple of darker tones on its chest.** As you do, you can see that you can select only small areas at one time. No matter where you click on the bird's chest, you end up with a partial selection, as shown in Figure 8.8.

# tip

When you're using the Magic Wand tool, you can deselect a current selection by moving the cursor inside the selection and clicking once.

**4** **Deselect the Contiguous option from the Options bar to turn it off, and then click the bird's chest again in the same spot.** Now more tones are being selected

because they no longer need to be touching one another, but the selection is still inadequate.

**5** **Increase the Tolerance setting by increments of 20, and experiment by clicking the bird's chest.** You might get lucky and eventually stumble across the magic number. However, there's a much faster way to build this selection with multiple selections.

**6** **Reset the Tolerance value to 30, and deselect any selections.**

**7** **Click the bird's chest to get the selection started Hold down the Shift key.** A small plus sign (+) appears next to the cursor, indicating that another click will add a new selection to the current selection.

**8** **Click somewhere else on the bird to add to the current selection.** Notice that more pixels have been added to the first selection.

**9** **Continue Shift+clicking different areas of the bird until you eventually get all of it selected.**

**Figure 8.8**

It's easy to accidentally select pixels you don't want to select when the tolerance is set this high. If that happens, use the Alt key to Alt+click the areas you want to remove from the selection. When you hold down the Alt key, you see a small minus sign (–) next to the icon, indicating that you're about to remove something from the selection.

You also can use the icons on the left side of the Options bar, shown in Figure 8.9, to change the tool to automatically add or subtract from the selection. The advantage to using the keyboard modifier keys is that they're faster. The advantage to using the tool options icons is that you can turn on a setting and leave it turned on. Just remember to turn it off when you're finished so you don't get confused later.

**Figure 8.9**

There are a couple of important lessons to be learned here. First, you can always do things in more than one way in Photoshop. Second, some methods are much more efficient than others. In the previous example, the difference was in the selection strategy, rather than the choice of tools. So remember, using the right tool for the job is important, but using that tool in the most efficient way is equally important.

When you're first starting out, these distinctions may not be so clear. Being able to simply get the job done, in some cases, is cause for celebration. That's okay. Just allow yourself to continue learning about the main tools you use so you become familiar with their various nuances. Eventually, you'll learn to quickly recognize situations that lend themselves to one particular tool or technique.

# The Quick Selection tool

The Quick Selection tool, introduced in Photoshop CS3, is the latest smart selection tool in the Tools panel. This new tool combines the smart technology behind the Magic Wand with the flexibility of a brush tool, allowing smart selections to be painted into the image. The Quick Selection tool also does a nice job of creating boundaries around the selected area, providing more defined selection boundaries than selections with the Magic Wand.

1  **Open the practice file, Spring_Flowers. tif, from the downloadable practice files on the Web site (www.wiley.com/ go/photoshopcs4ats).**

2  **Select the Quick Selection tool from the Tools panel.** (It's fourth from the top in the single column Tools panel.) It's stacked with the Magic Wand.

3  **Make sure that Auto-Enhance is selected on the Options bar.** It adds some of the selection edge fine-tuning that results in a smoother edge. This setting also allows the selection to flow more easily toward the edges of the content being selected.

4  **Adjust the Brush size of the Quick Selection tool to 100 px, leave Hardness set to 100, and Spacing set to 1 percent.** Try to select only the orange and yellow flowers in the foreground. Begin painting in the lower-right section of the image. As you paint, notice how the tool seeks similar colors.

# note

By default, the Add to Selection button on the Tool Options bar is selected, which means that every stroke adds to the last.

**5** **Continue painting until all of the flowers in front of the fence are selected.** Decrease the size of your brush when you get to the edges where the flowers and the fence overlap. If some of the fence is accidentally selected, press the Alt key while you paint to subtract it. Soon, your selection should look like the image in Figure 8.10. Leave this image open as you will continue to work with it more in the next section.

# Secrets of selection success

Each of the selection tools I've discussed so far has strengths and weaknesses. Some tools are smart: One might be good at selecting similar colors, while another is good at finding edges. Other tools, like the Lasso, are great when you want complete control over the tool.

Knowing about these differences — and choosing selection tools based on them — is the foundation of successful selection strategies. After you're comfortable with these differences,

**Figure 8.10**

you can take your selections to the next level by combining selection tools, based on their strengths, to quickly create perfect selections.

For example, in the example from the previous set of steps, there's still a problem. You can see it in Figure 8.10. Background areas, showing between and behind the foreground flowers, were also selected when the flowers were selected. You could use the Subtract selection button on the tool options of the Quick Selection tool (or hold down the Alt key) to go back and remove each of these areas from the selection. However, I want to show you a much faster

approach that takes only one or two clicks on the image with the Magic Wand tool and builds from the previous set of steps:

1  **Starting from Step 5 in the previous section, choose the Magic Wand tool, and set its Tolerance value to 28 and make sure that Contiguous is unchecked so that all similar tones are selected.**

2  **Alt+click in the large dark area that's just left of the middle of the image to deselect all the dark areas in the foreground as shown Figure 8.11.)** If too much is deselected, back up by undoing and try again with a slightly lower Tolerance value.

Figure 8.11

**3** If by chance a couple of floating pixels are still not deselected when they should have been, Alt+click them, or switch to the Lasso tool and remove them by holding down the Alt key and drawing a loose shape around them. With only a few clicks, all of the flowers in the foreground are selected. Now you could use the Hue/Saturation command to change them to a different color, or use the Levels command to lighten or darken them.

Mixing and matching tools to quickly piece together a great selection is the key to selection success. Use one tool that's suited to quickly building 90 percent of the image. Then use other selection tools to add and remove the bits and pieces they're most suited for working with. This strategy is much more efficient than fiddling with a particular tool's settings, trying to set its options so it creates the perfect selection all by itself.

# Fine-Tuning Selections

Selecting the right information is the first part of creating a great selection. The second part is adjusting the edge of the selection so that modifications made to selected pixels blend with the surrounding, non-selected pixels.

## Feathering a selection's edge

One of the most used methods of modifying a selection's edge boundary is the Feather command. As I mentioned earlier, with some tools it's possible to feather a selection before creating it, but it's more flexible to leave that decision until after the selection is created.

Here's a look at how that's done:

**1** Choose File → New to open a new file, and give it the following properties:

- Width = 6 inches
- Height = 4 inches
- Resolution = 300
- Color Mode = RGB Color / 8-bit
- Background = White

**2** Select the Rectangular Marquee tool and create a selection on the left side of the image. Make sure that the feather value on the Options bar is 0 px before you draw.

**3** Select the Paint Bucket tool (G) from the Tools panel. It's stacked with the Gradient tool, twelfth from the top. Click inside the rectangular selection to fill it with the foreground color. I used black, the default foreground color.

**4** Draw another selection with the Rectangular Marquee on the right side of the image that is similar in size to the selection on the left.

**5** Choose Select → Modify → Feather. The Feather Selection dialog box opens.

**6** Enter a value of 30, and click OK. Use the Paint Bucket to fill the new selection with the foreground color. Your two boxes should look something like Figure 8.12.

**Figure 8.12**

I want to point out a couple of things here. First, when the selection is feathered, the angular corners are rounded off. This shows that feathering tends to smooth edges around sharp detail. Second, the feathering takes place on both sides of the marching ants. That means the feathering effect is feathering outward and inward, with respect to the selection boundary.

Feathering a selection allows changes in a selected area to transition into unselected areas. The amount of feathering for a particular job depends on the size of the file. Thirty pixels is a lot for a small file like the $4 \times 6$ at 300 ppi (pixels per inch) file you just used. On a larger file, like a $16 \times 20$ or $20 \times 30$ at 300 ppi, a feather of 30 pixels would have much less of an effect. Sometimes when you use the Feather command, it takes a little trial-and-error to find the right

amount of feathering. You try one setting and follow through with whatever adjustments you want to make in the selected area. If you don't like the selection boundary transition after your changes, back up and try a different amount of feathering and redo the effect until you find the right formula.

## Using the Refine Edge command

The Refine Edge button appears on the Options bar whenever a selection tool is active. You can see it back in Figure 8.7. When you click the Refine Edge button, the dialog box shown in Figure 8.13 opens. (The Refine Edge dialog box can also be opened by choosing Select ➔ Refine Edge.)

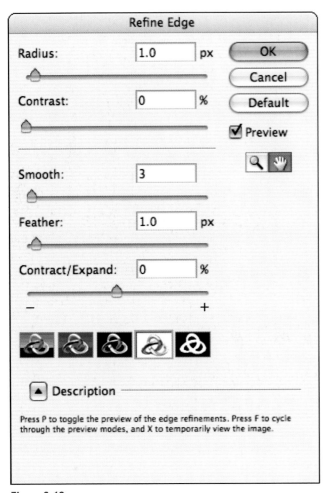

Figure 8.13

The Refine Edge dialog box features five sliders for modifying the edges of a selection. You can use these tools individually or together:

- **Radius.** Designates the size of the area around the selection's boundary where changes will occur. You can increase it to create more precise selections around soft detail such as hair and fur.

- **Contrast.** Removes any fuzziness in a selection's edge. It's often used to remove any noise that's picked up by increasing the Radius setting. Noise is caused by random fluctuations in pixel values. In its purest sense, it usually looks like film grain.

- **Smooth.** Removes the hills and valleys in a selection's boundary. Higher settings create a smoother edge.

- **Feather.** Softens edge transitions on either side of a selection (as you've already seen).

- **Contract/Expand.** Makes a selection larger or smaller.

# tip

There's a very useful area at the bottom of the dialog box called Description. It gives you a description of the various sliders and viewing options when you hover the cursor over them. If you don't see any descriptions, click the button with a triangle on it to show them.

In the past, Smooth, Feather, Expand, and Contract were options in the Select menu that were used to modify a selection. Using them was anything but intuitive because the effects of changes to these settings couldn't be seen until after the selection process, which resulted the trial and error I mentioned earlier. When these settings were combined, the results became even harder to predict because they had to be applied in separate steps. The Refine Edge dialog box options provide an elegant solution to that problem by providing five different ways to preview all modifications to the settings before they're applied.

At the bottom of the Refine Edge dialog box are five preview thumbnails. When one of these buttons is clicked, it changes the way the selection is previewed.

# tip

Press the F key while the Refine Edge dialog box is open to cycle through the five preview modes. While in those modes, press the X key to temporarily hide the preview. Press the X again to reinstate it.

Here's what each is and does, from left to right:

- **Standard.** Shows the selection in the usual way with our friends the marching ants.

- **Quick Mask.** Previews the selection as a Quick Mask. The unselected area is seen toned with a reddish color.

- **On Black.** Places the selected area on a black background to isolate it from the rest of the image content.

- **On White.** Places the selected area on a white background to isolate it from the rest of the image content.

- **Mask.** Previews the type of mask that will be created by the selection. This is extremely handy when creating masks from selections. Figure 8.14 shows the Mask preview when the feather value is increased.

# see also

You learn about creating masks from selections in Chapter 9.

This preview feature is great. It allows you to create the selection you need without lots of trial and error. It also lets you see how one setting can be used to tweak the modifications of other settings. The biggest drawback I see is that I end up playing with this tool more than I need to because it's so much fun to compare and contrast different edge refinement scenarios.

# tip

When you get down to business with this tool, zoom in to take a closer look at the selection's edges. You can use the Zoom tool that's in the dialog box to click the image or use the standard keyboard shortcuts for zooming.

**Figure 8.14**

# Cutting and Pasting with Selections

You've seen how useful selections are for isolating parts of an image so that local changes can be made to its tone and or color. Selections also are used to isolate something and then copy it somewhere else or remove it altogether. Here's an example you can try:

**1** Open the Seagull1.tif practice file from the downloadable practice files on the Web site (www.wiley.com/go/photoshopcs4ats).

**2** Select the Magic Wand from the Tools panel, set the Tolerance to 30 in the Options bar, and check Contiguous.

**3** **Click the sky to select it.**

**4** **Choose Select → Inverse (Shift ⌘+I/ Ctrl+I) to invert the selection.** Now only the bird is selected. You have two options now for creating a new layer with just the bird in it — to copy or cut. The difference is that cutting leaves a hole behind in the original layer. Copying doesn't affect the original layer.

**5** To cut, choose Layer → New → Layer via Cut (Shift+⌘+J/Shift+Ctrl+J). This cuts the selected information and copies it to a new layer. The first clue that a new layer has been created is that the marching ants disappear. The second clue that a new layer, called Layer 1, appears in the Layers panel, shown in Figure 8.15.

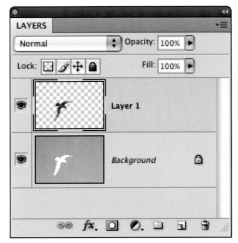

**Figure 8.15**

**tip**

A new feature in Photoshop CS4 is called spring loaded keys. When you temporarily need a tool like the Move tool here, press and hold its keyboard shortcut key — in this case, the V key. When you do, the tool switches to the Move tool temporarily while the key is depressed. Use the tool and then let go of the key when you're done. When the shortcut key is released, the tool reverts (springs back) to the tool that was active before the shortcut key was depressed.

**6** Select the Move tool (V) from the Tools panel, and move the bird to the right. Notice that only the duplicate bird on Layer 1 moves. That's because it's the currently selected layer, highlighted in blue in the Layers panel. When Layer 1 is moved, the hole left behind by the cut is revealed on the Background layer. The color of that hole will be the same as the current background color in the color swatches at the bottom of your Tools panel.

**7** Use the History panel to back up to the end of Step 3 to undo the Layer via Cut. This time you copy the selected information instead of cutting it. Choose Layer → New → Layer via Copy (⌘+J/ Ctrl+J). Move the duplicate bird to the right. This time, your image should look like Figure 8.16, with two birds visible.

**tip**

If you want to move the duplicate bird straight to the right, hold down the Shift key as you click and drag. The Shift modifier key restricts the movement of the Move tool to straight lines: up, down, and sideways.

**8** Open the Seagul2.tif practice file from the downloadable practice files (www.wiley. com/go/photoshopcs4ats) so you can move the duplicate bird to this image. You should now have two files open. You need to position the images so you can see both of them at the same time. Use the Arrange Documents menu on the Application bar and select the horizontal 2 Up view, shown in Figure 8.17.

Figure 8.16

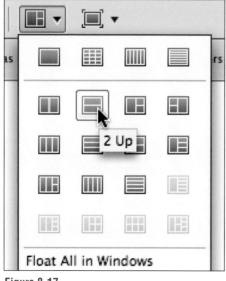

Figure 8.17

9 **Click the header of the Seagul1.tif photo to make sure it's the active image.** (The header is the top of the image that displays the name of the file.) When the file is active, you can see both layers in the Layers panel. Make sure that Layer 1 is still the active layer. If it isn't, click on the layer in the Layers panel to make it active.

## tip

If you hold down the Shift key as you drag and drop a layer, the new layer is dropped into the center of the image. Otherwise, it's placed wherever you drop it.

**10** **Select the Move tool (V) and click anywhere on the Seagull1.tif file and drag anywhere onto the Seagull2.tif photo.** When you release the mouse button, the dragged layer is dropped into place. By the way, when you drag a layer from one image into another, the first layer stays behind and a duplicate is created in the second image's Layers panel. I use this technique, without the selection, when I need the same adjustment layer on two files. Suppose I have two similar photos that are shots of the same subject taken at the same time. If I create a Color Balance adjustment layer for one, I can drag it onto the other image instead of building one from scratch for the second image.

**11** **After the duplicate bird is in the new image, use the Move tool to fine-tune its positioning until it looks something like Figure 8.18.** Note that the Background layer is a special layer and it's always locked by default, so you can't reposition it. This helps to prevent you from accidentally changing something on it. If you want to move it, all you have to do is rename it to anything other than Background. To rename the layer, double-click on it anywhere in the Layers panel. A dialog opens allowing you to change the name. It doesn't matter what name you use.

# tip

It's usually best to leave individual layers intact so that you can tweak them later if needed. However, sometimes it's necessary to merge them together. To merge all layers, choose Layer → Flatten Image. To merge the two layers without flattening other layers, select the top layer and choose Layer → Merge Down.

**Figure 8.18**

The general idea when using the technique you just used is to add a visual element to an image. However, you can also use the same technique to hide a visual element by copying information and placing it on top of the thing you want to hide. For example, you may want to hide an annoying light switch on a wall in the background of an image by copying a section of nearby wall and dropping it on top of the light switch and then merging the layers.

# Using the Transform Command

The two images in the previous example happen to have the same pixel dimensions. But if the dimensions were different, the incoming layer would have changed size relative to the difference in size between the two files. For example, if you drag a layer from an image with pixel dimensions of 2400 × 1600 into an image with pixel dimensions of 1200 × 800, the incoming layer — the bird in the last example — will look much larger in the new image than it did in its original image. If this were unacceptable, it would be necessary to scale down the bird's layer with the Transform command.

**note**

When dragging and dropping adjustment layers, you don't need to worry about any difference in size. That's because they re-size themselves to fit the entire image's pixel dimensions.

Figure 8.19 shows the commands in the Transform menu (Edit→ Transform). Each is used to change a different geometric aspect of a layer. You use the commands in the first group to make custom modifications where you have direct control. You use the second group to quickly perform common rotations. You use the last two choices to flip the orientation of the layer.

**tip**

If you want to flip or change the rotation of the entire image, rather than a layer, you need to use the Image→ Image Rotation menu.

Here's how to use the Transform command to transform the bird on Layer 1 in the last exercise:

**1** **Make sure nothing is selected (⌘+D/ Ctrl+D).**

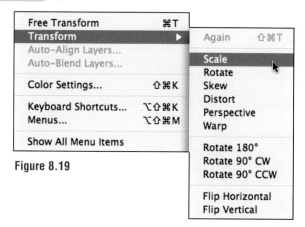

**Figure 8.19**

# Creating Flexibility with
# Layer Masks

Several years ago, when I first began my journey with Photoshop, the concept that seemed hardest to grasp was layer masking. I don't know how many times I read about it before the proverbial light turned on. When that light did go on, it illuminated not only a style of editing files, but also a philosophy of using a non-destructive Photoshop workflow based on the flexibility of layer masks. My goal here is to turn that light on for you so that you learn to master one of Photoshop's most powerful features — masking.

# What Is a Layer Mask?

Just about everyone has heard of masking tape. It's that papery tape that gets its name from the function it performs. If you plan to paint something, say a door for example, and you don't want to paint the doorknob or hinges, you cover them with masking tape first. That way you don't have to worry about paint getting on them when you apply the paint. The perfection of your work is revealed after the paint dries and the masking tape comes off.

This is very similar to the way layer masking works. Parts of a layer are masked off so that they're unaffected by modifications to the layer. Those areas become invisible, revealing the layer directly below. It's like using an eraser to remove part of the layer, with one major exception. Photoshop's Eraser tool is destructive because it makes permanent changes that can't be undone after the file is closed. As long as a layer remains intact, its mask can be changed completely at any time.

## note

When working with layers, it's always important to save master files with all of your layers intact. That means saving in the PSD (Photoshop document) or the layered TIFF file format.

The difference between masking tape and layer masking is that layer masking is applied with paint. The basic concept is that white paint is used to reveal information on the layer mask and black paint is used to hide it. The most common tool used to apply this paint is the Brush tool. Because of that, it's useful to explore the Brush tool before you begin creating your own masks.

## note

Black paint completely hides layer information and white paint reveals it. Gray paint partially hides and partially reveals layer information. The darker the gray is, the more information it hides. A lighter gray reveals more information.

# Working with the Brush Tool

You've used the Brush tool in a couple of exercises so far, yet those exercises haven't fully explored it. The following sections walk you through a couple of exercises that help you get a feel for setup options for this tool and how those options affect the application of paint.

## note

Several of Photoshop's tools, in addition to the Brush tool, use what's called brushes. A brush is the virtual equivalent of a real paintbrush. It's used to apply colors, tones, and even pixel information. Most of these settings explored here also apply to them.

# Changing Brush settings with the Options bar

One basic way of making adjustments to a brush is with the tool's options on the Options bar. Here's an exercise that will familiarize you with the Brush tool and how to use the Options bar to set its properties.

**1** **Choose File → New (⌘+N/Ctrl+N) to create a new document.** The New Document dialog box appears.

**2** **Set the following properties:**
- **Width = 6 inches**
- **Height = 4 inches**
- **Resolution = 300**
- **Color Mode = RGB Color/8-bit**
- **Background Contents = White**

**3** **Select the Brush tool (B) from the Tools panel, eighth from the top on the single-column Tools panel.**

**4** **Press the D key to set the foreground color to black.** The D shortcut key loads the default foreground and background colors — black and white. You can verify this by checking the two color swatches at the bottom of the Tools panel.

**5** **Click the Brush pop-up menu to the right of where it says Brush in the Options bar.** The menu, shown in Figure 9.1, has two sliders for Master Diameter and Hardness, as well as an assortment of brush presets below. The presets are specific brush settings that you can load by clicking the icons. (You can also access this menu by right-clicking on the image while the Brush tool is active.) Use the sliders to Set the Master Diameter for your brush to 100 px, and set the Hardness to 100%.

**Figure 9.1**

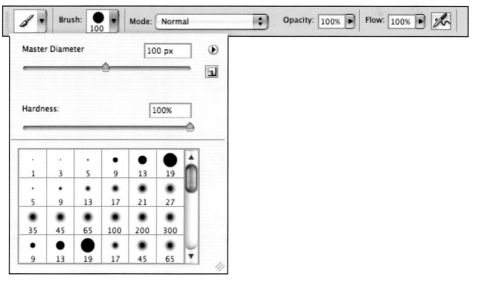

**6** Click one side of the new file you opened, and drag across the upper part of the white background while holding down the mouse button. You should see a heavy, black line appear on the white background.

## tip

If you want a perfectly straight horizontal or vertical line, hold down the Shift key while drawing.

**7** Right-click the image to open the Brush menu and change the Hardness value to 0%, and then draw a new line just below the first line. Notice is that the edges of the line are much softer. Notice also that the line isn't as thick as the first line. The softness of the edge fades in toward the middle of the stroke.

**8** Change the Opacity to 50% in the Options bar, and draw a third line below the second line. The new line is just like the previous line except that it's much lighter.

**9** Draw another line from top to bottom, as shown in Figure 9.2. Notice that when this line crosses the bottom line, the two strokes combine to create a tone that's twice as dark. If you want to verify this, use the Eyedropper tool to measure the bottom line where the lines cross and where they don't cross. Your values should be close to 64 and 128 respectively. Recall that you have 256 tones at your disposal (black = 0 and white = 255). The vertical stroke darkened the horizontal stroke by 50%, lowering it from 128 to 64.

You may be wondering why two 50% opacity strokes that cross each other don't combine to create 100% opacity. That's because each of the 50% strokes is simply making the current darkness of the stroke 50% darker. Even ten 50% strokes on top of each other don't combine to equal 0 (black). Instead, they equal 1 because no matter how many times you reduce the brightness of the strokes by 50%, you can never halve the density to 0.

Another adjustment on the Options bar is the Flow setting. Flow controls the rate at which a color is applied as a stroke is drawn. The lower

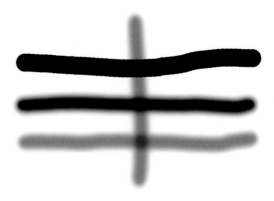

Figure 9.2

the value, the more spread out the color's application is. With a hard brush, this manifests as overlapping circles. I have to tell you that I rarely change the Flow value from 100%. I mention it here because students often ask what the Flow setting does.

One last thing to look at on the Brush tools settings on the Options bar is the Airbrush button, just to the right of the Flow setting (refer to Figure 9.1). When this setting is enabled by clicking on it, paint is continually applied while the mouse button is held down, much like holding a can of spray paint in one place while spraying. The results of painting with the Airbrush vary depending on the other settings on the brush. Because of that, I suggest leaving it turned off for now while you familiarize yourself with the Brush tool.

# Keyboard shortcuts for managing the Brush tool

There are some useful keyboard shortcuts that you should be aware of, in addition to pressing D to reset the default foreground and background color, when working with the Brush tool. You can use these shortcuts with any tool that uses a brush.

- **To change the brush size, use the bracket [ ] keys on your keyboard.** The right bracket makes the brush larger, and the left bracket makes it smaller.

- **To change the hardness in 25 percent increments, press the Shift key and the right or left bracket.** The left bracket reduces the hardness, and the right bracket increases it. If you are set at 100%, pressing Shift+[ four times reduces the hardness to 0%.

- **To change opacity, use the numbers on the keyboard.** Press 3 to set it to 30% or 5 to set it to 50%. If you want 55%, press 5 twice quickly. If the Airbrush feature is active, pressing numbers on the keyboard changes Flow instead of Opacity. To change the brush's opacity when using the Airbrush, use Shift plus the number.

# Using the Brushes panel

With the Tool Options bar and a handful of shortcuts, you can quickly change the main settings on a brush. Sometimes, though, those quick settings aren't enough to create the type of brush you need. When this happens, it's time to go to the main control center for the Brush tool — the Brushes panel.

You open the Brushes panel, shown in Figure 9.3, by choosing Window → Brushes, if it's not already on your desktop. Each menu on the left of the panel opens different options on the right, allowing for a huge amount of control over the Brush tool. In Figure 9.3 the Brush Tip Shape menu is shown. The preview window at the bottom shows how the current selection of settings is affecting the brush.

The Brushes panel is where Brush power-users come to create their special tools. These people usually are illustrators and painters who use Photoshop in very creative ways. Even though I use Photoshop tools that use brushes almost every day, I rarely go to the Brushes panel because I don't often need such sophisticated brushes. I pointed out the Brushes panel here in case you decide to explore some of the custom settings — and maybe become a brush power-user yourself.

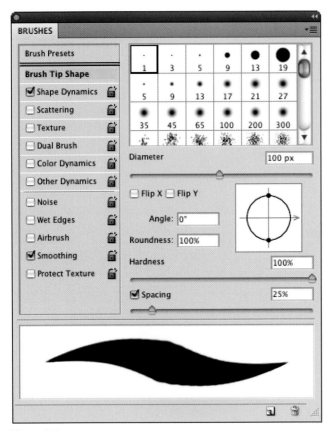

Figure 9.3

# Working with a graphics tablet

I don't know about you, but I can't draw very well with a mouse. Mice are great for moving around and clicking things quickly, but they don't do well when it's time to work on the details. You can see this by trying to use the Brush tool to write your name with your mouse. It's really hard for most people. Mice just aren't built for fine detail and articulation.

This raises another point. Because mice aren't built to be used in the way they're often used, they aren't ergonomic. (I know there are ergonomic mice out there, but they still don't offer the mobility needed.) This can lead to repetitive stress injuries. When we use mice in a very controlling way, we tend to tense the muscles in our hand, and sometimes those all the way up our arms and our necks.

When I really got serious about Photoshop several years ago, I began developing pain in my wrist and neck because I was spending so much time editing. The pain began to diminish the pleasure I was getting from Photoshop. I tried a trackball, but that wasn't any better. After I bought a graphics tablet, my Photoshop life changed. I can now work long hours with much less stress to my body.

# tip

When you spend a lot of time in front of a computer, you have to be conscious of your working environment. I've met many digital photographers who pour lots of money into their equipment, but never consider the health consequences of working in a non-ergonomic environment. To learn more about ergonomics, see the U.S. Department of Labor's Safety and Health Topics Web site at www.osha.gov/SLTC/ergonomics/.

A graphics tablet consists of a special pen called a stylus and a sensitive tablet that can sense when the pen touches the tablet. Because the action of holding a pen and drawing with it is more natural than using a mouse, the tablet requires much less strain. This natural motion also lends itself to fine articulation and detail work. I often work with mine in my lap to give my arm a rest.

Wacom tablets, like the one shown in Figure 9.4, are the industry standard for graphics tablets. Wacom makes a variety of tablets with different features and sizes under two main lines: Graphire and Intuos. They come in sizes from $4 \times 6$ inches to $12 \times 19$ inches. Keep in mind, though, that this is one case where bigger isn't necessarily better. For one thing, a large tablet takes up lots of room on your desk. When navigating the stylus around the tablet, you have to cover more distance on a large tablet, requiring more hand and arm movement. I have used the $6 \times 8$ tablet for many years and am completely satisfied with that form factor.

**Figure 9.4**

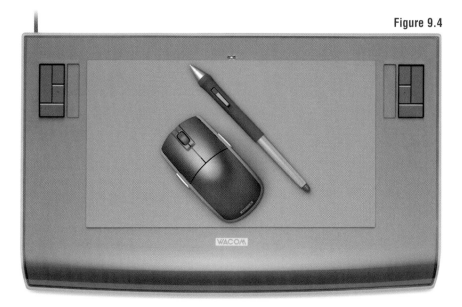

**Photo courtesy of Wacom**

Be aware that beginning to use a graphics tablet can be a little disorienting. For one thing, the tablet is mapped to the screen. That is, if the pen is touching the tablet in the lower-left corner, the cursor is in the lower left of the screen. To move the cursor to the top right of the screen, move the pen to the top right of the tablet. This learning curve can take a little time, but it's well worth the effort.

# Creating a Layer Mask

Okay, now that you know all about setting up the Brush tool, it's time to get down to business and create some layer masks. You begin by using a mask to combine elements of two different photos.

**1** **Open the two practice files, Canadian_Geese1.tif and Canadian_Geese2.tif, from the downloadable practice files on the Web site (www.wiley.com/go/photoshopcs4ats).** The photo of the two geese in Canadian_Geese1.tif is nice, but it's a little empty in the lower right corner. The object of this exercise is to add one of the geese in Canadian_Geese2.tif to that corner.

Naturally, you could use a selection to copy a goose from the second image and paste it into the first one, like you did with the seagulls in Chapter 8. But if you later found a mistake in the selection, you would have to back up and repeat the entire procedure. Also, because of the background detail, it

would be difficult to make a clean selection of the goose that would allow it to be seamlessly dropped into the image without being obvious.

**2** **Choose 2-up from the Arrange Documents menu on the Applications bar.** This positions the files so you can see both of them at the same time. Zoom out on both photos so you can see the entire image in each frame.

**3** **Click the Canadian_Geese2.tif file's header to make it the active file, select the Move tool (V), and then click and drag the photo into the Canadian_Geese1.tif photo.** Remember to hold down the Shift key if you want to place the new layer in the center of the image. Now the images are combined into a single file. The Canadian_Geese2.tif image (Layer 1) is on top of the Canadian_Geese1.tif image (Background), completely hiding it. This is confirmed by looking at the Layers panel, shown in Figure 9.5. You can close the Canadian_Geese2.tif file because it's no longer needed.

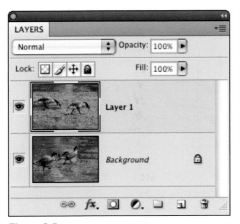

Figure 9.5

**Go to the Opacity setting on the Layers panel and lower the opacity to about 50%.** This makes Layer 1 translucent so that you can see the geese on the Background layer.

**Select the Move Tool (V) and click and drag Layer 1 down and to the right until the goose on the right is positioned in the lower left of the frame, similar to Figure 9.6.** Don't worry about the goose on the left of Layer 1 because it will be hidden by the mask.

Figure 9.6

**6** Go to the Masks panel (it's usually grouped with the Adjustments panel) and click the Add a Pixel Mask button at the top of the panel, shown in Figure 9.7. Notice that the thumbnail on the top left turns white and that a new thumbnail appears next to the image thumbnail on the Layers panel. If you don't see the Masks panel, choose Window → Masks.

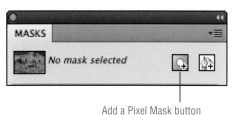

Add a Pixel Mask button

**Figure 9.7**

## note

The Add a Vector Mask button to the right of the Add a Pixel Mask button is used to create a different kind of mask. A vector mask uses mathematics to describe a mask, rather than pixels, which are used in digital photos. In all of my years using Photoshop to edit photos, I've never needed a vector mask, so they aren't covered in this book.

**7** Select the Brush tool, and set its Master Diameter to somewhere around 500 px, Hardness to 25%, and Opacity to 100% in the Options bar. Make sure that the foreground swatch color is black. When you create a layer mask, the color swatches are reset to — black and white. Use the X key to swap them if white is the foreground color.

## note

When a layer mask is active, you can't select any colors other than black, white, or gray in the Color Picker. Even if you click red in the Color Picker, the swatch on the Tools panel is gray. That's because only black, white, and shades of gray can be used on a mask.

**8** Start painting the left side of the image by clicking and dragging. Notice that as you paint the mask on Layer 1, you begin to see the geese in the Background layer. Keep painting until both of the geese are completely visible.

**9** Look at the thumbnail in the Masks panel to verify that the black paint is on the mask. Even though you're painting with black and white paint, you don't see any paint on the image. That's because it's being applied to the mask.

**10** Go back to the Layers panel and return the opacity of Layer 1 to 100% so that both layers are at full opacity.

**11** Reduce the size of your brush to paint the area between the birds.

**12** Lower the opacity of the Brush tool as you move in close to the bird on Layer 2. This allows you to partially mask some of the surrounding area so that it blends better with the background detail on the Background layer. If too much information on Layer 2 is removed, switch the foreground color to white (X) and paint some of it back in. When you're through, your image should look something like Figure 9.8.

**Figure 9.8**

**13** **Alt+Click on the mask in the Layers panel to see the actual mask displayed on the image.** This helps you identify areas that should be masked, but didn't get painted. In Figure 9.9 you can see where I missed a small area on the left. When you see this it's easy to fix. Just paint right on the mask. When it looks good, press Alt+Click to return the image to its normal view.

That's how easy it is to create a layer mask. Add the mask to the layer and use black paint to hide information on the layer and use white paint to reveal information. The easy way to remember this is to recall that when the new mask was created in Step 6 it didn't affect the layer and it was white.

A white mask is called a reveal all mask and a black mask is called a hide all mask. A reveal all mask is converted to a hide all mask by using the Paint Bucket tool (G) to fill it with black paint. The Paint Bucket tool with white paint is used to convert a hide all mask to a reveal all mask.

# caution

If you want to come back to a mask later to refine it, be sure to go to the Masks panel to select the mask with the Select the pixel mask button before painting. Otherwise, you end up painting directly on the image instead of the mask. You'll know when this happens because you'll see your black or white paint stroke, instead of it being hidden on the mask.

Figure 9.9

# Using a Selection to Create a Mask

Applying paint with the Brush tool is the way masks are usually created. However, you can also use selections to help speed up the process. This can save you lots of time when the image lends itself to creating a quick selection.

Sometimes it's difficult to paint around an object in an image with precision, especially when you're painting with a mouse. That's why it's a good idea to look for ways to quickly create a mask that's at least 90 percent perfect and then use the Brush tool to fine-tune it if necessary. One of the fastest ways to accomplish this is to use one of the smart selection tools to quickly create a near perfect selection and then turn it into a high quality mask. Here's how:

1 **Open the two practice files, Black_ Baloon.tif and Sky.tif, from the downloadable practice files on the Web site (www.wiley.com/go/ photoshopcs4ats).** The sky in the balloon photo is a beautiful blue sky, but it's almost too perfect. It's as though the balloon was shot against a blue screen. I want to add drama by replacing it with the more active sky in the Sky.tif file. This is done by placing the balloon photo on top of the sky photo and then masking out the sky in the balloon photo to reveal the sky below.

**2** Use the Move tool (V) to drag the balloon photo into the sky photo, just like you did with the geese photos in Step 3 of the last exercise.

**3** Select the Magic Wand tool (W) and set its Tolerance value of about 30 and make sure Contiguous is checked.

**4** Click on the blue sky to create an initial selection and continue to click on the sky while holding the Shift key to add to your selection. It should only take two to three clicks to select the entire sky. Because the balloon doesn't have any blues on it perimeter, none of it is selected.

**5** Choose Select → Inverse (Shift+⌘+I/ Shift+Ctrl+I) to invert the selection. The balloon is now selected instead of the sky.

**6** In the Masks panel click the Add a Pixel Mask button. The mask uses the selection and instantly creates a near perfect mask around the balloon. Figure 9.10 shows what the final effect looks like.

**7** Zoom in and look closely at the area between the basket and the hot air balloon. You can see that some of the original sky in the opening above the people wasn't removed because you used the Magic Wand with Contiguous checked.

**8** Use the Brush with black paint to hide the areas of original sky that weren't removed in Step 5.

Figure 9.10

**9** **Take a moment to look for any other inconsistencies that need to be touched-up.** Leave this file open for now so you can try a few other things with it in a moment.

As you can see, when a selection is combined with a mask it not only saves lots of time, but it also helps to create a high quality mask that can be fine-tuned with the Brush tool. In addition to this touch-up, there are some other things that you can do to fine-tune a mask. Most of them are in the Masks panel.

# Refining a Mask with the Masks Panel

Now that you've created a couple of masks and you understand the basic concept, take a closer look at the Masks panel and how it's used to fine-tune a mask. The Masks panel, shown in Figure 9.11, is new in Photoshop CS4. This panel is a welcome addition because it brings several features to the surface that used to be hidden.

## note

The commands in the Masks panel are only active when a mask is selected using the Select a Pixel Mask button in the Masks panel.

Here's a look at them and how they're used:

- **Density.** This new control is used to modify the opacity of the mask. Its effect is similar to changing a layer's Opacity value. If you still have the Black Balloon file open from the previous exercise, try lowering the Density value in the Masks panel to about 50 percent. Now the two skies begin to blend with one another. This lowered mask opacity wasn't as easy to accomplish in earlier versions of Photoshop.

## note

The red color of the Quick Mask goes back to the days when masks were hand cut, with a razor blade, on orange or red plastic sheets called Amber-lith and Ruby-lith. If you want to use a different color or change its opacity, choose Mask Options from the Masks panel menu.

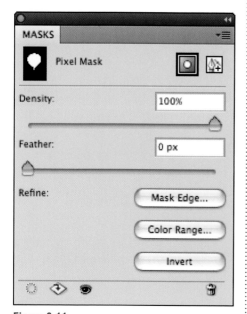

**Figure 9.11**

- **Feather.** As you learned in the previous exercise, selections and masks are closely related because you can easily convert a selection to a mask. This Feather command works much like the Feather command you learned about in Chapter 8. The easiest way to see the effects of the Feather slider is to switch to viewing the mask as a quick mask by pressing the \ key. Figure 9.12 shows the effect a 100 px Feather value has on the balloon mask. You can see that the Feather value affects the edge of the mask on both sides of its boundary, just like the Mask preview you saw when using the Refine Image command in Chapter 8.

- **Refine.** The Refine section of the Masks panel contains three options. They are

  - **Mask Edge.** The Mask Edge button is another reminder of the similarity of selections and mask. That's because it opens the Edge Mask dialog box which is identical to the Refine Edge dialog box that you learned about in when working with selections in Chapter 8. The controls in the dialog box, shown in Figure 9.13, are used in the same way to affect the edges of a mask.

**Figure 9.12**

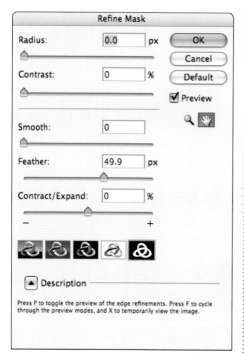

**Figure 9.13**

- **Color Range.** The Color Range button opens a dialog box, shown in Figure 9.14. This dialog box allows you to select similar colors to fine-tune your mask. It works in much the same way as the Magic Wand tool, except that any changes directly affect the mask. The first Eyedropper tool is used to sample the color you want to mask out. Then the two other eyedroppers are used to add or remove colors from your sample. Use the Select menu to quickly isolate specific colors or tones. The Fuzziness slider is like the Magic Wand's Tolerance value. It's used to increase the range of similar colors being included in the sample that's used to create the mask.

- **Invert.** This button is used to invert a mask so you can flip its effect. You could have used this in the previous exercise after the mask was created instead of Step 4.

You already learned about the Delete Mask button, which is located at the far right (the trash can). Now take a look at the three other buttons on the bottom of the Masks panel:

- **Load Selection from Mask.** Located at the far left, this button is a circle made of dashed lines. A moment ago you learned how to create a mask from a selection. This button allows you to do the opposite — create a selection from a mask.

- **Apply Mask.** When this diamond-shaped button with a down-pointing arrow in it is clicked, the mask becomes a permanent part of the layer and all of the information it was hiding is deleted. This is useful sometimes because, like an adjustment layer, a mask affects everything below it. I recommend that you don't apply a mask unless you have to in order to retain the flexibility of the mask.

- **Disable/Enable Mask.** This eye icon is a handy way to hide the visibility of the layer mask. It's a great way to check your mask by alternately hiding and revealing it so you see its effect better.

It's entirely likely that you won't need to use many of these adjustments on the Masks panel very often; however, it's good to know about them so that when you do need one of these features, you know where it's located. Take a moment to explore some of these settings with the mask you created in the previous exercise.

**Figure 9.14**

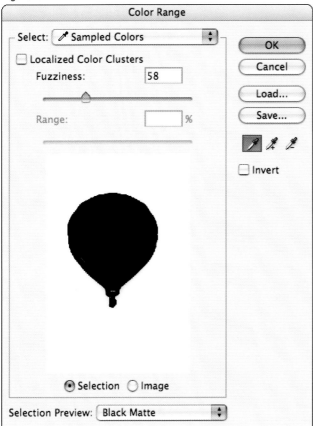

## Using Masks with Adjustment Layers

Something that you may not have noticed earlier in Chapter 6 when you learned about adjustment layers is that whenever you create an adjustment layer, a mask is automatically added to the adjustment layer. You can see it beside the image thumbnail in the Layers panel. This allows you to shape the adjustment layer to only affect the parts of the image that you want it to affect.

The goal in the next exercise is to turn the image into a black and white and then paint color back into one of the flowers. Follow these steps:

1. **Open the Tulips.tif practice file, shown in Figure 9.15, from the downloadable practice files from the Web site (www. wiley.com/go/photoshopcs4ats).**

Figure 9.15

**3** Select the Brush tool and begin painting the center flower with black paint to hide the effect of the adjustment layer. It should only take a few moments to make the photo look like Figure 9.16.

Figure 9.16

**2** In the Adjustments panel create a Hue/Saturation adjustment layer by clicking on the Create a New Hue/Saturation Adjustment Layer button, the second button from the left in the second row of buttons. Set the saturation value to –100, which removes all color from the image.

# see also

In Chapter 11 you learn a more elegant way to create black and white images using the Black and White command/adjustment layer.

This technique is very common. You see it often in wedding photography with photos of the bride and her bouquet of flowers. The entire image is changed to black and white and then only the bouquet is revealed with a mask.

Here's another common way to use an adjustment layer and a mask together — the goal with this photo is to darken the snow, but not the dog:

1 **Open the Snow_Dog.tif practice file from the downloadable practice files on the Web site (www.wiley.com/go/ photoshopcs4ats).**

2 **In the Adjustments panel, create a Levels adjustment layer by clicking on the Create a new Levels adjustment layer button (the second button from the left in the top row) and change only the gray slider's value to .60, as shown in Figure 9.17.** This darkens the entire image, including the dog.

3 **Select the Brush tool and begin painting the dog with black paint to hide the Levels adjustment on the dog and bring her back to her original tones.** Don't worry about painting along the exact outline of the dog. The goal isn't to make an exact outline; it's to add an artistic flavor. If you're seeing too much of a distinct line along the edge of her, use the Feather slider on the Masks panel to blend the edge.

4 **If you want to adjust the tonal change of the snow, revisit the Levels adjustment layer settings in the Adjustments panel.** Leave the file open so you can use it in the next exercise.

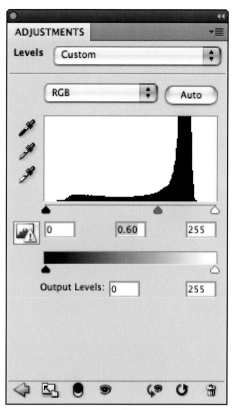

Figure 9.17

# Combining Selections, Adjustment Layers, and Masks

Now that you know about selections, adjustment layers, and masks, I want to show you how all three can be used together. A darkroom technique is to darken all corners on a photo with a soft vignette so that it helps bring the viewer's eye into the main subject. This is something that custom printers have been doing for years in color and black-and-white darkrooms. It's easy to do in Photoshop. You use a selection, an adjustment layer, and a mask in this technique on the photo of the dog, Ruby in these steps:

**1** Picking up where you left off with Step 5 in the previous exercise, select the Elliptical Marquee tool from the Tools panel.

**2** Make sure the Feather value is 0 px, the Anti-alias option is selected, and Style is set to Normal.

**3** Create an elliptical selection that covers most of the central area of the image, as shown in Figure 9.18. Remember that you can reposition the selection after it's drawn by placing the cursor inside the selection and then clicking and dragging into position. This way, you don't have to draw it perfectly the first time.

**4** Choose Select → Inverse (Alt+⌘+I/ Alt+Ctrl+I) to invert the selection so that the area outside the elliptical area is now selected.

**5** In the Adjustments panel, click the Create a New Levels Adjustment Layer button to create a Levels adjustment layer.

**6** Change only the middle gray slider to a value of .80, and click OK. This darkens the edges of the photo, but because the selection wasn't feathered, the transition between the dark edges and the middle of the photo is a hard edge.

Figure 9.18

**7** **In the Masks panel, adjust the Feather slider to a value of 50.** This smoothes out the edge transition and hides the selection's edge. Now your Layers panel should look like the one in Figure 9.19. If you want to change the amount of darkening on the edges, go back and adjust Layer 2. If you want to adjust the overall darkness of the snow, revisit Layer 1.

This simple effect combines three of the main Photoshop concepts covered so far: selections, adjustment layers, and masks. This is a good exercise to review whenever you need to refresh your memory about how these three important concepts work together to give you a huge amount of flexibility and control over your editing.

## tip

After you see the mask in place, you may want to adjust the size of the area being masked. If so, use the Contract/Expand slider in the Refine Mask dialog box. (Click the Mask Edge button on the Masks panel to open it.)

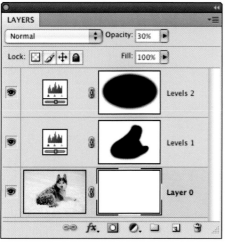

Figure 9.19

# 10

# Improving Your Photos with Retouching

When you hear the word "retouching," the first thing that often comes to mind is high-end fashion and beauty retouching we see in magazines. This kind of retouching is used to perfect an image of someone so that she appears flawless. Though retouching is used on a wide range of images beyond just fashion, the objective remains the same: to perfect the image so that weaknesses are eliminated and strengths are enhanced. Some of the techniques you've learned about in other chapters involving selections and masking are technically considered retouching. However, Photoshop has several tools that are collectively referred to as retouching tools because of the way they're used. In this chapter you learn about these tools and how to use them to improve your photos.

# What Is Retouching?

As I mentioned, retouching is about minimizing weakness and building on strengths. This comes in many forms when you use Photoshop. However in the most basic form, retouching is about covering the things you don't want to see, with things you do want to see. The process is straightforward — you copy pixels in one part of the image and you paint them over the existing pixels.

Figure 10.1 shows a photo I shot early one morning at a local dahlia farm. I really like the photo, but I can't stand the sign on the left, below the tractor. The sign takes away from the scene because it doesn't fit with the flowers. It also pulls the eye away from the tractor, which is where I want it to be, because it's the brightest thing in the image.

In addition to the sign, there are a three other things that compete for the viewer's eye. The bright orange vertical marker near the middle of the road that runs above the tractor, the bright vertical line just below it at the far end of the flowers, and a light cream-colored flower in the foreground that's in with a bunch of darker red flowers. When I look at Figure 10.1, my eye bounces around the image looking at these things and the tractor instead of focusing on the person in the tractor. My job here is to eliminate these distractions so that the viewer's eye goes where it's supposed to go. Figure 10.2 shows the image a few minutes of retouching. See if you notice the difference in where your eye moves as you compare Figures 10.1 and 10.2.

Figure 10.1

Figure 10.2

# Basic Retouching with the Clone Stamp Tool

The Clone Stamp tool has been part of Photoshop since the earliest days. It opened the door to digital retouching as we know it. In essence, the Clone Stamp tool is used to sample information from one part of an image so that it can be painted (cloned) into another part of the image.

## Removing distractions

Begin your exploration of this tool by retouching your own version of the photo in Figure 10.1:

1. **Open the Dahlia_Farm.tif file from the downloadable practice files on the Web site (www.wiley.com/go/photoshop cs4ats).**

2. **Zoom in to 100% and pan the image so that you can see the white sign.** The goal is to use the greenery in the group of flowers to the left to cover the sign.

3. **Duplicate the Background layer by choosing Layer → New Layer → From Background.** When the dialog opens, name the layer Retouching and click OK. The new layer is added to the top of the layer stack and becomes the active layer. All retouching is done on this duplicate layer.

4. **Select the Clone Stamp tool (S) from the Tools panel.** It's ninth from the top on the single-column panel. Make sure

that you're not selecting the Pattern Stamp tool that's stacked with the Clone Stamp tool, as shown in Figure 10.3.

The Clone Stamp tool has the same brush controls as the Brush tool on the Option bar. That's because it works in the same way. The difference is that instead of using paint, the Clone Stamp tool applies sampled portions of the image as you paint.

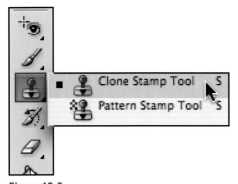

**Figure 10.3**

**5** **Set your Brush size to about 75 px and the Hardness to about 50% in the Brush section on the Option bar and make sure your Opacity and Flow are set to 100.** Also be sure the Aligned option is selected. This insures that the tool continues to sample pixels as you paint, even if you release the mouse button. When this option is deselected, only the initial sample point is used as a source for the brush. I almost always work with this option on and all of the exercises in this chapter assume that it's on.

# note

When the Aligned option is selected, the two Clone Stamp cursors stay in alignment each time you stop and resume painting. When the option is not checked, the sampled pixels from the initial sample area are used for every stroke.

**6** **Set a sample point by Alt+clicking the upper part of the greenery of the group of flowers directly left of the sign.** Try to insure that your sample point is level with the center of the sign. Now that you've sampled this spot, it will be used when you begin painting.

**7** **Release the Alt key, and move your cursor over the upper part of the sign, shown in Figure 10.4.** Notice that a preview appears on the cursor, to indicate what the cloned bush will look like when you begin to paint. This preview feature is called the Clipped Clone preview and it's new in Photoshop CS4. It's quite useful for critical alignment because it allows you to preview placement before you paint. It can be a bit disorienting when you're working on a complicated project, so I show you how to turn it off later.

**8** **Click and drag downward to begin cloning detail from the bush on the left over the sign.** Stop before you get to the bottom of the sign. Notice that a cursor appears on the cloned greenery that follows the painting cursor in perfect alignment as you moved the mouse. This is the effect of having the Alignment option selected on the Options bar. It allows you to sample the length of the bush as you cover the length of the sign.

**Figure 10.4**

## tip

When using any brush-based tool, be sure to use a stroking motion when painting even if the strokes are very short. This prevents you from getting what I call mouse-tracks. These circular tracks come from individual clicks with the mouse and they are sure signs that retouching has taken place.

## tip

Quite often it's a good idea to cover an area by sampling different areas. This prevents the cloning from being too obvious. You could do that here to break up the leaf pattern on the area you cloned.

**9** **Reduce the size of your brush and make a second stroke to complete the process by covering the bottom of the sign.** If necessary, go back to the greenery on the left and sample it again to clone the lower part of it so that your work is convincing. That's it. The sign is gone in two strokes.

**10** **Use the same technique to remove the orange marker, the tall bright flower below it, the bright cream-colored flower in the foreground, and any other elements you want to remove.** When working on the orange marker and the tall flower, be sure to use the clipped clone preview to insure that lines, such as the road, line up when cloned.

**11** **Hide the Retouching layer's visibility by clicking the eyeball next to it on the Layers menu to check your work.** Notice how much better this image looks after a few minutes of work with the Clone Stamp tool.

This is retouching in its most basic form. It was used to make a nice image presentable. Whenever you work on an important image, look for ways to fine-tune it by removing small distractions that have a big impact.

## Adding visual elements with retouching

In the previous exercise you learned to hide problem areas. Sometimes, though, the goal is to add additional elements to the image by cloning them. For example, if I had a photo of four ducks walking in a row and I wanted to add another to the end of the line, I could clone one of the original four.

Follow these steps to use the Clone Stamp tool to add an element to a photo, rather than remove one:

**1** **Open the Pink_Flower.tif file from the downloadable practice files on the Web site (www.wiley.com/go/photoshop cs4ats).** Figure 10.5 shows that there are a couple of empty areas in this photo that would look better if there were more flowers. The goal with this project is to add a flower to the empty area on the right by cloning one of the other flowers.

Figure 10.5

**2** **Duplicate the Background layer by choosing Layer → New Layer → from Background.** When the dialog opens, name the layer Retouching and click OK. All retouching is done on this duplicate layer.

**3** **Select the Clone Stamp tool (S) and set your Brush size to about 300 px and the Hardness to about 75% in the Brush section on the Options bar.** These are starting settings. You can vary the size and hardness as needed.

**4** **Set a sample point by Alt+clicking the center of the flower that's in the center of the photo.**

**5** **Click and begin painting in a circular motion, working your way outward to begin adding the new flower.** If you don't like the placement of the duplicate flower, use the Undo command to back up so you can resample and start again.

**6** **As you get closer to the outer edges of the flower, reduce the size of your brush and continue painting until you've added a duplicate flower.** Don't worry if it isn't perfect around the edges. I show you how to clean it up in a moment. Figure 10.6 shows the results I had with a couple of paint strokes. Leave this file open so you can continue with it in the next exercise.

**Figure 10.6**

# tip

When making an exact clone of something, you usually make one sample of the cloned material. All cloning begins with that point and ends with that point because the sample cursor stays aligned with the brush cursor.

The background in this project is quite forgiving so the lower part of the new flower blends in quite well. The main problem in Figure 10.6 is that I accidentally cloned part of the flower that's behind the main flower I was sampling. Parts of it now show behind the duplicate flower. This would have been avoided if I had been more careful and used a smaller brush. But even then it can be hard to follow both cursors while working. Fortunately, there's an easy way to paint out some of the things you don't want using the History Brush tool.

# tip

When painting with the Clone Stamp, let go of the mouse button once in a while to break up the process into more than one step. That way if you make a mistake near the end of the process, you only have to undo the last step, rather than the entire process.

# Undoing with the History Brush Tool

Directly below the Clone Stamp tool is another tool called the History Brush. The History Brush is perfect for solving the problem on the flower project. The way the History Brush works is that you pick a previous history state from the timeline on the History panel by clicking in the box to the left of that state. When you do that, a small icon of the History Brush is placed into the box to indicate it's the state you're working from.

After you select a history state, you can use it to paint that state back into the image. It's like using a paintbrush that samples a previous point in time. In this case, you want to pick any history state that is previous to the addition of the duplicate flower. By default, the History Brush is set to the opening thumbnail at the top of the History panel, which is also shown in Figure 10.7, which is exactly what you want for this exercise.

# caution

If you crop or change the size of the image, you won't be able to use a history state with the History Brush that's previous to that change.

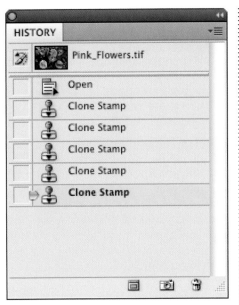

**Figure 10.7**

Here's how you use the History brush to clean up the cloning job from the previous exercise:

**1** **Go back to Step 6 in the preceding exercise.** Select the History Brush (Y) from the Tools panel. It's tenth from the top on the single-column Tools panel. Make sure you aren't selecting the Art History Brush that's stacked with the History Brush.

**2** **Select a small brush with a medium-hardness and paint out anything that you don't want to show around the outside of the duplicate flower, replacing it with the way the area looked when the file was first opened.** Zoom in to make it easier to see what you're doing. If your brush is too soft, you'll have a hard time getting a nice edge along the edges of the petals because the brush affects the edge of the flower. If this happens, increase the Hardness value until you get the kind of edge that you want.

Don't close this image yet, because you use it again in just a moment.

# note

Be aware that this tool is tied to the History panel. When a file is closed, all history states are lost. So be sure to use this tool, if necessary, before closing the file.

# Advanced Cloning Techniques

As you can see, the Clone Stamp tool is quite useful. You can quickly remove something or add something by sampling one area of the image and painting information from that area into the image. In this section I show you some of the advanced settings you can use with this tool to make it even more powerful.

## Cloning to a different layer

Photoshop's retouching tools are destructive by their very nature. That's because the things you do with them permanently change pixels in the image. In the first exercise in this chapter I had you duplicate the Background layer to isolate your retouching to its own layer. This was useful for making comparisons, and it protected the Background layer from having permanent changes made to it. The problem with this technique is that it doubles the file size. It also limits what you can do with the cloned information because it's not really isolated by itself.

# note

When you're working on an important project it's important that your editing does not permanently affect the Background Layer. This layer is not only your reference point for what the original image looks like, it also protects you from needing to back up to the beginning of the process and begin a project all over again because of a permanent change that can't be undone. This means that all tonal and color adjustments are done with adjustment layers and that when possible all retouching is on its own layer.

When the Clone Stamp tool is active, you may have noticed a menu on the Options bar that's called Sample. This menu is used to control which layer(s) is sampled when you Alt+click with the Clone Stamp tool. (This menu is also available for the Healing Brush and the Spot Healing Brush.) You have these three options in this menu, as shown in Figure 10.8:

- **Current Layer.** Only pixels from the current layer are sampled. With this default option, all cloning must be done on the same layer that samples are taken from.

- **Current & Below.** Only pixels from the current layer and layers below it are sampled. This option allows you to arrange the layers you're working with by dragging them into place so you sample only the layers you're interested in. After the retouching is done, the layers can be rearranged if needed.

- **All Layers.** All layers are sampled.

One of the most popular ways of using this multilayer sampling ability is to create an empty layer above the layer to be retouched so that all new retouching is added to the empty layer. That way, if you need to make changes to the retouching later, you can work with it on its own layer. Here's how:

1 **Open the Pink_Flower.tif practice file again.** If it's still open from the previous exercise, click the image icon at the top of the History panel to return the image to its opening state.

2 **Choose Layer → New → Layer to create an empty layer above the Background layer.** When the New Layer dialog box opens, name the layer Retouching and click OK.

# tip

You can also use the Create a new layer button on the bottom of the Layers panel instead — it's just to the left of the Delete layer button that looks like a trashcan.

**Figure 10.8**

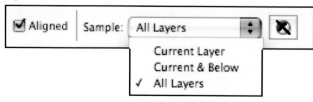

**3** Select the Clone Stamp tool (S) from the Tools panel, and choose All Layers from the Sample menu in the Options bar.

**4** Set the brush's Diameter and Hardness to the settings of your choice.

**5** Alt+click to sample the flower you cloned in the earlier exercise and begin painting it into the empty area to the right. When you finish, the image should look similar to the finished image in the preceding exercise, with the duplicate flower added to the right. The difference is that the cloned flower is on Layer 1 in the Layers panel.

**6** To see the Layer 1 by itself, click the eyeball icon next to the Background layer to hide the layer. Now the cloned flower should look something like Figure 10.9. The important thing here is that the Background layer is undisturbed, which you can verify by turning its visibility back on and turning off the visibility of Layer 1. If you need to fine-tune your cloning job and it's too late to use the History Brush, you can use the Eraser tool, or more preferably a mask, to refine the retouching on Layer 1.

**7** Sample the stem on the original flower and use a small brush to add it to the duplicate flower.

## Ignoring adjustment layers

There's an interesting nuance you need to be aware of when you retouch with multiple layers. Just to the right of the Sample menu is a button that allows you to ignore adjustment layers when using the Clone Stamp tool or the Healing Brush tool. When all layers are being sampled and adjustment layers are present, the effect of the adjustment layers is duplicated. This is really easy to see by doing a simple experiment.

Figure 10.9

Follow these steps:

**1** **Choose File → New to open a new file, and give it the following properties:**

- Width = 6 inches
- Height = 4 inches
- Resolution = 300
- Color Mode = RGB Color/8-bit
- Background = White

**2** **Choose Edit → Fill, and select 50% Gray from the Contents/Use pop-up menu.** At this point, your new file is 50% gray (red = 128, green = 128, blue = 128).

**3** **In the Adjustments panel, create a Levels adjustment layer by clicking the Create a New Levels Adjustment Layer button, (second from the left on the top row).** Change the middle, gray slider to 1.50 to lighten the image. Don't change the white-point slider or the black-point slider.

## see also

Adjustment layers are covered in detail in Chapter 6.

**4** **Click the Background layer in the Layers panel to make it active again.**

**5** **Select the Clone Stamp tool (S) from the Tools panel, change the brush diameter to 200 px, and use the Hardness setting of your choice.** Make sure that Opacity is 100%.

**6** **Choose All Layers from the Sample menu on the Options bar, and make sure the Ignore Adjustment Layers button is not clicked.**

**7** **Choose any spot you want, and Alt+click to sample it, and then scoot the cursor over a bit, and paint a small circle.** When you do this, notice that the circle you just painted is lighter than the gray you sampled, as shown in Figure 10.10. That's because the lightening effect of the Levels adjustment layer was doubled when it was sampled.

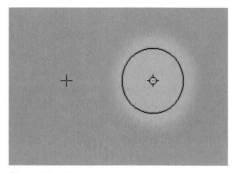

**Figure 10.10**

## note

Notice that the clone preview doesn't reflect this change. It shows the preview as the same tone as the sampled area.

**8** **In the Options bar, click the Ignore Adjustment Layers button and paint again.** The painted gray is the same tone as the sampled gray. The effect is the same as turning the adjustment layer's visibility off before cloning.

The inadvertent sampling of adjustment layers when all layers are selected for sampling has thrown many a novice retoucher for a loop because he didn't realize that the adjustment layer's effects were being multiplied. Now that you know what this problem looks like, you can take appropriate action when you see it happening by clicking the Ignore Adjustment Layers button on the Options bar.

## Cloning from one image to another

Sometimes the information you want to clone is in a different image. For example you want to add a flower to the Pink_Flowers.tif image by cloning a flower that wasn't in the original image. The steps to doing this are quite straightforward:

**1** Open both files.

**2** Select the image you want to sample from by clicking its header and use the Clone Stamp to Alt+click on the area you want to sample.

**3** Select the target image by clicking its header and begin painting the sampled information from the first image into the second image.

## Using the Clone Source panel

The Clone Source panel, shown in Figure 10.11, was introduced in Photoshop CS3 so it's still fairly new. This panel provides a number of features that enhance the performance of the Clone Stamp tool (as well as the Healing Brush tool). Here are some of the things you can do with this panel:

- **You can save up to five different sample sources.** Click the Clone Source buttons at the top before sampling with the Alt key. That way you can revisit a sample point in the image that was previously sampled.

- **Rotate or scale source material using the settings in the Offset area.**

- **Customize the overlay.** This helps you with positioning cloned data as it's applied. These settings also affect the Clipped Clone preview you saw while using the Clone Stamp tool in an earlier exercise.

**Figure 10.11**

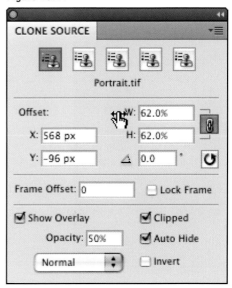

Saving multiple Clone Source points is pretty straightforward, so the focus here is on the other two features — the overlay and rotate/scale. First, work with the overlay section.

**1** Open the Pink_Flower.tif file from the downloadable practice files on the Web site (www.wiley.com/go/photoshop cs4ats). Return to the Pink_Flowers.tif practice file. Use the History panel to return it to its opening state. If you already closed it, choose File → Open Recent and select the file from the list to reopen it.

# tip

The Open Recent menu gives you access to the last ten files that were opened or saved. You can change the number of files that appear in this menu with the File Handling preferences.

**2** **Select the Clone Stamp tool, and open the Clone Source panel.** If you don't see it, choose Window → Clone Source.

**3** **Sample the flower in the middle using the Alt key, just as you did in an earlier exercise.** After the sample is made, the clone overlay appears, just as it did before, indicating where cloned information will be pasted when you paint.

**4** **Deselect the Clipped option at the bottom of the Clone Source panel, and notice what happens.** Instead of a small preview of the size of the Clone Stamp's brush you get a preview of the entire image. Lower the Opacity value to 50% so that you can see through the preview, as shown in Figure 10.9. This helps when you're trying to place the cloned data in a particular spot. It also helps when you want to see the area that's being sampled behind the preview.

**5** **Select the Auto Hide option to temporarily hide the preview whenever you're painting.** This is the way I like to set up the clone preview. (You can also use the Alt key to temporarily hide the preview at any time instead of setting it to Auto Hide.)

The Blending Mode menu at the bottom of the panel is used to change the way the clone preview blends with the image. The options are Normal, Darken, Lighten, and Difference. These blending modes, as well as the Invert option, are used to assist you with exact placement when it's necessary. The settings are most useful when your sample and target areas are very similar. For example, when you're cloning someone's face from one photo into another photo where she has a bad expression, the clone preview allows you to align the faces more accurately.

# Adjusting geometry as you clone

The settings in the Offset area of the Clone Source panel are used to change the geometric relationship between the sampled pixels and the pixels that are applied with the Clone Stamp tool. There are a number of options. Explore some of them so that you get a feel for when offsetting the clone tool is useful.

**1** **Pick up where you left off in Step 5 in the previous exercise.** If you did any cloning, undo it by backing up to the opening state in the History panel.

**2** **In the Clone Source panel, change the scale of the width to 50% and begin painting again.** Now the sampled data should be half the size in the overlay. This time the flower is smaller. A cloned flower that's half the size of the original flower looks more convincing than cloning the original flower exactly because it looks like it's further away.

# tip

The Clone Source overlay is extremely useful. However, not everyone likes to use it. You can turn it off completely by unchecking Show Overlay. You can temporarily display it if you need it by pressing Shift+Alt.

**3** Position your cursor over the W on the width setting to activate the *scrubby slider,* and adjust the width and height percentages while you're working with the tool. Notice that the cursor changes to a hand with an arrow on each side of it, which is a scrubby slider. Click and drag to the left to lower the value and drag to the right to increase it. Experiment with cloning different sized flowers into the image.

# tip

Photoshop is loaded with scrubby sliders. Use them when you want to make fine adjustments without having to type exact numbers into a number box.

**4** Type a value of 180 into the Rotation box just below the W and H boxes. Notice that the preview in the Overlay is upside down, which is not such a convincing effect for this flower photo.

**5** Reset all transform settings by clicking the Reset Transform button to the right of the Rotation box — the one with a circular arrow on it — and change the width setting to 100%. Now the preview is a mirror image of the flower as shown in Figure 10.12. Making either the width or height a negative value flips the cloned content on its vertical or horizontal axis.

In this exercise, the Rotation values don't help because they make the flower look odd. However, sometimes when you're trying to hide something with retouching, it can help to be able to break up the pattern of something you're sampling by changing its orientation as it's cloned.

**Figure 10.12**

# Using the Healing Brush Tool

The Healing Brush tool (J) is very similar to the Clone Stamp tool. Targeted information is sampled by Alt+clicking and then painting it into other parts of the image. The big difference is that the Healing Brush tool attempts to make the sampled data match the lighting and shading of the area to which it's being applied. In other words, it looks at the area where the sampled data is being applied and tries to make the sampled information match the target area. This is extremely useful when you're more interested in blending your retouching than getting a literal copy like the Clone Stamp tool does.

1 **Open Portrait.tif from the downloadable practice files on the Web site (www. wiley.com/go/photoshopcs4ats).**

2 **Select the Clone Stamp tool and try to remove the four dots that I placed on the forehead, shown in Figure 10.13.** Notice that if you don't sample skin that is exactly the same tone and color of the target area, your strokes are noticeable. This has always been one of the issues with using the Clone Stamp tool for retouching.

**Figure 10.13**

©Dave Hutt

**3** **Undo any work you did with the Clone Stamp tool, and then switch to the Healing Brush tool (J).** It's seventh from the top on the single-column Tools panel and is stacked with the Spot Healing Brush tool, the Patch tool, and the Red Eye tool, as shown in Figure 10.14. (Be sure not to choose the Spot Healing brush.)

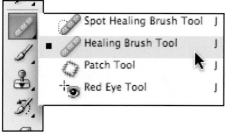

**Figure 10.14**

**4** **Set the brush to similar size and hardness settings for your attempt at using the Clone Stamp tool in Step 2.**

**5** **Alt+click to sample some skin and then paint over one of the dots.** Notice that as you paint, the sampled information looks similar to the way it did in Step 1. However, when you release the mouse button the Healing Brush tool takes over and intelligently blends the tone and color of the sample so that it matches the target area.

**6** **Alt+click on the background to the left of the man to sample the dark tones, as shown in Figure 10.15, and then use the Healing Brush tool to paint on one of the dark spots on the forehead.** Notice that the Healing Brush is able to

**Figure 10.15**

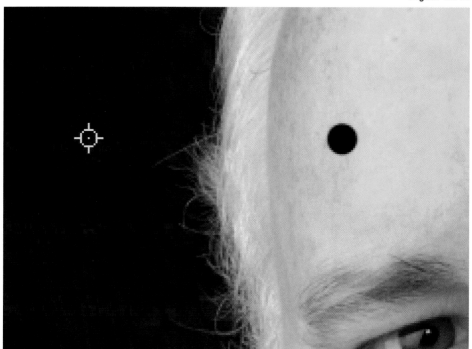

blend these tones even though they are very different. That's because there isn't much of a difference in the texture of the two tones. This simple step reveals the power of this retouching tool.

Though the Healing Brush tool is powerful, there are situations where it totally fails. It fails when it is used to retouch areas that are near an edge with strong contrast; for example, if you try to retouch the man's skin next to his light colored hair. That's because the tool doesn't know how to blend the tones because it sees light and dark.

There are two ways to deal with this scenario. The first is to switch to your old friend, the Clone Stamp tool. The other is to use a selection to isolate the area so that tones outside of the selection are not used in the Healing Brush's calculations.

Even though the Healing Brush is a brush tool, the options for setting it up are a little different than the Clone Stamp tool or the Brush tool. The first thing you notice is that it doesn't have an Opacity setting. Another big difference is that the Brush pop-up menu on the options bar isn't the same. Figure 10.16 shows what it looks like. (Refer to Figure 9.1 to see the Brush tool's Brush pop-up menu.)

## tip

The Clone Source panel can also be used with the Healing Brush.

Something else you might have noticed is that when the Healing Brush tool is selected, all the options on the Brushes panel are grayed out. That means that you can't use the Brushes panel with this tool. The few features that are available have been moved to the Brush pop-up menu in Figure 10.16.

**Figure 10.16**

There are two other settings on the Option bar that affect how this tool functions:

- **Source.** This option determines where source data comes from. When set to Sampled, the Alt key is used to sample image information. When set to Pattern, a pattern from the Pattern pop-up menu (which is activated when this option is selected) next to the Pattern is used. I always leave this set at Sampled.

- **Aligned.** This is the same as the Aligned setting in the Clone Stamp options. When this option is selected, sample points are aligned with the brush as it moves. When it is deselected, the original selection is used for every new stroke.

The main difference between the Clone Stamp and the Healing Brush tools is that the Clone Stamp tool makes a literal copy of the sampled information. The Healing Brush, on the other hand, attempts to blend sampled data into the target area.

# Busting Dust with the Spot Healing Brush

The Spot Healing Brush is a close cousin to the Healing Brush. They're both stacked together, along with the Patch tool and the Red Eye tool. The Spot Healing Brush has the same smart blending abilities as the Healing Brush. The main difference is that sampling isn't done with the Alt key. This tool automatically creates a sample from around the area that's being retouched. This lack of control can cause problems when detail you don't want to sample is inadvertently sampled. The Spot Healing Brush works best in areas that are low in detail, such as backgrounds. This tool is most useful when cleaning up dust on scans, or removing dSLR sensor dirt from a background that doesn't have a lot of detail in it.

The Spot Healing Brush has two tool options of note:

- **Proximity Match.** Uses pixels around the selection to generate the sampled data.

- **Create Texture.** Uses the pixels in the selection to create a texture that is used to fill the area being painted.

When using this tool to remove dust, you may have to try each of these settings to find the one that best suits your needs for that particular image.

# Using the Patch Tool

As useful as the Healing Brush tool is, I find I use the Patch tool for a large percentage of my retouching. The Patch tool is stacked with the Healing Brush tool and the Spot Healing Brush tool, and it works in a similarly intelligent manner. The main difference is in the way image information is sampled and applied. This tool uses a selection instead of a brush. You draw a selection and then drag it to the area to be sampled. When you release the mouse button, the sampled information fills the original target selection and blends in the same way as when you use the Healing Brush tool.

To see how this tool works, follow these steps:

**1** Open the Portrait.tif file from the downloadable practice files from the Web site (www.wiley.com/go/photoshopcs4ats). If it's already open from the last exercise, you may continue working with it.

**2** Select the Patch tool (J) from the Tools panel and make sure that Source is selected on the Options bar next to Patch. In this example, you want to tone down the lines under the man's eyes.

## tip

To quickly select a tool that's stacked underneath another tool, press Shift along with the tool's shortcut key to cycle through the stacked tools. In this case, press Shift+J. (To make this work, be sure to select the Use Shift for Tool Switch option in Photoshop's General preferences; it is already selected by default.)

**3** Click and drag your cursor to draw a selection around the lines under the left eye. Keep the selection a little loose around the outside so it's not too close to the detail that's being removed.

**4** Click inside of the selection and drag it to a clean area of skin that has a similar texture so you can sample it. In Figure 10.17, you can see that I used the central forehead area. Notice that as you drag the selection, the originally selected area is updated with a preview of the information in the sample selection you're dragging.

**5** When you like what you see in the preview, release the mouse button to replace the original selection with the information in the sample selection.

## tip

You can create selections using any of the selection tools covered in Chapter 8. You just have to switch back to the Patch tool to use it after creating the selection.

**Figure 10.17**

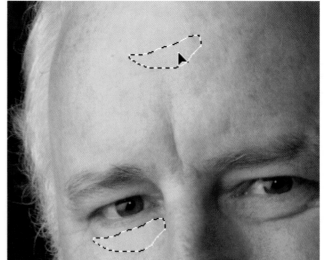

**6** Choose Select→Deselect (⌘+D/Ctrl+D). This deselects the selection and completes the Patch tool's application. The only problem with what you just did is that the effect is too strong because it removed all of the lines and took away some of the definition around the man's eye, making the retouching obvious. Because the Patch tool, like the Clone Stamp tool, doesn't have an Opacity setting as an option, you have to use something else to reduce the effect of the tool.

**7** Go back two steps in the History panel's timeline. You should now be at the point where the selection was first created with the lines showing under his eye.

**8** Drag the selection to the skin on the forehead again, and release the mouse button — just as you did previously in Steps 4 and 5.

**9** Choose Edit→Fade Patch Selection (Shift+⌘+F/Shift+Ctrl+F). The Fade dialog box opens.

**10** Move the slider to the left until you see just enough of the lines reappear to give the eye socket some shape. You can use the Fade command after just about anything you do in Photoshop, which is extremely useful. It allows you to overdo something and then fade it back to the point where you like it. The key to using Fade is that it must be the very next thing you do. For example, if you deselect the selection first, the Fade command under the Edit menu is grayed out.

**11** Back up again to Step 3 of this exercise using the History panel and this time, drag the selection to the dark background to the left of the man and release the mouse button. Notice that the background tones are blended in to match the skin tones. The effect is even softer than when you sampled the skin on the forehead because the background doesn't have as much texture as the skin you sampled earlier. Use the Fade command to tone it down. This is a useful technique for a situation like this when there isn't any clean skin to work with.

# note

Instead of using Fade, you could do all retouching on a separate layer and then lower the opacity of the layer. However, the Fade command allows you to adjust the opacity of individual actions instead of everything on the layer at once.

**12** Follow the same procedures to retouch the lines under the left eye, giving it approximately the same amount of fade.

The tool options for the Patch tool on the Options bar, shown in Figure 10.18, are fairly simple. On the left, just to the right of the Tool Presets, are four small buttons. These allow you to modify your selection by adding or subtracting to it, just like the tool options for the main selection tools. To the right of these buttons are two radio buttons that control how the patch is applied.

Figure 10.18

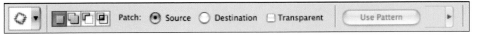

These settings do the following when selected:

- **Source.** The originally selected area is patched with the sampled pixels.

- **Destination.** The information from the original selection is dragged and dropped when you move the selection — sort of the opposite of the effect of selecting the Source button.

- **Transparent option.** Only the texture of the sample area is used as a sample. None of the color and tone information is sampled. (I have to say that I never use this option on an actual retouching job.)

You should be aware of a couple of other things when using the Patch tool. Quite often, you need to do a little cleanup around the edges of the patched area, using the Healing Brush tool or the Patch tool itself, so that the edges blend a little better — especially when patching large areas. Another issue with the Patch tool is that it suffers from the same smudging problem as the Spot Healing Brush tool when patching areas that are near edges of high contrast or the edge of the image frame. When working in areas like this, try to create the original selection away from these edges.

One other thing to be aware of with this tool is that it doesn't have the Source menu on the Options bar that allows you to sample one layer and patch onto another layer. I get around this by duplicating the layer (Layer ➜ Duplicate Layer) I want to work with and doing all retouching on it. This allows me to keep the original layer intact so that I can occasionally hide the retouching layer to make a before and after comparison. It also allows me to trash the retouching layer and begin again if I want to without affecting the rest of the image.

# Fixing Red Eye in a Flash

Red eye is caused by light reflecting off the retina and bouncing back into the lens of the camera. It usually appears when a camera's flash is on or near the same plane as the lens. The effect is more pronounced in subjects who have gray or blue eyes, as well as children.

Figure 10.19 shows a photo of Ruby, our Siberian Husky. Whenever I point a camera with an on-camera flash at her, red eye shows up in the photo. (I've noticed this with other blue-eyed dogs as well.) Fortunately, this is easy to fix in Photoshop.

To fix this, I select the Red Eye tool and draw a selection that encompasses the entire eye, as shown on the eye on the left in Figure 10.20.

Because this tool works only on red, I don't have to be very careful with the selection. After the selection is in place, I release the mouse button and the red eye is instantly eliminated, as shown in the eye on the right. Something that would have taken a bit of doing with other techniques a few years ago now takes a few seconds with the Red Eye tool.

The Red Eye tool has only two settings on the Options bar:

- **Pupil Size.** Increases or decreases the area affected by the tool.

- **Darken Amount.** Sets the amount of darkening that's added.

By default, both of these are set to 50%. Try adjusting these values if you're not getting the results you want.

## note

My other two dogs reflect green in their eyes when a flash is used. Unfortunately, this tool won't work for them.

Figure 10.19

Figure 10.20

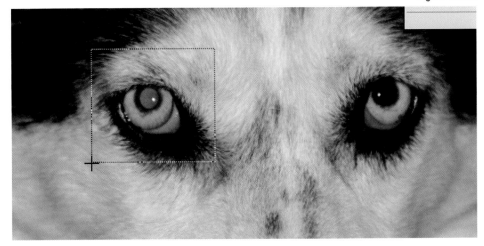

# Sculpting with the Liquify Filter

You began this chapter by learning about Photoshop's most fundamental retouching tool, the Clone Stamp tool. You wrap this chapter up by learning about one of Photoshop's most exotic retouching tools, the Liquify filter. This tool is so specialized that I rarely use it. However, it's a powerful tool, so I want make you aware of it so that you can take a closer look at it as your Photoshop skills improve.

The Liquify filter works by distorting the image with tools like Warp, Pucker, and Bloat. To access the Liquify filter, go to the top section of the Filters menu and choose Filter → Liquify. Figure 10.21 shows the Liquify dialog box. As you can see, the options in this dialog box are quite comprehensive. On the left side is a set of tools that affect the filter's distortion in different ways. On the right side are a number of options for fine-tuning the effects of those tools.

The woman in Figure 10.21 didn't like the way her bottom looked because the camera angle distorted it. This is the sort of problem that the Liquify filter is well suited for solving. The goal here is to distort the image so that the protruding bottom is minimized.

For this job, I selected the Push Left tool from the Tools panel on the left, sixth from the top. The Push Left tool moves pixels to the left when you click and drag straight up. When the cursor is dragged downward, the tool moves pixels to the right. Here, I want to move the pixels around her bottom to the right, so I drag the tool downward while holding down the mouse button. The left image in Figure

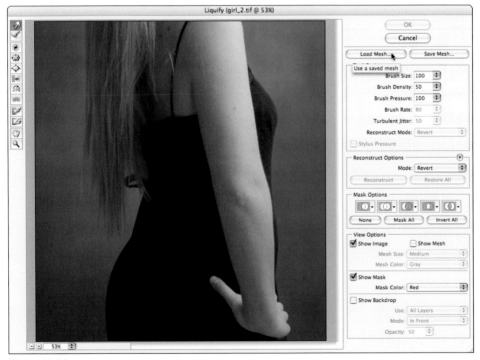

**Figure 10.21**

10.22 shows the effect of dragging and moving pixels to the right. The right image shows what the girl looks like after the application is completed. This was all done with a single stroke.

# tip

Use Liquify's Freeze tool to paint a mask onto areas you don't want to affect. An existing mask can also be used.

This filter works so well here because the background is simple. If the background contained lots of detail — like an outdoor portrait in a garden — adjustments like this would require more work. As it is, the only area that needs to be cleaned up with the Clone Stamp tool or Healing Brush is where the bottom tips of her hair were also distorted to the right. This kind of cleanup is quite common when using the Liquify filter.

# note

The Liquify filter is a resource hog. If you're working on a large file, it can take quite a while to load and execute. When working with a large file, use a selection to isolate the area being worked on before opening the Liquify filter. That way, only the selected area is loaded into the Liquify filter's dialog box, which speeds up the process quite a bit.

Again, I'm barely scratching the surface of what this filter is capable of. I encourage you to spend time exploring it in more depth. When you get playful with it, you can also create some really interesting visual effects.

Remember that every tool in this chapter can be used in countless ways!

**Figure 10.22**

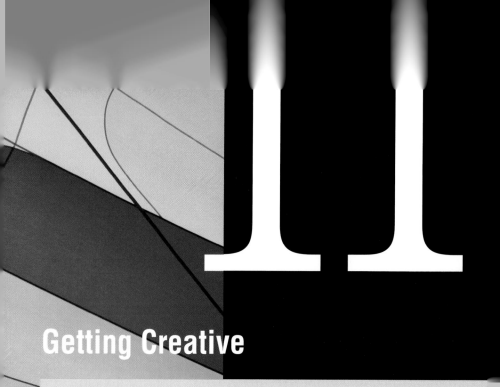

# Getting Creative

**M**uch of what you've learned up to this point is geared toward managing image fundamentals. These fundamentals are the foundation of a solid workflow that consistently produces quality results. After you master those skills you're ready to begin working with your images on a more creative level. On this level you begin to add additional elements to your photos that help you express your creative vision. After you master these techniques, it will change the way you work. The biggest change will be that you begin visualizing the possibilities before you even click the shutter button.

With Photoshop, the creative options seem limitless because of the things you can do with this amazing technology. However, there are some fundamental image enhancements that have been around since the earliest days of photography. One of them is burning and dodging.

# Burning and Dodging

The terms burning and dodging refer to techniques that are used to locally darkened and lighten portions of a photo without affecting the rest of the photo. They allow the image's maker to shape and massage the image's tones to help guide the viewer's eye through it — showing her what's important and what isn't.

In the traditional darkroom, when printing a negative onto a piece of light-sensitive paper with an enlarger, the longer the light from the enlarger hits the paper, the darker the tones on the paper become. If an area of a print needs to be darker than the rest of the print, the printer makes a second exposure onto the paper using a sheet of cardboard with a small hole between the enlarger and the printing paper (or even his cupped hands with a small opening between them), allowing the light to hit only the area to be darkened. This way, he controls where the additional light strikes the paper. This process is called burning-in or burning.

Dodging is the opposite. If something needs to be lighter than the rest of the print, the printer uses a tool to block some of the light passing from the enlarger to the printing paper. The tool the photographer uses is often a circular piece of cardboard taped to the end of a piece of thin wire. This way, he holds back some of the light from hitting the sensitive paper; less light means lighter tones on the print.

In the days of the traditional darkroom, burning and dodging was a hit-and-miss operation. You never really knew how well you did until the photo paper was developed later. Fortunately, the process is much easier and more controllable in the world of digital imaging and Photoshop.

There are numerous ways to approach burning and dodging in Photoshop. In the following sections I show you two of them. The first uses Photoshop's standard Burn and Dodge tools. The second method presents a more flexible technique using the Brush tool that isolates the burning and dodging to its own layer.

## Using Photoshop's Burn and Dodge tools

Photoshop's Burn and Dodge tools (O) are stacked together (along with the Sponge tool), fourteenth from the top on the single-column Tools panel. The icons for these tools, shown in Figure 11.1, are reminders of the traditional darkroom methods of burning and dodging — a cupped hand for burning and a circular piece of cardboard on a wire for dodging.

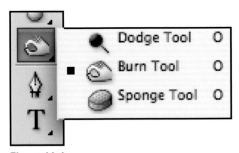

Figure 11.1

note

The Sponge tool is used to locally control color saturation. It's okay when you're in a hurry, but when you work on a serious image, use an adjustment layer and a mask.

These tools have been part of Photoshop for many years. However, they received an upgrade with the release of Photoshop CS4. A new algorithm is now being used that provides more natural results and prevents the tools from shifting a region's color as its tonality is modified. The resulting effect is subtler than previous versions of the tools, especially when dodging.

Both the Burn and Dodge tools use a standard brush to apply changes to the image. If you want to lighten something, paint with the Dodge tool. If you want to darken something, use the Burn tool. The more you paint over an area, the darker or lighter it gets. Use the following tool settings in the Options bar, shown in Figure 11.2, to modify the tool's effect on the image:

- **Brush.** This menu is the usual brush menu. It's best to use this tool with a very soft brush unless you're working along a hard edge.

- **Protect Tones.** Select this to help minimize clipping in the shadows and highlights by protecting them. This also helps to keep colors from shifting hue as tones are modified.

Though the Burn and Dodge tools are useful, the biggest problem I have with them is they're destructive by nature. The only way to isolate the effects of these tools to a separate layer is to duplicate the image layer (doubling the size of the file) and use them on that duplicate layer. Even then, if you change your mind later, it's difficult to back up and make minor modifications to their effects. If you're working quickly, it's fine to use the Burn and Dodge tools. However, when you're working on an important project, it's best to find a way to burn and dodge on a separate layer.

**Figure 11.2**

- **Range.** Use this menu to select the tonal range to be modified. Use Midtones to change mid-range tones, use Shadows to change dark tones, or use Highlights to affect the lighter areas.

- **Exposure.** Use this setting to adjust the amount of the effect. The setting is similar to the Brush tool's Opacity setting. It's always best to begin with a low Exposure amount and build up the effect you want with consecutive strokes.

- **Airbrush.** This is the same as the Airbrush setting in the Brush tool's options. I prefer to leave it off when burning and dodging.

# Burning and dodging without Photoshop's Burn and Dodge tools

There are a few different ways of locally lightening and darkening regions of an image. Here's the system I use:

**1** Open the practice file Downtown_ Portland.tif from downloadable practice files on the Web site (www.wiley.com/ go/photoshopcs4ats). This photo, shown in Figure 11.3, was shot from the International Rose Test Garden in Portland, Oregon. The view is looking back toward downtown Portland with

Figure 11.3

Mt. Hood in the background. In this image, there's quite a discrepancy between the dark tones of the trees and foliage in the foreground and the light tones on the mountain in the background, which is barely visible. If you attempt to darken the entire image to make the mountain more visible, the overall tonality becomes too dark.

The goal here is to balance the tones in this image by darkening the mountain and its foothills, as well as some of the buildings downtown, while maintaining the tonality of most of the greenery in the foreground.

**2** Choose Layer → New → Layer (or click the New Layer button on the bottom of the Layers panel) to add a new layer.

**3** Name the new layer Burn & Dodge and click OK.

**4** **Choose Soft Light from the drop-down menu at the top left of the Layers panel.** This changes the blending mode of the Burn & Dodge layer. This important step affects the way the Burn & Dodge layer blends with the layer below it.

# caution

The painting on a burn and dodge layer is affected by any adjustment layers above it. When you have an adjustment layer that's applying a strong tonal correction, place the burn and dodge layer above it so it will be unaffected by the adjustment layer.

**5** **Select the Brush tool from the Tools panel and change its size to about 100 px in the Options bar.** You can change the size as you work so that it suits the area where you're working.

**6** Decrease the Hardness value to 0 percent, set the Opacity to 2%, and set Flow to 100 percent. You're going to be painting with black and white, so make sure the color swatches on the toolbar are set to their defaults by pressing D. (Remember that you can use the X key to swap the colors of the foreground and background swatches.)

**7** Begin with black and start painting the mountain and the foothills in front of it. Paint with white where you want to lighten parts of the image, and paint with black to darken. Try not to paint the buildings just yet. The effect should be slightly noticeable. This is the reason you're working with such a low opacity on the Brush tool. It's much better to reach the desired tonality by building up a few strokes than it is to try to nail it with one stroke at a special opacity. Notice that the darkening effect is stronger on the darker tones of the hills in the foreground than it is on the mountain. That's because the mountain is so much lighter to begin with.

## note

Though you're painting with white and black paint, the effect is different than working with a layer mask. In this case, you're painting content onto the layer instead of using a mask to modify existing layer content.

**8** Increase the Opacity of the Brush tool to 50 percent and paint the mountain and the distant foothills to darken them a bit more. Occasionally, click the eyeball next to the layer to turn the Burn & Dodge layer's visibility off and on to check your work.

**9** When you're happy with the mountain, decrease the Brush Opacity to 15 percent and paint some of the buildings to darken them. Most of the objectionable light tones are beginning to come into line.

## tip

If you don't like some of your burning and dodging, use the Eraser tool (E) with a soft brush to remove any painting from the Burn & Dodge layer and try again with the Brush tool. (Yes, this is one of those rare times when using the destructive Eraser tool is okay within the non-destructive workflow.)

**10** Change the Brush color to white (press X) and paint some of the dark areas in the foreground. Now see what you can do about some of the dark foliage in the middle foreground. Don't lighten any of the foliage that's near the edge of the frame. Notice that if you lighten an area too much, the foliage takes on a ghostly gray appearance. Be careful when you begin to see this because it can be distracting if overdone.

**11** Switch the color back to black (press X), and change the brush size to 500 px and increase the Opacity to about 40 percent.

**12** Paint across the top of the image and down both sides of the sky. The sky is still so light and I don't like the way it draws the eye away from the main subject matter. The objective here is to darken all of these edges, helping to contain the viewer's eye within the frame. Build up the strokes at the top and sides so that the tone gets darker as it gets closer to the edge of the frame. Figure 11.4 shows what the final image looks like.

# tip

If you plan to crop the image much, you'll have to revisit this layer after cropping to check the edges. If some of your darkening was removed, add more to balance the image.

**13** **Choose Normal from the drop-down menu at the top left of the Layers panel.** This sets the Burn & Dodge layer's blending mode back to Normal. The image should look something like Figure 11.5. This is a good way to check your strokes to see if you missed something obvious. This also reinforces the idea that all of your brush strokes actually added layer content in the form of paint.

When burning and dodging, be aware that if the detail is already gone from a blown-out highlight, no amount of burning will bring it back. The same goes for detail completely lost to a shadow. If you try to recover it, you'll end up flattening out the tones by making them too gray.

Before moving on, here's a quick review of this easy, nondestructive burning and dodging technique:

**1** **Create an empty layer above the main image layer(s).**

**2** **Change the new layer's blending mode to Soft Light.**

**3** **Use the Brush tool at a low opacity.** I usually begin with 15–20 percent, increasing the value only when I can't see any effect. Paint with black to darken and white to lighten.

**Figure 11.4**

**Figure 11.5**

# Using the Black and White Command

A couple of years ago, out of curiosity, I began to write down all of the various methods that digital photographers were using to convert color photos to black and white. In a few minutes I was able to list at least a dozen. Some of these techniques are crude, while others produced great results. When Photoshop CS3 was released this all changed because Adobe introduced a powerful new command called Black and White. This is now the only method most photographers are using.

tip

Black and White is also available as an adjustment layer.

Figure 11.6 shows the Black and White command's dialog box (Image → Adjustments → Black & White). This dialog box has six sliders, one for each of our six main colors: Reds, Yellows, Greens, Cyans, Blues, and Magentas. These sliders allow you to adjust the brightness of different colors so that you choose which tones in the black and white image are light, and which are dark. This allows you to customize the tones in the black and white based on their actual colors.

In the following exercise I show you how to use this command to create a black and white from a color image. Follow these steps to learn how to quickly make your own black and white conversions.

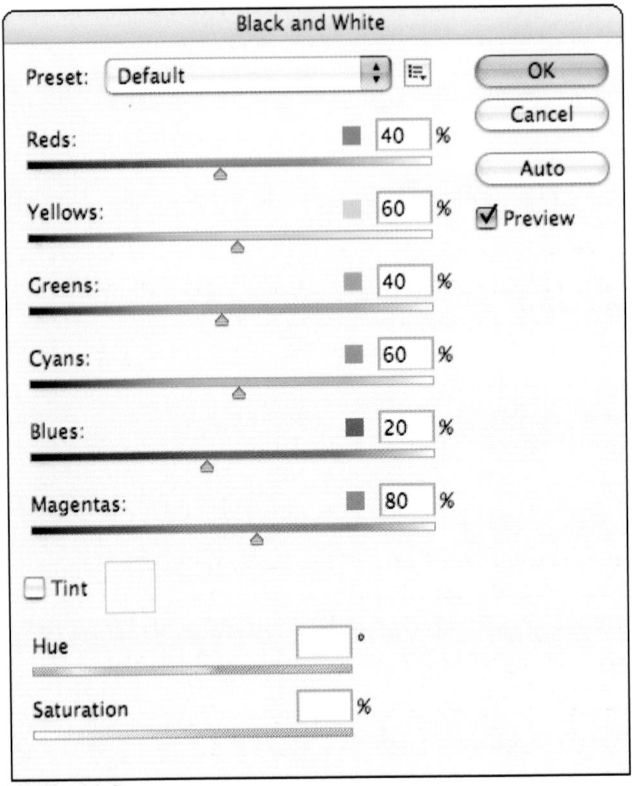

**Black and White**

Preset:  Default

Reds:           ■  40  %

Yellows:        ▢  60  %

Greens:         ■  40  %

Cyans:          ▢  60  %

Blues:          ■  20  %

Magentas:       ■  80  %

▢ Tint

Hue                      °

Saturation               %

OK

Cancel

Auto

☑ Preview

## tip

If you find you use this four-key shortcut, to open the Black and White dialog box often, consider changing it using Edit→Keyboard Shortcuts.

Figure 11.6

**1** **Open the practice file titled Gargoyle.tif from the downloadable practice files from the Web site (www.wiley.com/go/photoshopcs4ats).**

**2** **Choose Image→Adjustments→Black & White (Shift+Alt+⌘+B/Shift+Alt+Ctrl+B) to open the Black and White command.** Your image preview turns to grayscale when the Black and White dialog box opens with its default settings. Grayscale is another way of saying that the image has no color in it and only tones of gray are used to describe image content.

**3** **Click the Auto button to let the command evaluate the colors in the image and make its own adjustment.** Generally, I'm not a big fan of auto adjustments in Photoshop. However, this one does a pretty good job of getting you into the ballpark. It maximizes the distribution of gray values in the image. Because of this, it almost always gets you closer than the dialog box's default settings. In the case of the practice image it helps a little, but the contrast of the image in Figure 11.7 still looks flat. Because you know the dominant colors in this photo are red and blue, you can use that information to modify the tonality to the image.

**Figure 11.7**

**4** **Adjust the Reds slider to a value of 130%.** This lightens the red bricks without affecting the blue bricks.

**5** **Adjust the Blues value to –50%.** This darkens all of the blue bricks that frame the face. Now the image, shown in Figure 11.8, is much more appealing because of the increased contrast of the red and blue bricks. Notice that neither of the adjustments changed the tonality of the face of the white wall on the right

because these two areas don't have either red or blue in them. You can use these six sliders to customize the way each color is converted to black and white. If you want a certain tone to be lighter, raise the value. If you want it to be darker, lower the value. If you don't remember what a particular color is (because the preview is black and white), click the Preview box to temporarily hide the black-and-white effect. In this case,

**Figure 11.8**

the colors that needed to be changed were simple. Sometimes, though, it's hard to tell exactly which slider to use for a particular color.

6 **With the Preview check box checked, move the cursor over the image.** When you do, you notice that the cursor becomes an eyedropper. When you click a color, you notice that the associated color swatch is highlighted in the Black and White dialog box. If the color is a combination of two colors, both those

swatches are highlighted. All you have to do is click the tone you want to lighten or darken to see which slider to use. But that's not all. There's something even cooler that you can do.

## caution

Be aware that all the similar tones in the image change together. If you click one person's skin tone, similar skin tones on other people also are affected by any changes.

**7** **Click and hold your cursor on the face, and drag the cursor to the right.** Notice that the cursor changes to a hand with double arrows pointing sideways. Notice that the tones for the underlying color you clicked starts getting lighter. In this case the face has yellow in it so the Yellows value in the Black and White dialog box also begins to increase. When you click and drag the cursor to the left, the tones darken and the values decrease. It doesn't get much more intuitive than this.

Leave this file open because you'll be adding one more effect in the next exercise.

When it's time to convert a color image to black and white, you can't beat the new Black and White command for creating custom conversions. Remember that this command is also available as an adjustment layer. That means that you can convert an image to black and white and then use a mask to go back and reveal some of the color, like the image of the tulips you worked with in Chapter 9.

# Toning a Black and White Image

Adding a tint to a black and white is another technique that's been around since photography's earliest days. In the days before digital photography this was accomplished by using dangerous and stinky chemicals to apply a sepia tone. Sepia is a faded brown color that results from using specific darkroom chemicals to tone a black and white print.

There are a few different ways to tone an image in Photoshop, but now, with the Black and White command, it's never been easier. Here's how to quickly add a tint to the photo from the previous exercise:

**1** **Go back to the Gargoyle.tif practice file and pick up where you left off in Step 7 of the previous steps.** Open the Black and White command again.

**2** **Select the Tint option at the bottom of the dialog box, shown in Figure 11.9.** When you do, the Hue value is set to 42

and the Saturation value is set to 20%. These default values are intended to approximate a sepia tone.

**3** **Use the Hue slider to change the color of the tone and the Saturation slider to modify the intensity of that color.** Alternatively, you can click on the color swatch beside Tint to open a color picker that allows you to choose a specific color. Then you can use the Hue and Saturation sliders to tweak that color. When you like the color of the tone, click OK to complete the procedure and close the Black and White dialog box.

## tip

Try using a blue instead of a warm brown and notice how much cooler the feeling of the overall image becomes.

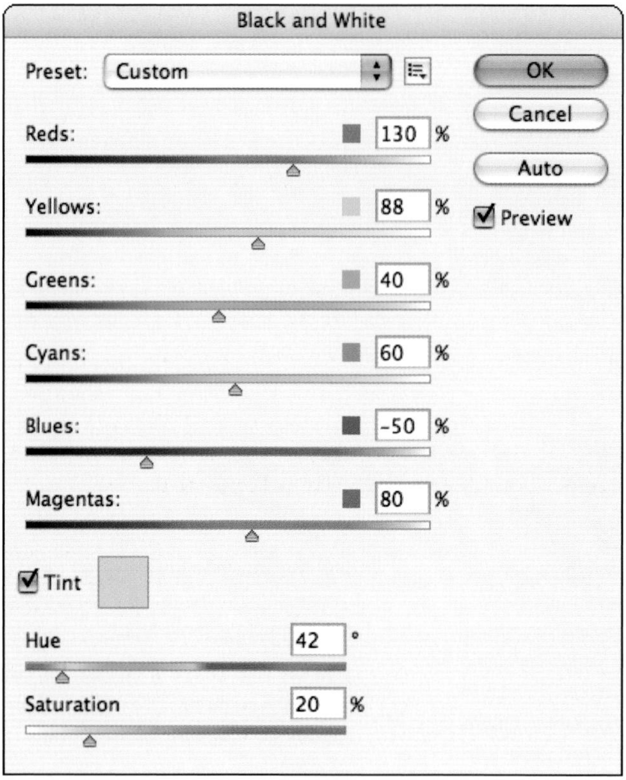

Figure 11.9

# Introduction to Photoshop's Filters

Photographers have been using filters for years. Typically, these are glass filters that are screwed onto the front of the lens to modify the image as it's captured. Examples of this kind of filter are starburst and soft focus filters. In the digital age it usually isn't necessary to use these filters when shooting because these effects can be added in post-production. This ability allows the photographer to make creative decisions after the image is captured, which leaves the door open for all sorts of changes.

Photoshop has so many filters that it would take an entire book to cover them all. The goal here is show you filters that I use all of the time: the

Gaussian Blur and Radial Blur filters. After you understand how to work with these two filters, you'll be able to apply this information to any of the other filters you want to explore.

## note

Photoshop comes with a wide range of filters located in the Filter menu. Some of these filters, such as the Sharpening and Blur filters, are used often. Others, such as the Artistic and Brush Stroke filters, are used only when special effects are needed.

# Using the Lens Blur filter

Sometimes a photo has a greater depth of field than what you might prefer. Background detail is so sharp it distracts from the main subject. One way to fix this is to blur the image with a filter and then mask out the main subject so that it's in focus.

Follow these steps to learn how to do this yourself:

**1** **Open the practice file titled Beach_ Dog1.tif from the downloadable practice files on the Web site (www.wiley.com/go/photoshopcs4ats).** This is a nice photo of Hazel, but the background is so sharp that it leads the eye away from her.

**2** **Choose Layer → Duplicate Layer and click OK.** A duplicate Background layer is created, named Background copy. You use this layer for the blur effect.

**3** **Choose Filter → Blur → Gaussian Blur.** The Gaussian Blur dialog box opens shown in Figure 11.10.

**4** **Increase the Radius value to 4.0 and click OK.** This blurs the entire layer, including Hazel. Click OK to run the filter. Now you need to mask Hazel so she isn't affected by the blur.

**5** **In the Masks panel, click the Add a Pixel Mask button.**

**6** **Choose the Brush tool (B) and set the Hardness value to about 50%, the Opacity value to 100%, and set your foreground color to black and begin painting Hazel to mask her.** Vary the brush size as appropriate while you paint. If you have trouble getting a clean line along her outside edges, lower the Opacity to 50% to help blend the edges. When you have Hazel completely masked, she'll be back to her original sharpness. You need to take one more step to make this effect convincing.

Figure 11.10

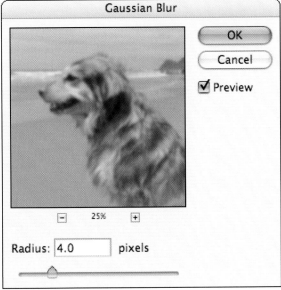

**7** Mask the foreground and the ground around her with your brush set to 100%, and then lower the opacity of the brush (begin with 50%), and paint the ground that is just on the other side of her to fade the effect. The foreground and the ground around her should be in focus, just as she is.

**8** Click the eyeball icon to hide the visibility of the blurred layer to compare before and after versions. Make the layer visible again and make any necessary adjustments to the mask to complete the effect.

# tip

Blurring the background around a subject is a great way to rescue an image that has less than optimal sharpness. That's because it makes the subject relatively sharper than its surroundings, causing it to appear sharper than it is.

## Adding motion with the Radial Blur filter

Photoshop has a filter called Motion Blur that's great for creating a motion effect from side to side, but another, less known, filter that's used to create motion is the Radial Blur filter. Give it a try on a different photo of Hazel at the beach:

**1** Open the practice file titled Beach_ Dog2.tif from the downloadable practice files on the Web site (www.wiley.com/go/photoshopcs4ats). In this photo, shown in Figure 11.11, Hazel is running toward the camera. It's a cute photo, but it's kind of boring because everything in the image is in focus — arresting her motion.

**Figure 11.11**

**2** **Choose Layer → Duplicate Layer and click OK.** A duplicate Background layer is created, allowing the blue effect to be on its own layer.

**3** **Choose Filter → Blur → Radial Blur.** The Radial Blur dialog box opens, shown in Figure 11.12.

**4** **Choose Zoom, set the value of Amount to 20, and leave Quality set to Good for this example.** When you work on something important, change it to Best. Just be aware that the filter takes longer to run on this higher setting.

**5** **Click and drag the Blur Center preview so it is centered on Hazel's face, and then click OK to run the filter.** Centering the filter on the main subject is the trick to using it. You can see where I'm doing this in Figure 11.12.

## tip

To re-run a filter with its last settings use ⌘+F/ Ctrl+F. To reopen the dialog with the last settings, use Alt+⌘+F/Alt+Ctrl+F. This Alt key modifier works with other dialogs too. For example, if you want to open the Levels dialog with its last settings use Alt+⌘+L/Alt+Ctrl+L.

**6** **If the position isn't just right, undo the effect (⌘+Z/Ctrl+Z), and then reopen the filter dialog with its last settings using Alt+⌘+F/Alt+Ctrl+F.** Make any adjustments to fine-tune the positioning.

**7** **Create a layer mask using the Masks panel and paint her with black.** This prevents Hazel from being affected by the blur, just as you did in the previous exercise.

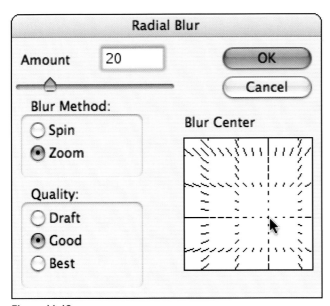

**Figure 11.12**

**8** **Lower the opacity of the Brush tool as you paint around her edges.** Consider allowing some of her edges to blur, as shown in the detail in Figure 11.13.

# tip

Remember, when a filter is run on a separate layer, you can reduce the opacity of the layer to fine-tune a filter's effect. Also, don't forget about the Fade command (Edit→Fade), which allows you run a filter a little stronger than you like and then fade the intensity until it's perfect.

The final effect adds some pizzazz to an otherwise boring photo. This technique is quite common in wedding photography. It's a great way to spice up a photo of the bride and groom as they walk down the isle after the ceremony or when they're leaving the church. It also has the added benefit of minimizing distractions in the background so that the bride and groom are the center of attention.

Though you only brushed the surface of the choices in the Filter menu in this section, you should now have a good idea of how filters can be combined with masks to produce interesting and controllable effects. After you learn to use the Smart Sharpen filter in the next chapter, consider revisiting this section to use Smart Sharpen to selectively sharpen image content. This is commonly done to sharpen only the eyes in a close-up portrait image. Also realize that it's possible to have more than one filter layer. For example, blurring the background after you sharpen the eyes.

**Figure 11.13**

# Creating Panoramas from Multiple Photos

Sometimes it's difficult to capture the wide range of a scene in a single photo. This is especially true for elongated horizontal scenes. A technique that's used to solve this problem is to shoot a series of photos and then let Photoshop stitch then together into a single image by matching overlapping detail. These images are called panoramas because they show a wide view. Panoramas can be horizontal or vertical.

## Using the Photomerge command

The Photomerge command allows you to select a series of photos and then let Photoshop automatically combine them into a single image. After Photoshop completes the heavy lifting, you can fine-tune the image to fix any anomalies created during the assembly. Figure 11.14 shows

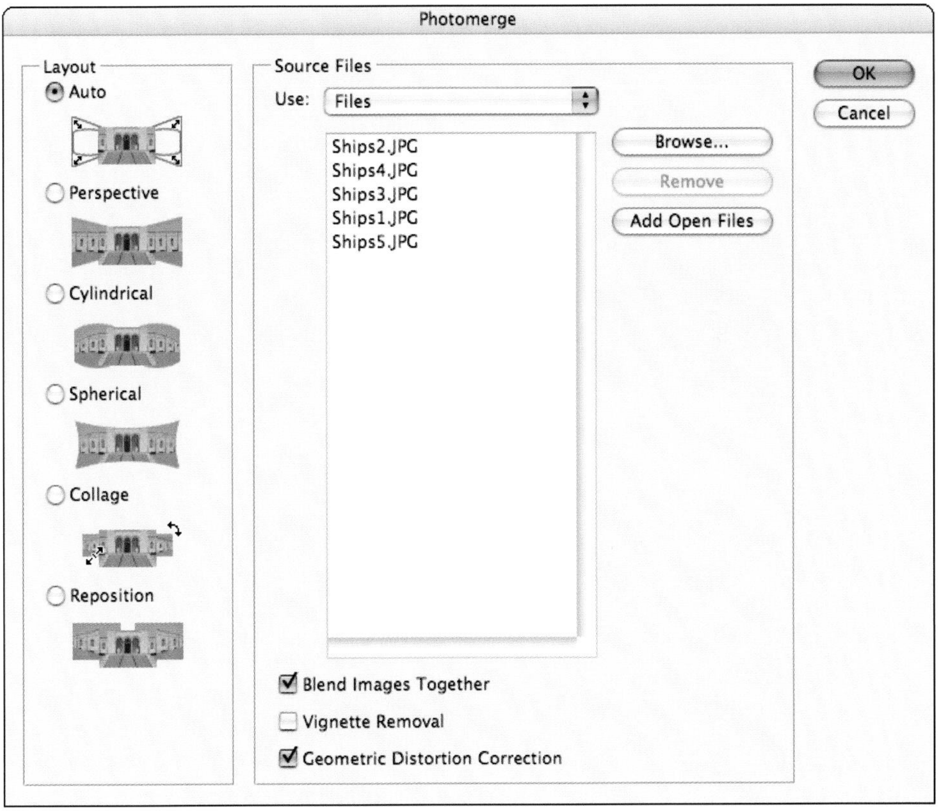

**Figure 11.14**

the Photomerge dialog box that's opened by choosing File → Automate → Photomerge. Consider some of the options here, beginning with the Layout options, before taking the command for a test drive:

- **Layout.** This section of the Photomerge dialog box offers several layout options. They are:

  - **Auto.** This setting lets Photoshop analyze the images and choose the best layout option (Perspective, Cylindrical, or Spherical) for combining them.

  - **Perspective.** The middle image is designated as the main source image. The rest of the images are then transformed and repositioned to match the geometry of the source image.

  - **Cylindrical.** This layout option reduces distortion that can be caused by using the Perspective layout. This distortion is called "bow-tie" distortion because the ends of the image tend to be stretched vertically more than the middle source image. This selection is best used for creating wide panoramas.

  - **Spherical.** Use this layout option when the panorama is extended vertically, as well as horizontally; for example, when you photograph the inside of a building, from side-to-side and floor to ceiling.

  - **Collage.** This layout option is more flexible than Reposition. Images are aligned to match their best locations, orientations, and sizes.

  - **Reposition.** This option aligns the photos and matches overlapping content, but does not transform the geometry of the images.

- **Source Files.** This section is where you choose your files to be merged. There are three other options that are used to adjust the images after they're combined that are in this section of the dialog box:

  - **Blend Images Together.** Use this default option to let Photomerge find the best places to overlap images and create seams between them. This option also attempts to match the color of the images as they're merged together. This reduces the amount of touch up that's often necessary when the option is turned off.

  - **Vignette Removal.** This option is used to reduce any vignetting that's in individual photos. This helps the overlapping seams to matchup more accurately.

  - **Geometric Distortion Correction.** Select this option to reduce any distortion caused by the focal length of the lens. This option is grayed-out when Collage or Reposition layouts are used.

# note

If Photomerge can't automatically assemble your photos, you'll get a message informing you that some images could not be automatically aligned.

At first all of the options in this dialog box can seem overwhelming. However, after you try it out you'll see that Photomerge is easy to use:

1. **For this exercise open five different practice files from the downloadable files on the Web site (www.wiley.com/go/photoshopcs4ats): Ships1.jpg through Ships5.jpg. If any other files are open, close them now. I shot this series**

of photos as two tugboats escorted a container ship out of port. I intentionally overlapped each photo so that Photomerge would have enough content to work with as it lays out the panorama. I also was careful to include one photo that shows all of the industrial plant on the right so that Photomerge doesn't have to re-create the detailed building with overlapping pieces.

**2** **Choose File → Automate → Photomerge.** The Photomerge dialog box opens.

**3** **Choose Add Open Files to add the ship files to the list and select Auto as the Layout method.**

**4** **Select Blend Images Together and Geometric Distortion Correction options, and then click OK.** This command can take a minute or two to work its magic, especially on large files and an older system. Figure 11.15 shows the assembled panorama.

**5** **Open the Image Size dialog box (Image → Image Size).** When you do, you notice that the panorama's overall length is about 25 inches × 300 ppi (pixels per inch) and the file size is over 120 megabytes. I intentionally made

these files a bit smaller in size than their normal size in case you're working on an older system. When you plan to use Photomerge with large files, be prepared to create a very large panorama.

# tip

You can run Photomerge on selected files in Bridge by choosing Tools → Photoshop → Photomerge. This allows you to use raw files for the panorama. When using raw files, use Adobe Camera Raw to fine-tune them first to make their tone and color uniform to get the most from this command.

Come back after you finish this exercise and go through it again with these options turned off to compare the results of using Photomerge without them.

Photomerge places each of the original photos on separate layers as it assembles the panorama. Figure 11.16 shows these layers in the Layers panel. The really cool part is that layer masks are used to automatically blend the images together.

Figure 11.15

**Figure 11.16**

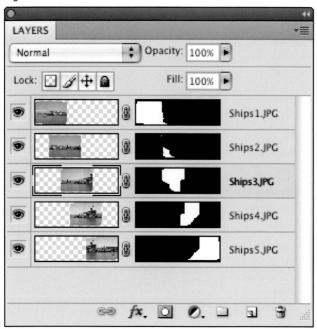

The combination of layers and masks gives you a great deal of control over the panorama. If one of the seams isn't perfectly lined up you can use the Brush tool and adjust the mask. You can also adjust the layer's geometry using the menu in the Transform command (Edit→Transform). Neither of these options should be necessary in the previous exercise.

Something else to notice is that the finished panorama is a little ragged around the edges where the gray and white checkerboard shows behind it. This checkerboard is Photoshop's way of indicating transparency — which means there's nothing there. The rough edges are created when the individual photos are rotated and transformed into position. You can use the Crop tool to trim the edges, or you can use the Clone Stamp tool to clone over the transparency.

## see also

The Crop tool is discussed in Chapter 12.

This image lends itself to the second option because the ragged edges are mostly in areas where there is little detail. This option also allows you to avoid cropping the edge of the ski boat on the right. Here are a couple of tips if you want to use the Clone Stamp tool to clean up the edges of the panorama.

- **Click on the top layer and add a new layer: Layer→ New→ Layer (Shift+⌘+N/ Shift+Ctrl+N).** Use this layer to isolate your retouching.

- **Choose All Layers from the Sample menu on the Clone Stamp tool's options so that you can sample the underlying layers as you clone.**

- **When working on the lower portions of the image, be careful about duplicating the patterns in the water.** Change your sample point often to add variety to the patterns.

# Tips for shooting photos for a panorama

Photomerge does a pretty decent job of automatically creating panoramas. You can help the process by providing original photos that are designed for assembly. Here are some of the things you should consider:

- **Provide at least a 25 percent overlap between the edges of the photos.** This gives Photomerge sufficient content to compare from image to image.

- **Use one focal length on your lens.** Don't zoom in for some photos and zoom out for others.

- **Maintain a consistent exposure.** When Blend Images Together is selected, Photomerge does a good job of matching images. However, when extreme differences occur, the final result suffers. The best way to maintain consistency when shooting is to shoot in manual mode instead of program mode. That way you're sure to shoot each photo with the same exposure settings.

- **Keep your camera level.** The best way to accomplish this is to use a tripod with a rotating head. It also helps to have a tripod with a leveling bubble so you can be sure the tripod is level.

- **Avoid extra wide-angle lenses.** Photomerge has trouble working with images made with fish-eye and other super wide-angle lenses.

Now that you know how easy it is to create a panorama with Photomerge, you can start looking for opportunities to create your own. Instead of zooming out and shooting one shot of a large scene, zoom in a little and shoot several shots and let Photoshop stitch them together.

# 12

# Finishing the Image

A fter you get a photo looking the way you want it to look, it's time to prepare it for final output. Whether that output is printing or online viewing, preparing it entails two things: final cropping and sizing, and output sharpening. I waited until now to discuss these topics because it's important that they be carried out late in the workflow. In fact, output sharpening is usually the last thing that's done to an image before printing it. That's because final sizing and cropping should be done before sharpening. In this chapter you learn all about how to carry out these procedures so that you know that your finishing touches improve your images, rather than degrade them.

# Changing an Image's Resolution and Size

I've met many photographers who don't understand how to change an image's size or resolution correctly. The problem usually stems from a lack of understanding about image resolution and how it affects image size.

# caution

Always save a master file with all layers before changing size or cropping. Otherwise it may be hard to back up and resize the file for a different output use later.

## Understanding resolution

One of the things that can be the hardest to get your head around when you start down the digital path is resolution. This confusion is compounded by the fact that there are two different kinds of resolution in the digital world. One is *dots per inch,* and the other is *pixels per inch.*

- **Dots per inch (dpi).** This refers to the number of dots per inch that an inkjet printer is capable of applying to a sheet of paper. It can range from 720 to 2800 and more. The closer these dots are to each other, the more

they blend together forming continuous tones on the print. Naturally, this depends on the paper that's being printed on. If the paper is porous watercolor paper, the dots soak in and blend just fine at lower dpi settings like 720. On glossy photo papers, a higher setting — such as 1440 — is needed because the ink dries on the surface. About the only time people discuss dpi is when they are talking about a printer.

- **Pixels per inch (ppi).** This is what is usually discussed when talking about resolution in digital photography. It refers to the distance between the pixels that make up digital images. Pixels per inch is an important setting because it determines what digital images look like when they're displayed and printed. Sometimes a lower value is desirable, and other times a higher value is preferred.

If you have a file with a resolution of 120 ppi or lower, you run the risk of seeing the space between the pixels when you print. This causes edge detail, which should be smooth in the print, to look jagged. The goal is to get the pixels close enough together so that these single dots form continuous tones and lines. Figure 12.1 gives

**Figure 12.1**

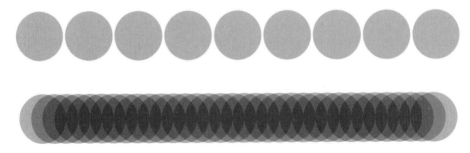

you an idea of how this works. As the dots get closer to one another, they begin to form a line. When you zoom out, the individual dots disappear. (It's similar to the idea of getting ink dots close together on a printer (dpi).

# tip

Keep in mind that some people mistakenly use the terms dpi and ppi interchangeably, saying dpi when they really mean ppi. If they're not specifically talking about a printer's output, then they probably mean ppi.

The thing to keep in mind when it's time to change resolution is that if you have an image file that's 150 ppi and you simply change it's resolution to 300 ppi for printing at a lab, the new image's dimensions are affected because the distance between the pixels is cut in half. An 8 × 10 becomes a 4 × 5 at 300 ppi.

# Doing the simple math

I know I just said the dreaded M word, but please keep reading because in the next few paragraphs I show you how to use simple math to understand what Photoshop is doing when you resize your photo files. Begin by getting a better handle on how resolution works. Follow these steps:

1  **Choose File → New to create a new file.** The New dialog box appears.

2  **Set the following attributes, as shown in Figure 12.2, and then click OK to open the new file:**

- **Width = 8 inches**
- **Height = 10 inches**
- **Resolution = 150**
- **Color Mode = RGB Color, 8-bit**

**Figure 12.2**

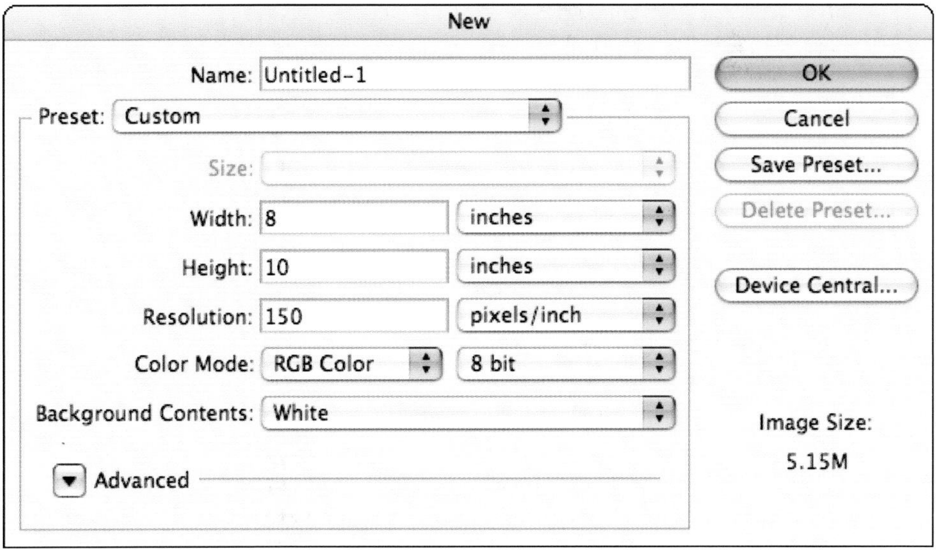

**3** **Choose Image → Image Size (Alt+⌘+I/ Alt+Ctrl+I).** The Image Size dialog box appears. Notice that the starting dimensions are the same as what you specified with the New File command.

**4** **Deselect the Resample Image option.** Notice that the Pixel Dimensions area at the top of the Image Size window goes gray when Resample Image is turned off. That means that the number of pixels being used in your image is fixed at 1200 × 1500 pixels.

**5** **Change the resolution setting to 300.** Leave the measurement at pixels/inch. Notice that the size of the image goes from 8" × 10" to 4" × 5", as shown in Figure 12.3. That's because you're only changing the distance between pixels as you modify the resolution of the file. You have fixed overall pixel dimensions of 1200 × 1500. When you set your resolution to 300 ppi, the math dictates

that the image is 4" × 5" (4" × 300 ppi = 1200 pixels, and 5" × 300 ppi = 1500 pixels). When the resolution is set to 150 ppi, the image must be 8" × 10" in size (8" × 150 ppi = 1200 pixels, and 10" × 150 ppi = 1500 pixels).

## Resampling the image size

In the previous example, you were asked to turn off Resample Image because Resample Image has a special function that affects the math involved in resizing an image. When you turned off Resample Image, the Pixel Dimensions remain fixed when you changed the resolution value. Take a look at what happens when Resample is turned on:

**1** **Begin with the file you created in the previous set of steps, and return to its original state using the History panel.** If you closed it, then go back and complete Steps 1 and 2.

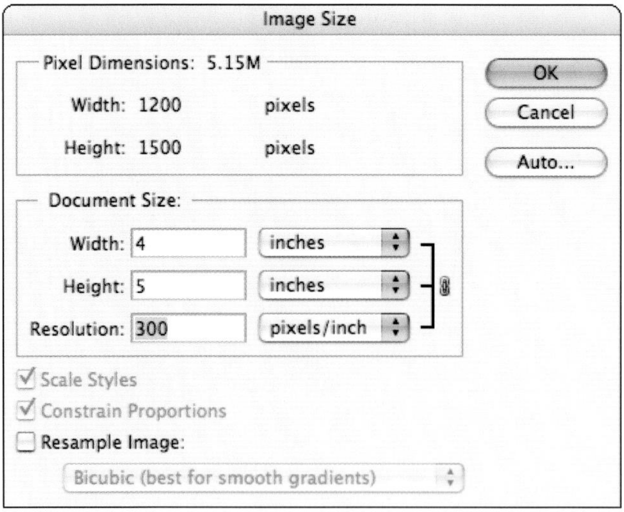

| Image Size | |
|---|---|
| Pixel Dimensions: 5.15M | OK |
| Width: 1200 pixels | Cancel |
| Height: 1500 pixels | Auto... |
| Document Size: | |
| Width: 4 inches | |
| Height: 5 inches | |
| Resolution: 300 pixels/inch | |
| ☑ Scale Styles | |
| ☑ Constrain Proportions | |
| ☐ Resample Image: | |
| Bicubic (best for smooth gradients) | |

**Figure 12.3**

# tip

If you still have the Image Size window open from the preceding example, you can reset it to the settings it had when you opened it by holding down Alt and clicking Reset —where the Cancel button used to be. This works with almost every dialog box where you see a Cancel button.

**2** **Choose Image → Image Size (Alt+⌘+I/ Alt+Ctrl+I).** The Image Size dialog box appears.

**3** **Leave the Resample Image option selected or select it if it isn't already checked.**

**4** **Change the Resolution to 300.** Leave the dimensions at pixels/inch. Notice that the Image Size remains at 8" × 10". What changed was the Pixel Dimensions at the top of the window. They went from 1200 × 1500 to 2400 × 3000.

**5** **Change the Resolution to 600.** Now the Pixel Dimensions changes to 4800 × 6000, but the Document Size remains fixed, as shown in Figure 12.4

Something to notice when comparing Figure 12.3 and Figure 12.4 is the little chain icon that appears to the right of the Document Size settings. This icon indicates that these values are linked. When one value is changed, the other linked value is affected. In Figure 12.3, where Resample is off, the Width, Height, and Resolution settings are all linked. In Figure 12.4, where Resample is on, only the Width and Height values are linked. Resolution is not be affected by changes to these values. This is a great way to remember which Resample setting to choose.

When Resample Image is turned on, modifications to Resolution or Document Size in the Image Size dialog box affect only the Pixel Dimensions. When you make an image's width and height dimensions smaller, or reduce its resolution, resampling takes pixels from the image. This is called *downsampling*.

**Figure 12.4**

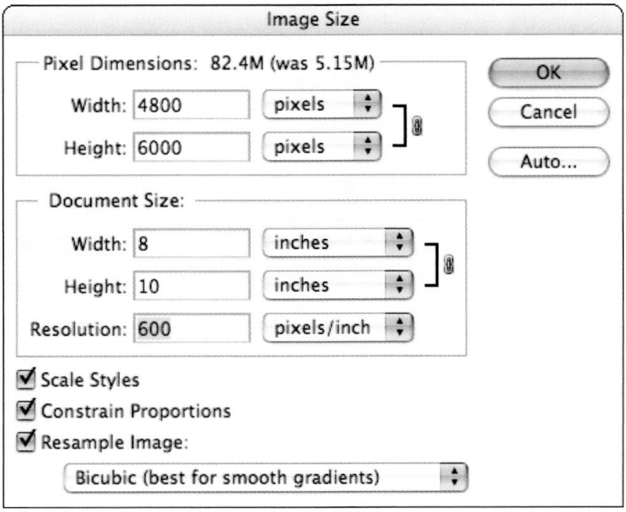

If you make the Document Size larger or increase the Resolution value, resampling adds pixels to the image. This is called *upsampling.* You can verify that this is taking place by looking at the file size readout next to Pixel Dimensions in Figure 12.4. The original file size was 5.15 megabytes (M). Now, with the addition of all the new pixels being added by Photoshop, the file size is 82.4M.

# tip

There are two different ways to measure a photo file's size in megabytes. One is the size of the photo when it's open. This size is determined by the pixel dimensions — width × height × three color channels. This is the size shown next to Pixel Dimensions in the Image Size dialog box. The second measurement is for when the file is saved to disk. Naturally, this varies by the type of file that's saved. For example, a saved TIFF file is always bigger than a JPEG saved from the same file because the JPEG is compressed. This size is the size shown when you look at the file in your Mac Finder/Windows Explorer.

Keep in mind that adding lots of pixels to an image can affect the image's quality. Photoshop is pretty good at upsampling, but only so much can be done. Lots of guesses need to be made on Photoshop's part when deciding what color to make a new pixel. The quality of the outcome depends on the size and quality of the original file. When a quality file is used, it's easy to double, and even triple, the size of the file. However, if you push it too far and try to upsample an image beyond Photoshop's capabilities, you can hit a point of diminishing returns where quality begins to suffer. For projects that require massive upsampling beyond Photoshop's abilities, look to a plug-in like Genuine Fractals by onOne Software (www.ononesoftware.com). This plug-in uses fractal math to accomplish some amazing upsampling feats.

So remember, if you only want to change the resolution of the file, uncheck Resample. If you need to make the image smaller or larger, then Resample must be checked. Use Table 12.1 as a recap of the relationships you covered in this section:

**Table 12.1**

Relationship Among Inches, Resolution, Pixels, and File Size

| Size in Inches | Resolution | Pixel Dimensions | File Size |
| --- | --- | --- | --- |
| 8 × 10 | 150 | 1200 × 1500 | 5.15M |
| 4 × 5 | 300 | 1200 × 1500 | 5.15M |
| 8 × 10 | 300 | 2400 × 3000 | 20.6M |
| 8 × 10 | 600 | 4800 × 6000 | 82.4M |

# Using the correct image interpolation method

There's one more wrinkle to throw at you before moving on. In the previous examples, you probably noticed a pop-up menu next to Resample Image in the Image Size dialog box, as shown in Figure 12.5.

The two interpolation methods that are of most interest are Bicubic Smoother and Bicubic Sharper. These are the two you'll use almost exclusively when resampling photographic images in Photoshop. When you're upsampling, or increasing the number of pixels in an image, choose Bicubic Smoother. When you're downsampling, or decreasing the number of pixels, choose Bicubic Sharper.

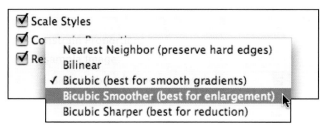

**Figure 12.5**

This box allows you to change the *image interpolation* that's used when you resample an image. Different interpolation settings affect the way new pixels are assigned color based on the pixels that surround them. There are five options in this menu:

- **Nearest Neighbor.** Fast, but not very precise; best for illustrations with edges that are not anti-aliased rather than photos. It preserves hard edges.

- **Bilinear.** Medium quality results with most types of images.

- **Bicubic.** Slower but more precise; produces smoother graduations than the two previous methods.

- **Bicubic Smoother.** Based on Bicubic Interpolation, but designed for enlarging images.

- **Bicubic Sharper.** Based on Bicubic Interpolation, but designed for reducing image size because it maintains the detail of the original image.

# Changing size and resolution together

Sometimes it's necessary to change the document size and resolution at the same time. For example, suppose you have a file that's sized to 8" × 10" at 250 ppi, and you need to change it to a 4" × 5" at 300ppi. Making this change with the Image Size command requires two steps. You can carry out both in one use of the Image Size command:

**1** Choose File → New to open the New dialog box; make the file measure 8" × 10" at 250 ppi.

**2** Choose Image → Image Size (Alt+Ctrl+I). The Image Size dialog box appears.

**3** Deselect the Resample Image option, and change the resolution to 300. Notice that the Document Size changes to 6.67" × 8.33" because you're moving the pixels closer together.

**4** Select Resample with the Bicubic Sharper option from the Resample Image menu, and change the Document Size Width to 4 inches.

**5** Click OK. Now you have a file that is 4" × 5" at 300 ppi.

# Using the Crop Tool

Because cropping in Photoshop is considered destructive — it can't be undone after the file is closed — I always leave master image files uncropped. The reason I waited until now to discuss this basic tool is because this permanent step shouldn't be performed until most of the editing work on the image is complete.

There are two ways to use the Crop tool. You can use it to crop to a predetermined aspect ratio, (like 5 × 7), or you can use it to create a custom crop to suit special needs. Take a look at how this tool can work for you:

**1** Open the Beach_Dog3.tif from the downloadable practice files on the Web site (www.wiley.com/go/ photoshopcs4ats). Before doing anything, check the document size of this image so you know what you're working with (Image → Image Size or Alt+⌘+I/Alt+Ctrl+I). This file's size is 7.787" × 11.68" at 300 ppi.

**2** Select the Crop tool (C) from the Tools panel; it's fifth from the top on the single-column Tools panel. Go to the Options bar, shown in Figure 12.6, and click the Clear button to clear any settings from the Crop tool's options. When all settings are cleared, the tool is ready to handle any kind of cropping aspect ratio.

**3** Click near the upper-left area and drag downward to the lower right. Notice that you can create any aspect ratio you want while dragging. When you let go of the mouse button, you use the control handles at the sides or corners of the selection to change the dimensions of the cropping boundaries.

## tip

If a setting called Snap is turned on, you may have trouble with the cropping selection trying to jump to the image boundary when you work near the boundaries of the image. Snap allows the cursor to move in smart ways so that it quickly lines up with other things in the image. Sometimes, though, it's not smart enough. To solve this problem, choose View and click Snap to deselect it. (Notice that this is one of the few commands you can access while the cropping selection is active.)

**Figure 12.6**

**4** **Click anywhere inside the cropping selection to drag and move it to a different location.** You can also use the cursor keys to nudge the box a small amount. Hold down Shift when you use the cursor keys to nudge by a larger amount.

**5** **Move the cursor outside of the cropping selection until it turns into a curved, double-headed arrow icon.** The horizon isn't straight, but you can fix it from here.

**6** **Click and drag to rotate the crop box to any orientation.** Try to match the line of the horizon with the top line of the crop box (make them parallel), as shown in Figure 12.7.

## tip

Rotation is centered around the crosshair in the center of the crop box. If you want to rotate around a different area — like a corner — click and drag the crosshairs to that location.

**7** **When you like the crop, press Enter or Return and you should see something similar to Figure 12.8.** If you want to cancel the crop and begin again, press Esc. You can also commit a crop by clicking the check mark button on the options bar. And you can cancel the cropping action by clicking the Cancel button, which is also in the Options bar.

Figure 12.7

A third way is to right-click and choose from the contextual menu. This free form cropping works fine when you don't need a specific size, but most often at this point in the workflow you do. Trying to create an exact size using the Crop tool like this is very hard to do. It's more a matter of trial and error and lots of luck. Fortunately, you can specify a particular size before cropping.

**8** **Return the file to its opening state by clicking the image icon at the top of the History panel.**

**9** **In the Options bar, type** 5 in **into the Width field and** 7 in **into the Height field, and then type** 300 **in the Resolution field.** This is the most common resolution for printing.

**Figure 12.8**

**10** Draw your crop box again and rotate the crop until you like it and then commit the crop. This time notice that the aspect ratio is locked and that there are no control handles at the top, bottom, or sides. Now you have a file that's sized for 5 × 7 at 300 ppi.

# tip

If the reading beside the numbers says something other than "in" (inches), then your ruler preferences are set to something other than inches. This is easy to fix. If the ruler isn't currently visible, choose View → Ruler (⌘+R/Ctrl+R), right-click the ruler, and select Inches from the pop-up menu.

# caution

By default the Crop tool uses bicubic resampling to change the size of the image. When you decrease the size, you're downsampling, and when you increase the size, you're upsampling. If you need to increase the size more than 10–15 percent, it's best to use the Image Size command with the Bicubic Smoother option to increase the image size so that it's close to what you want before final cropping.

Consider non-standard options when using the crop tool, especially when an image lends itself to this treatment. For example, if you have a photo with a great horizon-line in it, think about cropping out most of the top and bottom regions of the image to create a panorama of the horizon.

# Professional Sharpening Strategies

I work with lots of photographers, most of them professionals. When I first begin to work with a new photographer, one of the first questions I ask is how she handles sharpening in her workflow. That's because sharpening is one of the most misunderstood aspects of the post-production workflow. When it's done incorrectly, it can have a detrimental effect on the final image. If someone is making this mistake, I want her to know before moving on to other things.

## Understanding sharpening

Digital photo sharpening is nothing more than enhanced edge contrast. Photoshop tricks you into thinking a photo looks sharper by isolating edge detail and enhancing contrast along those edges. One side of the edge is lightened while the other side is darkened. The enhanced edge contrast is referred to as haloing because of the effect it causes along these edges.

There is no magic formula for sharpening because the amount of sharpening for a particular image depends on two very different things — the content of the image and its overall dimensions. Images with lots of edge detail, like the bowl of silver rings in Figure 12.9, can handle more sharpening than images with fewer hard edges, such as photos of people or a photo of a landscape on a foggy morning. This is because lots of sharpening adds to the feel of the ring photo, while it would detract from the softer feeling of the portrait or foggy landscape. Additionally, a smaller print of this shot doesn't need as much sharpening as a larger version would require.

**Figure 12.9**

©Jordan Sleeth

## Three kinds of sharpening

At first thought, sharpening seems like a no-brainer. Who wouldn't want their photos to be sharp? However, the subject is much more complicated. The main reason is that there are three different kinds of sharpening. Each type of sharpening needs to be applied at the appropriate time.

- **Capture sharpening.** By their very nature, digital image files need to have some sharpening applied. This sharpening pass is considered baseline sharpening. When you shoot raw this is addressed during conversion with Adobe Camera Raw. When you shoot JPEG, this baseline sharpening is applied by the camera.

# caution

Most cameras have a sharpening setting that allows you to apply different sharpening presets to your photos as you capture them. If you're shooting raw, this setting has no permanent effect on the image. However, if you shoot JPEG, it does have a permanent effect. I always recommend turning off all in-camera sharpening when shooting JPEG because it's easy to add sharpening later, but impossible to remove it after the original file is created.

- **Creative sharpening.** This type is used to fine-tune an image creatively by selectively modifying the sharpness of selected areas of the image using selections or masks. When I use the term sharpening here, I am also referring to its opposite, blurring, which is the lack of sharpness. What this means is that creative sharpening can be used in the same image to sharpen something of interest, such as someone's eyes, and to blur something else, like the background around the subject. The image does not need to be resized before this sharpening is carried out.

The main thing to understand about creative sharpening is that its effect is relative to the rest of the image. The goal isn't to make part of the image perfectly sharp. The goal is to make part of the image stand out from its surroundings by sharpening it or blurring the detail surrounding it.

- **Output sharpening.** This is overall sharpening that's designed to prepare an image for final output, such as printing or onscreen viewing. This sharpening is applied to the entire image with the intent of getting it ready for a particular output option. One of the things to understand here is that size matters. A file that's being prepared for printing as a $5 \times 7$ requires a completely different sharpening scenario than the same file being prepared for a $16 \times 20$. Otherwise, if the sharpening on the $5 \times 7$ looks great, the $16 \times 20$ will not be sharp enough.

The reason sharpening is divided into these three areas is because oversharpening degrades the quality of a photo by introducing unwanted artifacts. Oversharpening occurs when output sharpening settings, which are stronger, are used for capture sharpening. Later when the image is sized and prepared for output, it's necessary to sharpen again because the resizing affects the first sharpening pass. When the second sharpening pass is carried out on a previously over-sharpened file, it can adversely affect the quality of the image.

This also means that any creative sharpening will be further sharpened during the output sharpening process. Knowing this is important because it means you need to avoid overdoing the amount of creative sharpening.

# caution

Something you especially want to avoid when possible is sharpening an image for output, changing its size, and then resharpening for a new output size. Sharpening on top of previous sharpening adversely affects the image by introducing unwanted artifacting — distortions introduced by the digital process — causing image details to look "crunchy" instead of smooth.

On more thing to keep in mind about sharpening is that it's not used to fix severely blurred images. It's used to compensate for some of the effects of digital capture — whether by camera or scanner. If your photo is a little soft in focus, then you may be able to help it with sharpening. But you'll never be able to make it look the way it would have looked if it had been shot in focus.

# Photoshop's main sharpening tools

No matter if you're doing creative sharpening or output sharpening, you'll use one of Photoshop's two sharpening tools: the Unsharp Mask (USM) and the Smart Sharpen filters. These filters are very similar to one another. I'll compare and contrast them as you explore how they're used.

## Using the Unsharp Mask filter

People are often confused when it comes to using the USM filter because the name is totally counterintuitive. Why would someone want to use something named *unsharp* to sharpen an image? The reason this sharpening filter has such an odd name is that it refers to a sharpening method that was used with film before digital editing was an option. In that method, a negative that needed to be sharpened was duplicated. The duplicate negative was intentionally created just a bit out of focus. The two negatives — the original and the new one — were then sandwiched together slightly out of registration and then printed. The effect increased contrast around edge detail and made the resulting print look sharper. This is the same way the USM and the Smart Sharpen filters work.

The Unsharp Mask dialog box, shown in Figure 12.10 is found in the Filter menu (choose Filter→Sharpen→Unsharp Mask). This filter doesn't detect edge detail per se; instead it looks for pixels that have different tonal values than surrounding pixels. It then increases the contrast of those surrounding edge pixels, causing the lighter pixels to get lighter and the darker pixels to get darker, creating the sharpening halos I mentioned earlier. The sliders in the USM dialog box are used to control the size of these halos. Here's a closer look at the controls:

**Figure 12.10**

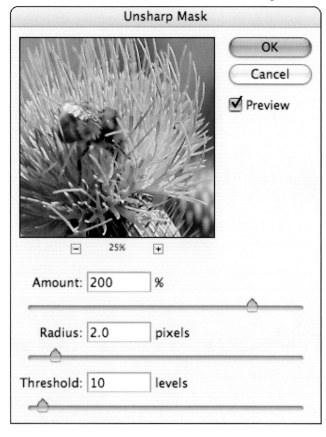

# note

You may notice that there are two other sharpening filters in the Sharpen menu, named Sharpen and Sharpen More. One would think that these are the main sharpening tools, but they aren't. They are blunt instruments that can't be controlled. In the many years that I've been using Photoshop, I've never used either one.

- **Amount.** The Amount slider is used to control the amount of contrast between differing pixels, which affects edge contrast. Higher values equal more contrast and lower values equal less contrast.

- **Radius.** The Radius slider is used to determine the number of pixels that are changed when the filter sees tonal variation. Higher values increase the size of the halos, causing the sharpening to be obvious. Because of this, the Radius slider is the most important slider in this dialog box. Exercise caution when using it because too high of a value creates sharpening halos that are noticeable. To high of a Radius value combined with a high Amount value causes the image to look oversharpened.

  Keep in mind that this value is going to vary depending on the subject matter. A lower value works best with photos rich in edge detail, while a higher value can be used for photos that don't have as much detail in them.

- **Threshold.** The Threshold slider is used to determine how different in tone the surrounding pixels need to be before they're considered edge pixels, causing them to be sharpened. For example, a value of 5 affects only neighboring pixels that have a tonal difference of 5 units or more (on a scale of 0 to 255). The default value of 0 causes all pixels in the photo to be sharpened.

# tip

Apply creative sharpening to a duplicate image layer in the master layered file. This insures that you can undo any sharpening later by discarding the layer.

Using the Unsharp Mask requires a bit of a balancing act among these three sliders. The best way to understand how they're used is to take the USM filter for a test drive. Follow these steps:

1. **Open High_Desert_Flower.tif from the downloadable practice files on the Web site (www.wiley.com/go/ photoshopcs4ats) and zoom to 50 percent.** This photo has lots of edge detail on the main subject, with little edge detail in the background. Remember that the USM filter, like the rest of Photoshop's filters, only affects the currently selected layer.

2. **Choose Filter → Sharpen → Unsharp Mask.** The Unsharp Mask dialog box appears.

3. **Type 200 for Amount, 2.0 for Radius, and 10 for Threshold, as shown in Figure 12.11.** Notice how much sharper all of the edge detail becomes.

4. **Change the Amount value to 300.** This oversharpens much of the edge detail on the flower and makes the image too contrasty.

# tip

Though the USM dialog box has a preview window, you won't be using it. It's much better to use the actual image for evaluation purposes. So go ahead and drag the dialog box to the side so you can get a good look at the flower.

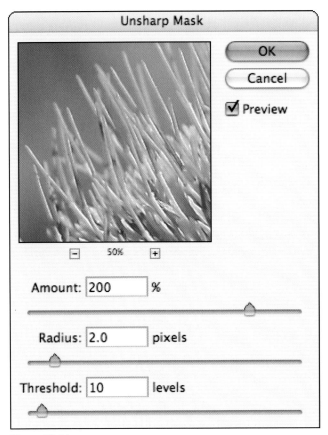

Figure 12.11

**5** **Now increase the Threshold setting to 25 and notice that the sharpening tapers off.** This is especially noticeable in the middle of the crown of the flower where there are so many similar colors. That's because only edge pixels with a tonal difference of 25 or more are sharpened.

**6** **Increase the Amount value to 300.** The sharpening increases, but it's still more subtle than the Step 2 setting.

**7** **Now increase the Radius value to 4.** Notice how much this small adjustment affects the flower's edge detail. It's beginning to look too crunchy, which means it's becoming over-sharpened.

**8** **Decrease the Amount value to 200.** The crunchiness is reduced, bringing the edge contrast back into line. As you can see, there isn't necessarily an exact set of sharpening values for this image because of the way these settings affect one another. If this photo were being printed, it would benefit from the settings in Step 3 or Step 8. Something else to notice here is that the out-of-focus bee is still out of focus, even though its edges are sharpened.

I find that low Radius and Threshold settings and higher Amount settings are usually the best place to start when using the Unsharp Mask. In the previous exercise you began with 200 for Amount for this 6 × 9 photo. If the photo were larger, then a higher starting Amount value (such as 300 for an 11 × 14) would be appropriate.

Then adjust the Radius and Threshold values to match the subject content of the photo.

When the sharpening is complete, take one more look at the tonality and contrast of the image. That's because large amounts of sharpening affect tonality and contrast. If you're using adjustment layers for managing the tones, make any further adjustments to them before flattening the file and/or saving it.

# tip

Sometimes sharpening causes a color shift. When this happens, it's easy to fix. If the sharpening is applied to a duplicate layer, change the layer's blending mode to Luminosity. If the sharpening is applied to the main image layer, choose Edit→Fade and change the Mode to Luminosity in the Fade dialog box. (Just remember that Fade must be the very next step after sharpening is applied.)

## Using the Smart Sharpen filter

One of Photoshop's newer filters is the Smart Sharpen filter introduced in version CS2. This filter is considered smart because it treats various regions of the image differently based on the content of those regions. The Smart Sharpen filter attempts to sharpen only the areas of the image that have detail without affecting areas that don't. This is different from the USM filter that affects all areas of the image equally. Figure 12.12 shows the Smart Sharpen dialog box. Notice that this dialog has Basic and Advanced modes. The difference is that the Shadow and Highlight tabs are added in the Advanced mode. This dialog box doesn't have a Threshold slider because it isn't needed. It also has some controls that aren't in the USM dialog box.

Take a closer look:

- **Amount.** This slider is used to control the amount of contrast between differing pixels, which affects edge contrast. Higher values equal more contrast and lower values equal less contrast. It functions the same as the sliders in the Unsharp Mask.

- **Radius.** This slider is the same as the Radius slider in the Unsharp Mask dialog box. It's used to determine the number of surrounding pixels that are changed when the filter sees tonal variation.

- **Remove.** This is a cool feature that adjusts the way the filter works, depending on the problem. The pop-up menu has three options: Gaussian Blur, which is the same algorithm used by the USM filter; Lens Blur, the best choice for most digital camera files; and Motion Blur, which attempts to compensate for blur caused by motion during the exposure. When Motion Blur is selected, the Angle setting is activated. This allows you to input the direction of the motion that caused the blur. For example, if the blur is from a sideways motion during the exposure, use a value of 0.

**Figure 12.12**

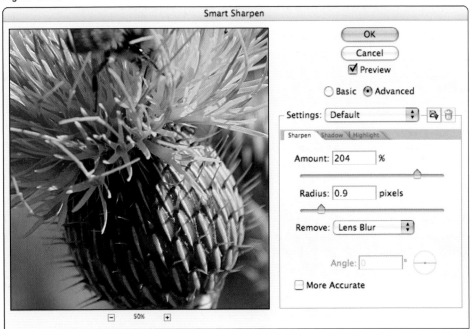

- **Advanced.** Selecting this radio button gives you more control by allowing you to work with the shadows and highlights independently of the rest of the image. It adds two new tabs to the dialog box, Shadow and Highlight. Figure 12.13 shows the Shadow tab, which is identical to the Highlight tab. You can use Fade Amount to adjust the amount of sharpening and Tonal Width to restrict your adjustments to the shadows with the Shadow tab, and to the highlights with the Highlight tab. This is quite useful when you have lots of noise in the shadows that you don't want to sharpen.

- **More Accurate.** Selecting this option provides a more accurate sharpening effect, but the process takes longer.

# note

The only thing I don't like about this filter is that the dialog box is huge, which can make it hard to see the image while using the filter — especially when working on a computer with a smaller display. Because I don't use the dialog's display, I scoot the dialog to the left until I can't see the dialog's display, freeing up more room for viewing the image.

## Sharpening for output

In Step 1 of the previous exercise, I asked you to zoom to 50 percent before using the USM filter. There are two reasons I specified that zoom ratio. The first reason is that historically, Photoshop does the best job of drawing the

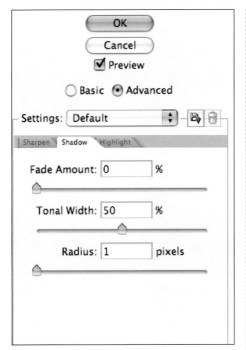

**Figure 12.13**

image onto the screen with zoom ratios that are multiples of 25 percent. This has changed with the introduction of OpenGL image processing in Photoshop CS4. When OpenGL is in effect, the screen is drawn with equal accuracy at any zoom level. However, if you're using Photoshop CS4, but your system doesn't support OpenGL, then this won't be the case for you.

# see also

OpenGL is discussed in Chapter 5.

The second reason I specified 50 percent is because it is the zoom ratio that usually comes closest to approximating the actual size of the printed image on your screen, while meeting the multiples of 25 percent rule I describe previously. One would think that zooming to 100 percent

would display the image at its actual size. However, because a computer monitor isn't capable of displaying an image at 300 ppi, it has to spread the pixels out to the resolution it can display — usually between 70 and 90 ppi. (That's why 72 ppi is a common resolution for photos intended for the Web.) This causes a photo with a resolution of 300 ppi to look bigger on the computer monitor than the actual print. If you're viewing at 100 percent while sharpening, you probably will be disappointed in the results because your preview doesn't match reality. You're seeing the photo at a much larger size than the final output size.

The optimal zoom ratio can vary from system to system. Here's how to find out which zoom ratio is closest to the actual size for your particular viewing environment:

**1** **Choose View → Rulers to turn on the rulers.** Figure 12.14 shows a photo with the rulers displayed. If your rulers are already turned on, you don't have to do this.

**2** **With the Photoshop rulers showing, hold a real ruler up to the screen while zooming the image using the keyboard shortcut presets (⌘++/Ctrl++ to zoom in and ⌘+−/Ctrl+− to zoom out).** When Photoshop's ruler and the real ruler match, the file is displayed at its actual size. If OpenGL isn't functioning on your system, you want a multiple of 25 percent. Try 25 percent and 50 percent to see which is closest to reality. On all of my monitors, 50 percent is a little bigger than reality and 25 percent is a little smaller. I use 50 percent because an image that displays a little bigger is easier to look at and evaluate. If OpenGL is functioning, you may find that 33 percent, the preset between 25 percent and 50 percent, comes closest.

**Figure 12.14**

note

When sharpening for the Web, zoom to 100 percent to display the image at actual size because the output is intended for a computer monitor.

Following these guidelines helps insure that the sharpening you see on your screen more closely matches the final output size. However, be advised that there are a couple of other variables that come into play when adding output sharpening.

- **Display versus Print.** Even in a perfect world, the sharpness shown on a monitor won't always translate to printed output. That's because the way a computer displays an image is different than the way the image looks on paper. In fact, different monitors often look different from one another. When I first switched from a CRT monitor to an LCD flat panel monitor I noticed that everything looked sharper on the new monitor. That's because of the resolving power of this newer style of LCD monitors. I had to make a mental adjustment to compensate for this.

# see also

Print and screen matching is further discussed in Chapter 13.

- **Printing Processes.** Different kinds of printers and printing paper affect the way an image looks. Prints on glossy paper always look a little sharper than prints on matte. Some inkjet papers, such as fine-art papers, are very absorbent and really soak up the ink, which diminishes the effects of sharpening.

- **Size Matters.** Sharpening is dependent on the dimensions of the print. That's why it's important to do all final cropping and sizing before output sharpening is applied.

The thing to take away from this section is to experiment with your intended output process until you're comfortable predicting how your computer's display translates to a printed image. Make some prints and compare them to the images on your monitor until you feel comfortable predicting any discrepancies between the way the monitor displays the image and the way it looks when printed.

# 13

## Printing Your Favorite Photos

Creating quality prints from your special photos is one of the most rewarding aspects of being a photographer. It allows you to take your original vision to its full fruition, completing the cycle that began when you clicked the shutter. These prints give you the chance to share your work with others in a way that isn't possible on a computer screen. The good news about printing is that you don't have to do your own inkjet printing to get quality prints. There are lots of great photolabs out there that do a great job of printing your images on traditional photographic papers. In this chapter I guide you through both options so that when you choose a favorite image for printing, you'll know the best way to prepare the file, no matter if you're printing on an inkjet printer or taking the file to a lab.

# Soft-Proofing Your Prints on Screen

Printing your favorite photos is fun, but it can get expensive if you end up reprinting photos to get the color right. That's why it's important to get color as close as possible before the first test print is made. This can be difficult because a printer's color gamut is much more limited than what is typically displayed on a computer monitor.

One way to deal with this discrepancy is to print a proof to get an idea of what the output looks like, make adjustments, and print another proof. This process goes on until the proof's tone and color are just right. Then you use the same settings to make a larger print. This is a useful way to approach color management when the tone and color is really close to begin with. However, when it isn't, you end up wasting paper, ink, and time.

Photoshop provides a much more economical way of evaluating color through a system called soft-proofing. This system allows you to color manage your photo's color by providing you with an onscreen proof that mimics the way the print will look when printed with a specific printer/ink/paper combination. This is accomplished by informing Photoshop of that specific printing scenario so that images are displayed in a way that mimics them on the screen.

In order to use soft-proofing, you need to have profiles for the printer/ink/paper combination you're using. If you're using an inkjet printer, its profiles should have been installed on your system when you installed the printer's driver and other associated software. If you don't have these profiles, go to your printer manufacturer's Web site to see if they are available online.

## see also

Color profiles are discussed in Chapter 7.

If you're using a photolab for printing, you need to get a profile from the lab if you want to soft-proof for that printer. Not all labs provide these profiles, but it never hurts to ask. These profiles give you invaluable insight into what a finished lab print will look like. It allows you to make any color changes that are necessary before committing to a print. For example, when I was writing this book, my project editor provided me with a profile for the offset press that was used for printing so I could adjust my images accordingly for the best results in the final printed product.

## tip

In order for soft-proofing to be reliable, you must have a calibrated monitor and your printer profiles must be accurate and up-to-date. Monitor calibration is discussed in Chapter 7.

Fortunately, soft-proofing is as easy as it sounds. To set up a soft-proofing scenario for your printer, follow these steps:

**1** **Open a file you intend to print.**

**2** **Choose View → Proof Setup → Custom.**
The Customize Proof Condition dialog box, shown in Figure 13.1, opens. This dialog box allows you to create a soft-proof setup for a specific printer by choosing various printing and display settings.

**Figure 13.1**

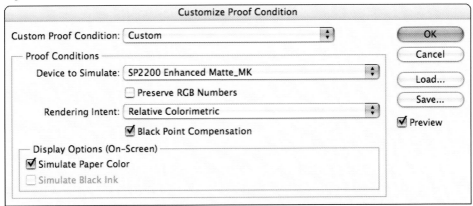

---

③ **Click the Device to Simulate menu and scroll through it to find the profiles for your printer.** In this example I plan to print a photo on Epson Enhanced Matte paper with an Epson 2200 inkjet printer. The Epson 2200 profiles are listed together in the menu, as shown in Figure 13.2. I selected the SP2200 Enhanced Matte _MK profile because I intend to use the matte black ink, which is what Epson recommends. The MK at the end of the profile name indicates this profile is for matte black. (The profiles with PK are intended to be used with the Photo Black ink cartridge.)

*note*

Printer profiles are specific to the printer. Sometimes, depending on the printer's manufacturer, these profile names can be difficult to decipher. If you have trouble understanding yours, contact the manufacturer.

④ **Check the Preserve RGB Numbers check box to simulate how the colors will look without actually converting them to the color space of the output device.** It's most useful when working with offset presses that use the CMYK color space, so leave it unchecked.

⑤ **Use the Rendering Intent menu to specify how colors are converted to the device you're simulating.** When Preserve RGB Numbers is checked, the Rendering Intent menu is grayed-out. Take a closer look at the rendering intent options and how they affect color mapping, which is how individual colors are translated from one color space to another.

Rendering intent helps to compensate for differences between Photoshop's working color space, and the printer's color space. Of these rendering intents, photographers tend to primarily work with Relative Colorimetric and Perceptual, which act as follows:

- **Relative Colorimetric rendering intent.** Keeps all in-gamut colors as they are and only moves the out-of-gamut colors (the colors the printer can't print) into the printer's gamut. It's usually the best choice.

- **Perceptual rendering intent.** Tries to manage those out-of-gamut colors by preserving the relationship of all of the colors as it compensates for out-of-gamut colors. In some cases, that means that in-gamut colors will shift. This rendering intent is a good choice when your image contains lots of very saturated (out-of-gamut) colors.

Figure 13.2

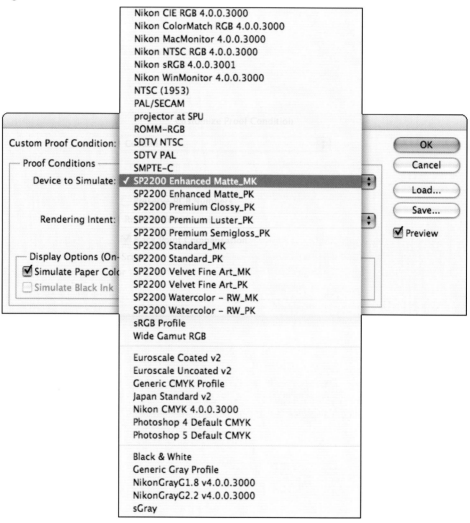

Sometimes, changing the rendering intent affects colors, and sometimes, it doesn't. It really depends on the tones and colors in a specific image and the printer/ink/paper combination you use. If you use an inkjet printer, you can specify this when you print.

**6** **Select Black Point Compensation to insure that the image's shadow detail is preserved by simulating the dynamic range of the printer — the total range between black and white that it can reproduce.** For the soft-proof to be accurate, this same rendering intent must also be selected later on in the Print dialog.

*note*

Some paper manufacturers create profiles without black point compensation so they instruct you to turn off this setting. Be sure to check the documentation for the papers you use.

**7** **Select Simulate Paper Color.** This setting is used to simulate the white of the printing paper that's being used. At first it seems that this setting has a detrimental effect on the image you're viewing because it makes the image look dull and flat. That's because your monitor is capable of displaying bright whites that can't be printed. It's best to look away from the monitor when choosing this option so that you don't notice the big change. Otherwise, it can

be disorienting because of the way it affects the display to match the print conditions.

**8** **Select Simulate Black Ink to make the black on your monitor look more like the black that's reproducible on the printer.** This is similar to the Simulate Paper Color option. As you can see in Figure 13.1, this option is grayed out because it isn't an option for the profile being used.

**9** **After you fill out the Customize Proof Condition dialog box for a particular printing condition, click Save.** The Save dialog box opens. It is a good idea to save the settings so you can easily access them again without having to repeat this setup.

**10** **Type a name that describes the setup and click Save.** Now when you go to the Proof Setup menu, the saved setup displays at the bottom of the list, as shown in Figure 13.3.

*note*

The Simulate Paper Color and Simulate Black Ink options are not supported by all profiles. If they aren't supported by your profile, they're grayed out.

After you have a custom proofing setup, you can use it by selecting it from the Proof Setup menu. If it has a check mark next to it, like the one in Figure 13.3, you can switch to it using ⌘+Y/ Ctrl+Y. This keyboard shortcut acts as a toggle, alternately turning the most recently used proof setup on or off every time it's used.

**Figure 13.3**

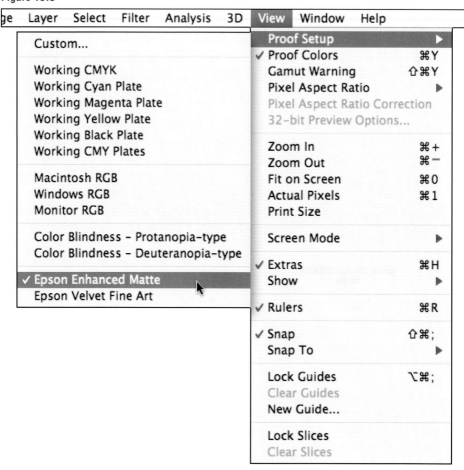

# Bringing Out-of-Gamut Tones and Colors into Line

When you first adjust the tonality of an image using Levels or Curves, the goal is to maximize the dynamic range without clipping shadows or highlights. However, even if you're careful about clipping early in the process, it can still become a problem when it comes time to print. That's because many printers are unable to discern the deep tones in the shadows that are almost black, and the lightest tones in the highlights that are almost white — even when you can see them on your screen. These out-of-gamut tones get clipped to either black or white.

To check your image for out-of-gamut tones and colors, follow these steps:

1. **Open the file titled Dog_Portrait.tif from the downloadable files on the Web site (www.wiley.com/go/ photoshopcs4ats).**

2. **Choose View → Proof Setup and select the proofing setup that most closely approximates your intended printing scenario.** If you created one in the last exercise, choose it now.

3. **Choose View → Gamut Warning.** Any out of gamut tones or colors are now displayed with a gray overlay, as shown in Figure 13.4, indicating that they're being clipped. When you see this overlay on a photo, you can adjust the tonality and color of the photo until it disappears. In Figure 13.4, the problem is that some of the dark colors are too dark, even though they weren't clipped when they were originally adjusted with Levels.

## tip

If you're working on an important photo that may get printed again with a different output device, it's a good idea to use a separate adjustment layer for printer specific adjustments so that you can turn it off or modify it or turn it off when you use a different output scenario.

**Figure 13.4**

**4** Choose Image→ Adjustments→ Levels
(or press ⌘+L/Ctrl+L). The Levels dialog
box opens, as shown in Figure 13.5.

**5** Use the black Output Levels slider to
limit the tonality of the blacks — if you
see gray in the gamut warning, click
and drag it to the right until the gray
disappears. This removes the out-of-
gamut tones by bringing them back into
range, but it also reduces the contrast,
making the image look flatter. I prefer the
image with some of the blacks being
darker because it adds more punch to the
image. Back the slider off and allow some
of the dark shadows in the dog's ears to
be clipped. This brings back some of the
deeper tones, increasing overall contrast.

**6** If any highlights are out of gamut, slide
the highlight Output Levels slider to the
left until the tones come into gamut. Try
to insure that they are in-gamut; otherwise
they receive no tonality and become the
color of the paper they're printed on.

# note

You may remember that in Chapter 6 I told you
to avoid using the Output Levels sliders when
adjusting the tonality of your image. That's
because they're used in this way for managing
shadow and highlight clipping caused by
specific output devices.

**7** Click OK.

The gamut warning is a great way to get a preview
of how a specific output scenario affects an
image. Use it when you want to know if the tones
and colors you see on your screen are reproducible,
or if they're out of the gamut of the intended
output device. Remember that color adjustments,
as well as tonal adjustments, can be used to bring
the image into gamut. For example, in the previous
steps, it was possible to bring the out-of-gamut
tones into gamut by using the Hue/Saturation
command to lower the overall saturation. In this
case, the final image looks better when the
shadows are lightened instead.

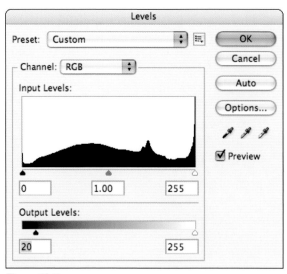

Figure 13.5

# Inkjet Printing with Photoshop's Print Command

Inkjet printing has come a long way since the technology's earliest days. The output from modern printers rivals traditional photographic printing in quality and longevity. Additionally, the variety of printing papers is way beyond the range of traditional photographic papers. With that in mind, inkjet printing isn't for everyone. The downsides are the cost per print and the amount of time involved. For many people, though, these issues are outweighed by the convenience and control of using an inkjet printer.

## Understanding the settings

When someone asks me to help solve an inkjet color-matching issue, I usually find that the problem is an incorrect setting. Though most of the Print dialog and driver settings are intuitive, three important settings must be correct for Photoshop and the printer to have an intelligent conversation about color. If any one of these is set incorrectly, the chances of a good color match become slim. As you go through this section, I point out each of these three special settings.

Figure 13.6 shows the Print dialog box that opens when you choose File→Print (⌘+P/Ctrl+P). Some of these settings are more important than others. The settings are as follows, from left to right:

**Figure 13.6**

# tip

The Print One Copy command is used to quickly make an additional print after all the following settings have already been applied to the Print dialog and the printer driver.

- **The Preview window.** Allows you to see how the image is positioned on the paper. This preview is very useful because it alerts you to sizing errors — which has saved me a number of times. There are three settings you can change that affect the Preview window.

  - **Match Print Colors.** Allows you to preview the color of the printed image. Changes made in the color management settings on the right affect this preview. This setting, as well as Gamut Warning and Show Paper White, allow you to soft proof your image in the Print dialog box.

  - **Gamut Warning.** The same as the Gamut Warning that I discussed in the previous section, except that modifications to the image cannot be carried out in the Print dialog. If you want to be sure that your image is in-gamut, make those adjustments before opening the Print dialog box.

  - **Show Paper White.** Simulates the color of the paper in much the same way as Simulate Paper Color in the Proof Setup dialog box.

- **Middle of the dialog box.** Mostly self-explanatory, this section includes options for number of copies, adjusting the page setup, changing the position of the image on the page, and scaling the print size. I stay away from using the Scaled Print Size section unless I'm doing a quick print. Normally, it's best to have all sizing done before opening the Print dialog box so that proper output sharpening can be applied.

Additionally, you can add a bounding box, which applies a black outlines to the image. The corners of the box can be used to resize the image. Again, I don't recommend resizing the image in the Print dialog. Finally, you can also change the units of measure. I leave this set at inches.

- **Color Management.** This section on the right is where the important settings are. If you don't see a heading that says Color Management at the top right of your Print dialog box, click beside Output to open the pop-up menu and select Color Management. These are your choices:

# tip

Notice that as you hover the cursor over different sections of the Color Management area, a contextual description appears at the bottom of the screen. Use this to learn more about the options here.

  - **Document.** Selecting this option informs Photoshop of the starting color profile for the document. In this case, it's Adobe RGB (1998). Be sure this radio button is selected instead of Proof.

  - **Proof.** This is used to make one output device simulate another output device; for example, to make an inkjet print that looks like it was printed on a particular offset press. This is useful when you want to know what an offset print will look like without going through the expense of offset printing a single proof print. Only use this option when working with that type of proofing scenario.

  - **Color Handling.** This tells Photoshop whether you want it to handle color management or if the printer is taking care of color. It's best to let Photoshop manage the color unless you're using *RIP* (raster image processor) software with your printer. This setting is one of the big three that people often get wrong. I discuss Printer Manages Color in a moment.

## note

RIP software replaces the driver software that comes with a printer. Its primary function is to make the interface between you and the printer — and the computer and the printer — more flexible and powerful. One of the primary advantages to using a RIP with your printer is that it's very good at handling color. RIP software also does a great job with black-and-white printing. One of my favorites is ImagePrint by ColorByte (www.colorbyte software.com). The software isn't cheap, but it pays for itself in no time if you do lots of inkjet printing.

- **Printer Profile.** This is the second important setting that can cause problems if it isn't set correctly. If this one's wrong, all bets are off for consistent color matching. By default, this is set to the color space that the image is currently in — in this case, Adobe RGB (1998). For the most part, that's useless information. What Photoshop needs to know is something about the way a specific printer reproduces color. This information is contained in a printer profile that describes the printer, the paper, and the ink used to make the print. The profiles in this pop-up menu are the same profiles you saw in the section on soft-proofing.

- **Rendering Intent.** This tells Photoshop what system to use for mapping colors from the computer to the printer. This helps to compensate for differences between the color space of Photoshop and the printer's color space. These rendering intents are the same as those I discuss in the section on soft-proofing earlier in the

chapter. Sometimes, changing this setting affects colors, and sometimes, it doesn't. It really depends on the image and the printing environment. If the Match Print Colors option is selected, any changes in Rendering Intent are reflected in the preview.

- **Black Point Compensation.** Selecting this option helps to map the black from the image in Photoshop to the black that the printer is capable of printing, instead of clipping out-of-gamut blacks. It's usually best to leave this checked so that the full range of your image's tones are used by the printer.

- **Proof Setup.** This section is grayed out unless Proof is selected in the Color Management area.

## note

If you choose Printer Manages Colors in the Color Handling section, most of the options below it are grayed out.

The two key settings so far are Color Handling and Printer Profile. These settings let Photoshop manage the color and give it useful information to describe the intended printing environment.

After you have set all settings in the Print dialog correctly, it's time to get the printer ready for printing by clicking the Print button. When you do, the print driver dialog box for your printer opens. This dialog varies depending on the printer's manufacturer, as well as platform: Mac or Windows. Find the page setup area and choose the type of paper you'll be using. Figure 13.7 shows the Print dialog for the Mac version of my Epson 2200 printer driver dialog box. Yours may look different, but you should be able to find the same settings I detail in the following section.

**Figure 13.7**

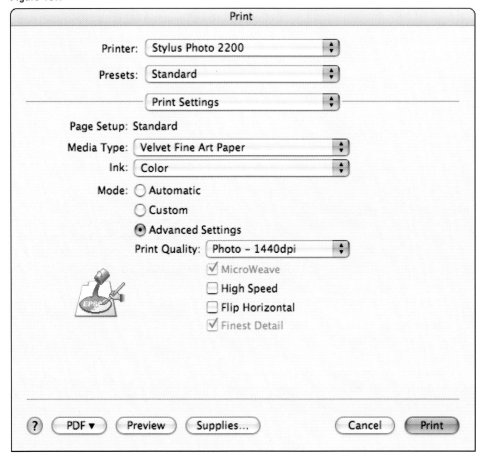

While you're in this section of the printer driver, it's also a good time to select the printing resolution you intend to use. In Figure 13.7 you can see that I chose Photo – 1440dpi from the Print Quality menu. As I mentioned earlier in the section on resolution, this setting determines how closely the dots of ink are laid down on the paper. The higher the number is, the closer the dots. When printing on matte or glossy paper, it's best to use 1440 dpi so that the dots are close enough that they form a continuous tone — you can't see the space between the dots. If 720 dpi is used on glossy paper, you could end up with some jagged lines.

When printing on fine-art papers that are absorbent, it's okay to use 720 dpi because the ink soaks into the paper and fills in the space between the dots. Using 720 dpi instead of 1440 dpi saves ink because fewer dots are being printed.

The higher setting of 2880 dpi is intended to bring the dots even closer together. However, you'll have a hard time discerning the difference between 1440 dpi and 2880 dpi without a magnifying glass. The main difference is that twice as much ink is used to print the extra dots. This not only costs more money, it can also have a detrimental effect causing the print to look muddy from the extra ink. I recommend that you test each of these settings with all of the papers that you use so that you'll know which is best for a specific paper.

You most likely also see a setting in this section that's called High Speed. When this option is selected, the print head sprays ink as it moves across the paper in both directions. Though this results in faster printing, it usually has a detrimental effect on the quality of the print. So, I always leave it off.

tip

If I need a low quality print in a hurry, I use my color laser printer.

After you've addressed your Print settings, you need to find the color management section of your printers driver software so that you can turn off the printer's color management. This is the third key setting that must be set to insure correct color on the print. If you don't include this step, the printer uses its color management settings on a file that's already being color managed by Photoshop. This step is not only unnecessary, it also has a detrimental effect on the print. Figure 13.8 shows this setting for my setup on a Mac.

Figure 13.9 shows the Epson 2200 driver in Windows with the same settings. I prefer this layout to the Mac version because just about everything is in one place so it's easier to check your settings. If you're using Windows, you can often find the No Color Adjustment setting by clicking the ICM button. ICM stands for Integrated Color Management. It's a color management module designed by Microsoft and part of the Windows operating system.

**Figure 13.8**

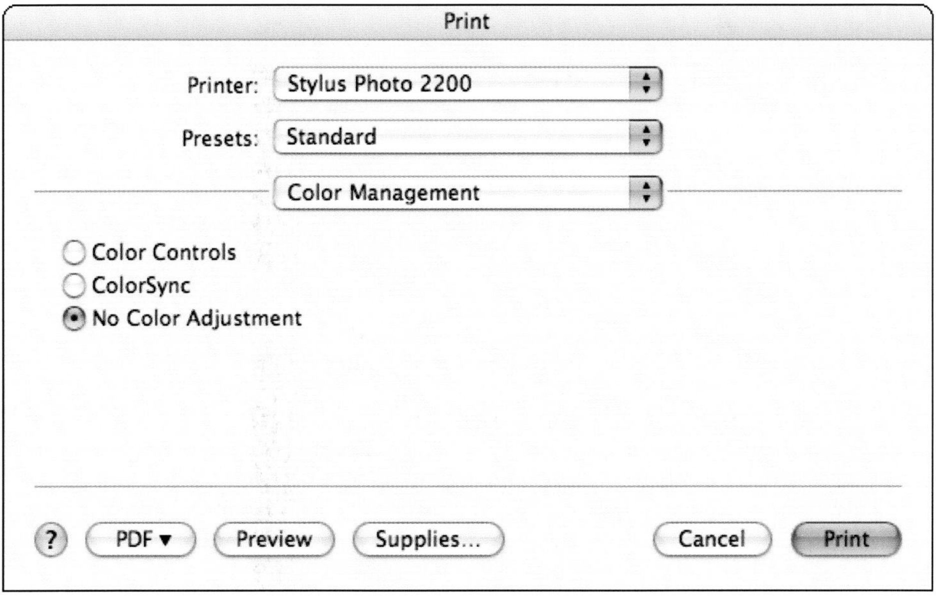

Print

Printer: Stylus Photo 2200

Presets: Standard

Color Management

○ Color Controls
○ ColorSync
◉ No Color Adjustment

(?)  ( PDF ▼ )  ( Preview )  ( Supplies... )        ( Cancel )  ( Print )

**Figure 13.9**

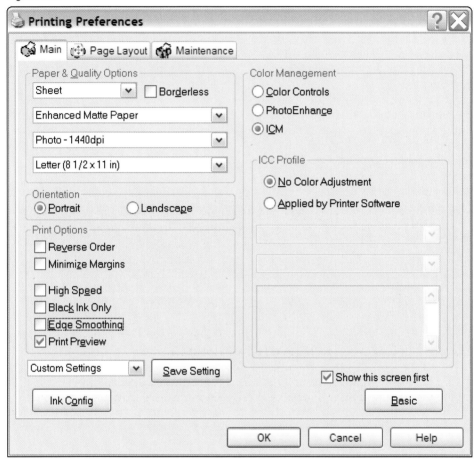

## tip

After you get all of the printer settings the way you like them for a particular paper, it's a good idea to save the setup as a preset in the printer driver. On a Mac, you do this using the Presets menu. On a Windows machine, you do it by clicking the Save Settings button.

## Letting the printer manage color

Earlier, when discussing the Color Handling section in the Print dialog box, I mentioned that you should choose Photoshop Manages Colors instead of Printer Manages Colors. I recommend this for a couple of reasons. The first is that if the Printer is managing color conversions, it becomes impossible to get a good soft-proof using the Proof Setup command.

The second is that a recent change in Photoshop changes the way color is managed for Windows users during printing. Now, in Photoshop CS4, when the printer manages the color, Windows ICM automatically converts the color space of the image to sRGB. In some cases, this can lead to colors in an Adobe RGB (1998) image being clipped to fit into the smaller space, even though the printer is capable of printing those colors. If you're printing sRGB files, this isn't a problem.

With that said, modern inkjet printers are getting much better at managing color. When you select this option, it reduces the number of settings you need to check before printing. If you have a newer printer, it's worth trying both Printer Manages Colors and Photoshop Manages Colors on separate prints of the same file to see how they compare.

If you're using Photoshop CS2 on a Mac with OS X Leopard, you may find that your printer driver doesn't allow you to turn off color management. When this happens you may find that choosing Printer Manages Colors in the Color Handling section of the Print dialog box gives you the best results. Another option is to check with your printer's manufacturer to see if a newer driver is available that works with Leopard.

## Evaluating the print

The goal with printing — whether it's done on an inkjet printer or by a lab — is to match the way the image displays on the monitor as closely as possible. Naturally, if the monitor isn't calibrated and profiled, it is hard to determine whether the print is a match to the screen. I have seen cases where a photographer's color matching problems disappeared when she calibrated her monitor.

# tip

Be sure to give inkjet prints time to completely dry before making a critical analysis of their color. Absorbent paper, like fine art paper, dries faster than less-absorbent paper, such as glossy paper.

The other key to determining if the print is a match to the display is to be sure that the print is being viewed under a daylight-balanced light source. If the viewing light being used is normal household light (incandescent), it appears warmer than it really is. If it's being viewed under florescent light, it appears cooler. If you aren't using daylight-balanced light, you can't evaluate the print's color in relation to the monitor because you won't be able to see it correctly.

There are a number of lighting solutions you can turn to when you need a daylight balanced light source. On the high end are custom viewing booths that can cost upwards of $2,000. A more affordable solution for someone just starting out are the daylight balanced lights made by Solux (www.solux.net). These lights are endorsed by the Nikon School of Photography and the Epson Print Academy.

## Saving money with test strips

Even when all settings are correct, you may still find that you want to adjust the color of your image after you see a print. Because of this, it's a good idea to make a test print before making a full-sized print. I use a test strip system, similar to what I used to use when I printed in the chemical darkroom, which allows me to print a strip of paper with a portion of the full image. I use this strip to evaluate the overall image and make any necessary adjustments before using a full sheet of paper and ink.

Here's how to do it:

**1** Open a file that you want to print. In this example the paper size being used is 8.5 × 11.

**2** Use the Crop tool to crop out everything except for a narrow strip that contains important image information, as shown in Figure 13.10.

**5** Click on the top center box in the Anchor preview, shown in Figure 13.11. This is perhaps the most important part of the process. When you do this, you're telling the Canvas Size command to add the new canvas below and to the sides of the current image.

**Figure 13.10**

**3** Choose Image → Canvas Size. The Canvas Size dialog box opens.

**4** Enter the dimensions for the size paper you're using. Use 8.5 inches wide and 11 inches high for this example. If you print the strip like this, it falls in the middle of the sheet of paper, wasting the entire sheet. Therefore, it's necessary to place the strip at the top of the sheet of paper. You do that by directionally expanding the canvas around the cropped strip.

**6** Choose White in the Canvas extension color menu. The printer now doesn't print anything on the surrounding canvas.

**7** Click OK. Now the test strip is at the top of the canvas, as shown in Figure 13.12. When you make a print, only this section is printed. After you evaluate it, you can trim off the strip and use the rest of the paper for addition test strips. At some point, the paper will be too short to feed through the printer, usually when it gets down to about three inches in height. When that happens, go ahead and discard the unused paper. Even though this portion of the paper isn't used, you're still saving money by using test strips to make critical color evaluations instead of wasting a whole sheet of paper.

**Figure 13.11**

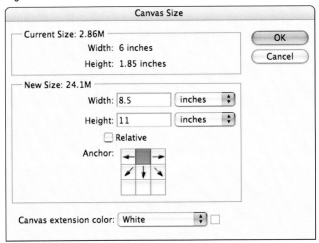

# note

If your printer isn't capable of printing borderless prints, the very top of the strip won't print. Also, you may get a warning telling you that some of the image area is outside of the printable area when you go to make a print. In this case, that's okay.

**Figure 13.12**

# Using a Photolab for Printing

As I mention earlier, inkjet printing isn't for everyone. It can be time consuming and expensive. Most photographers I know, especially the professionals, have their printing done by professional photolabs. Here are some of the main advantages to printing at a lab:

- **Real photo paper.** Although there's nothing wrong with using quality inkjet papers and inks, some people are not comfortable with them. Photolabs use the same types of printing paper that they've traditionally used. This gives you the opportunity to have your photos printed on quality papers like Kodak's Metallic or Fuji's Crystal Archive papers.

- **Finishing services.** Full-service labs offer a wide range of finishing services such as dry mounting and canvas mounting, as well as matting and framing.

- **Professional color management.** This is often the number one reason for using a lab, especially for photographers new to color management. That's because the people who work in photolabs, especially professional labs, are experts at seeing and correcting color. You can save time and improve your quality by letting these experts take care of your final color corrections until you're comfortable taking over the task.

When you work with a new lab, it's very important to ask lots of questions before placing your first order. That way you know exactly how to prepare your files. Find out what the lab prefers. For example, what color space does the lab use? Knowing the answer to this question allows you to make sure that you use the same color space when editing, enabling you to better predict what the final color will look like when the prints are made. For example, if you edit your file in Adobe RGB (1998) and the lab uses the sRGB color space, you are likely to be disappointed with the color of the print because you were viewing an unrealistic version of the photo on you monitor.

## tip

If you prepared a file in Adobe RGB (1998) and then find out that the lab uses sRGB, you can change the image to sRGB by choosing Edit → Convert Profile. When the dialog box opens, select sRGBIEC61966-2.1 as the Destination Space. (Leave the rest of the settings at their defaults.) This shifts the color numbers while attempting to preserve their appearance in the original color space.

Another question to ask is if the lab prefers JPEG or TIFF files. Most prefer JPEG, but I know of some labs that work with both. If you plan to deliver TIFF files, be sure to flatten them before taking them to the lab. Also, if you're working with 16-bit files, be sure to change the file to 8-bit. You do this by choosing Image → Mode → 8-bits/Channel.

Some labs prefer that you deliver files that are completely prepared for printing — that is, sized and sharpened — while others simply want a full-sized JPEG file. I always prefer to manage these variables myself, especially when I order large prints. I want to know that the image is cropped exactly as I want it cropped and that sharpening is done the way I like it. However, if you don't have the time or the experience to make these decisions, let the lab do it for you.

The most important thing to consider when working with a lab is communication. Discuss your needs and expectations with the lab before placing an order. Make sure that it is willing to listen. When your expectations aren't met, be sure to find out why. Quite often, a slight tweak to your workflow solves the problem. If the lab is doing something wrong, be sure to let it know so it can fix the problem on its end. Most labs are happy to listen to your concerns and make necessary adjustment if there's a problem. If the lab isn't willing to listen, start looking for another one.

# 14

# Creating Slideshows and Web Galleries

**P**rints aren't the only kind of output you can create from your digital photos. Because the photos are digital, they can be shared a variety of ways. In this chapter you learn to use the new Adobe Output Module (AOM) in Bridge (CS4) to create a variety of custom presentations from your photos. When you see how easy it is to create slideshows and Web galleries, you'll be ready to share your photos in ways you never thought possible.

You first encountered AOM in Chapter 2 when you explored Bridge. That's because AOM is part of Bridge, rather than Photoshop. Choosing the Bridge workspace named Output opens the module. Now that you know how to make your photos look just the way you like them to look, it's time to take a tour of this new feature and explore some of the fun things you can do with it.

# Overview of the Adobe Output Module

The AOM is shown in Figure 14.1. Because the top section and the Favorites and Folders panels on the left are the same as the rest of the Bridge workspaces, I've omitted them from the figure to give the module more space. In fact, when you're using this module, you may want to hide the panels on the left so you have more room for the other panels. To hide those panels, deselect them from the Window menu or drag the left edge of the preview area across them.

## note

AOM grew out of a separate download for Bridge CS3, called Adobe Media Gallery, which used to be available from Adobe.

Two of the panels in Figure 14.1 are familiar: the Content and Preview panels. They function the same way they do in the other workspaces for the most part. The Content panel displays the contents of the currently selected folder or collection. When you double-click a thumbnail, it opens in Photoshop, or Adobe Camera Raw if the file is a raw file. The main difference in the Preview panel is it has two different views you can access by clicking the tabs at the top left: Preview and Output Preview.

Here's how the difference between these two previews:

- **Preview.** This panel is the same as the standard Preview panel in all other Bridge workspaces and functions the same way as it does there.

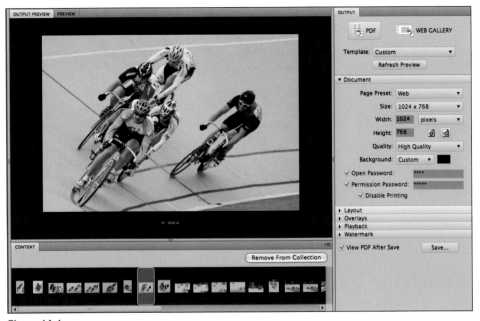

Figure 14.1

- **Output Preview.** This panel displays a preview with the current layout and design settings. The main difference in this version is that it doesn't automatically update when you click a thumbnail in the Content panel or change design settings. To see your changes, you need to click the Refresh Preview button at the top of the Output panel. At first, this is a little annoying. However, creating these previews takes time. It's better to choose a few settings and then update the preview than it is to sit around waiting for the preview to update every time you change a setting.

# note

If you don't see the Output Preview window, don't worry. If it's hidden, it appears when you click the Refresh Preview button at the top of the Output panel.

The most important panel in AOM is the Output panel on the right side. This is where you design your projects. It's loaded with features and has separate sub-panels that you can individually collapse. (All but the Document area are collapsed in Figure 14.1.) Two buttons appear at the top of the Output panel: PDF and Web Gallery. You use it to choose between the PDF presentation and Web gallery sections of the Output panel. When you click one, the sub-panels below dynamically change to fit the context of your selection. For example, when you click the Web Gallery button, a Site Info sub-panel appears with information formatted for a Web gallery. Most of the options in this Web Gallery sub-panel do not appear in any of the PDF sub-panels.

# Preparing Photos for Slideshows and Web Galleries

If you're creating a slideshow or Web gallery from previously edited images, then there's little you need to do to prepare your files. That's because AOM takes care of sizing files and preparing them for output. However, when you're creating a presentation from unedited original files, it's a good idea to take a few moments to add some polish to them. This is usually limited to any tonal and/or color adjustment that's required to make the image look uniform. Don't spend too much time with this polishing process when you share large amounts of files unless you have to. It's better to reserve your quality time for the special photos.

# note

I met a portrait photographer who spent 12 to 15 hours preparing photos for online viewing by his clients. He wanted them to look great, but the clients rarely ordered more than a couple of poses. If you're a professional, think about tweaking-out one or two images so that the client can see what's possible. They'll understand that you're saving your valuable time for the photos that matter most to them.

If the original photos are raw files, you can open all of them in ACR to quickly tweak the tone and color and to apply any cropping. When you finish, click Done so that ACR closes and saves your changes without opening the files in Photoshop. If you're working with JPEG originals, you need to open the files in Photoshop to adjust them. You can save time by opening groups of similar JPEG and TIFF files into ACR and using the synchronize feature to adjust them. To open these non-raw files in ACR, select them in Bridge, right-click one of them, and choose Open in Camera Raw from the pop-up menu.

## tip

Use a collection to group your presentation files together. That way you can rearrange their order without affecting the original thumbnails. It also makes it easier to keep the files together in case you want to re-create the presentation later.

# Creating a PDF Slideshow

There are numerous permutations of the way these sub-panels appear, depending not only on the presentation style you choose (PDF or Web Gallery), but also on settings in some of the sub-panels. Because of that, I walk you through a single scenario here for creating a PDF slideshow presentation that you can show onscreen or e-mail to someone. This is one of the most common ways photographers use PDF presentations. The major advantage to it is that the person who receives the PDF won't be able to extract the individual photos from it for unauthorized printing. This helps the photographers keep a handle on who's using their photos. After you learn this process, you'll be ready to explore some of the other Output panel options.

Follow these steps to create your own PDF Web Gallery:

**1** **Use your favorite Bridge workspace to select about twenty photos that you want to use for a slideshow.** Save them as a collection, as discussed in Chapter 3.

**2** **Use the Workspace picker to change your Bridge workspace to the Adobe Output Module (⌘+4/Ctrl+4).** Make sure you're in the PDF portion of the module by clicking the PDF button.

**3** **Open the Template menu near the top of the Output panel, shown in Figure 14.2.** The presets in this menu are used to quickly set up several common layouts. You can customize their settings in the sub-panels below. (When you customize settings, the preset name changes to Custom.) Choose the Maximum Size preset and click the Refresh Preview button, just below the Template menu to update the Output Preview.

Figure 14.2

# note

I changed the User Interface Brightness in the Bridge General preferences to lighten the interface so that the screenshots are easier for you to see.

**4** Move down the Output panel to the Document sub-panel, shown in Figure 14.3, go to the Page Preset menu and choose Web. Even though this presentation isn't intended to be uploaded to the Web, these presets allow you to prepare presentations sized for onscreen viewing.

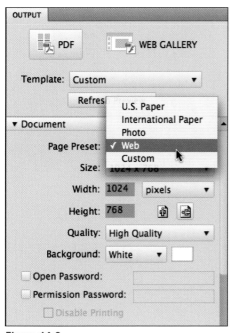

**Figure 14.3**

# tip

Only the images that are selected in the Content panel are used for the PDF presentation.

**5** Set the Size to 1024 × 768. This describes the pixel aspect ratio of the overall size of the presentation. If you plan to send the slideshow to someone with an older, smaller screen, use the 800 × 600 setting. If you know they have a large screen, think about using a larger size.

**6** Choose a quality setting in the Quality menu: Low Quality or High Quality. The difference between the two settings is the amount of compression that's applied to the files. High Quality creates larger files and Low Quality creates smaller files. If you plan to send the entire slideshow to someone via e-mail, use the Low Quality setting to reduce the overall size of the file. If you plan to show the slideshow on your system or burn it to a disc, use the High Quality setting.

**7** Use the Background menu to choose change the background color. The options are Black, White, and Custom. You can choose a custom color by clicking the color swatch to the right of the menu and opening the color picker.

**8** Select the Open Password option and type a password into the text box. This protects the PDF document because now no one can open your presentation without the password. Be sure to write your password down so you can open your project when you're through with this exercise! Now that the basic settings for this presentation have been established using the Document sub-panel, it's time to move down the Output panel to the next sub-panel, the Layout panel.

# tip

Remember to click Refresh Preview every once in a while to see the effect your changes have on your presentation.

# note

The Permission password allows the user to make modifications to the presentation. This password can be different from the Open Password. When you use a Permission password, you have the option of disabling printing. This prevents someone else from using the Print command in their viewing software to print your PDF slideshow.

Figure 14.4

**9** **Specify 30 as the spacing for the Top, Bottom, Left, and Right values in the Layout sub-panel, shown in Figure 14.4, and click the Refresh Preview button.** The default value is 12, which places the image too close to the edge of the image frame. Three other settings appear at the bottom of the sub-panel:

- **Use Auto-Spacing.** This setting lets AOM lay out the columns and rows according to the values you enter into the Columns and Rows text boxes. When you choose it, the spacing settings are grayed out.

- **Rotate for Best Fit.** This setting rotates images so that they are always as large as possible. If you do it now, your vertical images will be turned sideways to maximize the use of the page. Though the image will be larger, your viewers will have to turn their heads to see it so don't check it now.

- **Repeat One Photo per Page.** This setting is used to repeat a single photo in every cell on a page. For example, you can create a contact sheet with the same image in every cell.

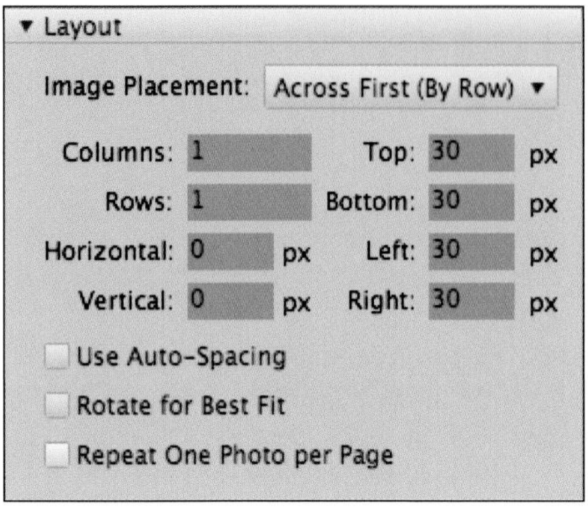

**10** **Move down to the Overlays sub-panel, shown in Figure 14.5, and select Filename if you want the name of each file to be displayed in an overlay on top of it's image.** If you don't want the file extension to show (jpg, tiff, psd), deselect the Extension option. Use the Font, Size, and Color settings to customize the look of the overlay type. Now the look and feel of your presentation is laid out and it's ready to move down to the Playback sub-panel to set up the timing of the slideshow and the way slides transition from one to the other.

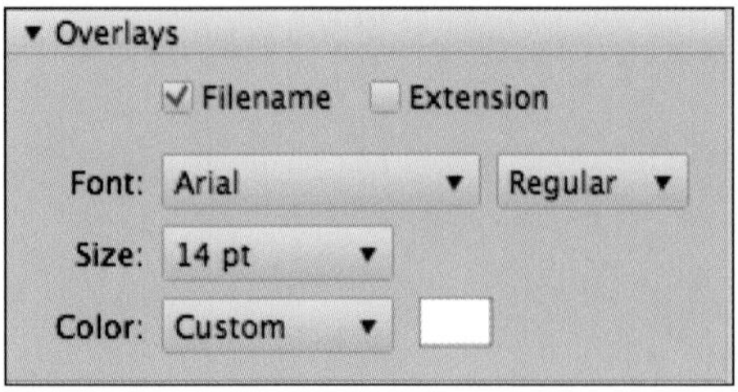

Figure 14.5

**11** **Select Open in Full Screen Mode in the Playback sub-panel, shown in Figure 14.6, so your slideshow is full-screen when it shows.** This doesn't increase the size of the images beyond what you chose in the Document sub-panel. It simply expands the window around the images so that everything else is hidden.

This sub-panel lets you control several other slideshow playback features. Use the Advance Every Seconds option to set the amount of time for image display. If you leave this blank, you have to advance the slides manually using the arrow keys on your keyboard. The Loop After Last Page option makes the slideshow begin again after the final slide plays. Use the Transition section to choose the type of transition you want and how quickly you want the transition to take place. Use the Transition Direction setting to control the direction in which the transition moves. (This setting isn't available for all transitions.)

**Figure 14.6**

**12** **Type the text for a watermark in Watermark Text field in the Watermark sub-panel, shown in Figure 14.7.** A *watermark* is text or a logo that's overlaid on the image to identify the image's maker. The way it's usually used is to add a Copyright symbol with your name behind it to every page. Use the Font, Size, Color, and Opacity adjustments to make the overlay look the way you like it. Be sure to choose Foreground at the bottom of this sub-panel. If you choose Background, the overlay is placed behind the image. This can be useful when lots of images are on a page. Adding a copyright symbol has its uses, but if you have already restricted printing, you shouldn't have to worry about protecting the images in your slideshow with it. Often the watermark is more useful for adding labels like "Proof" rather than ownership labels.

## tip

To create a copyright symbol (©) on a Mac press Alt+G. To create one with Windows, press Alt+0169.

## note

The Watermark section has some limitations. For one, you can't reposition the watermark. And, when multiple images are displayed on a page, you can't place the watermark on each image.

## Using Rows and Columns

You can also use the Layout panel to change the number of images on the page and the spacing around them. Changing the Columns and Rows values modifies the overall number of images by displaying them in separate cells. For example, choosing 2 columns and 2 rows displays 4 images on each page. You can use these values to create a traditional contact sheet layout. Changing the Horizontal and Vertical values adjusts the distances in pixels between these rows and columns.

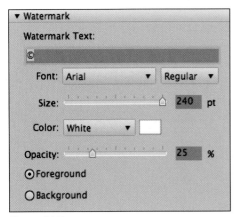

**Figure 14.7**

**13** Select the View PDF After Save option at the bottom of the Output panel if you want to preview the slideshow after it's created, and then click the Save button to save your presentation. This opens the Save As dialog that allows you to name your presentation and choose a location to save it to.

### note

Adobe PDF documents can be opened with a wide variety of image viewing and editing software. If you have trouble opening your PDF, download the free Adobe Reader at www.adobe.com/products/reader.

It takes a few moments for the PDF to be generated. While that happens, consider these AOM issues: Creating a slideshow in AOM is quite easy. However, this module does have some serious limitations. For example, you can't preview your slideshow while you're building it to see what transitions look like. Also, after you set up a specific layout, it's impossible to save it as a preset for future use. That makes it harder to use different layouts for different occasions. One more problem is that you can't add music to the slideshow using AOM. Adobe is aware of these limitations and I'm sure they're working hard to eliminate them. I expect to see major improvements to the PDF portion of AOM down the road.

### tip

You can manually advance the slides forward or backward while the slideshow is running using the right and left arrows on your keyboard. Press the Esc key to cancel the slideshow.

### note

Even though you can create layouts that are sized for printing, you can't print them directly from this module. That means that you first have to create a PDF and then open it in Photoshop and use Photoshop's Print command, as discussed in Chapter 13. I hope Adobe makes this easier in future releases.

# Building and Uploading Photo Galleries

You access the Web Gallery section of AOM by clicking the Web Gallery button at the top of the Output panel. Figure 14.8 shows the Web Gallery workspace with the Site Info and Create Gallery sub-panels collapsed. It's quite similar to the PDF workspace with the Content panel below the two Preview panels, and the Output panel on the right. The biggest difference is that the Output panel's sub-panels are different.

The Web Gallery has eight different layout options in the Template menu, shown in Figure 14.9. Each option affects how the thumbnails and the large view are positioned. (The layout shown in Figure 14.8 is the Standard layout with some modified colors.)

## tip

Remember to click the Refresh Preview button when changing templates.

The layout options fall into some general categories:

- **Filmstrip.** A filmstrip is used to display small thumbnails adjacent to a larger preview area. (Only the first ten thumbnails appear in the Output preview to save on rendering time when you click the Refresh Preview button.)

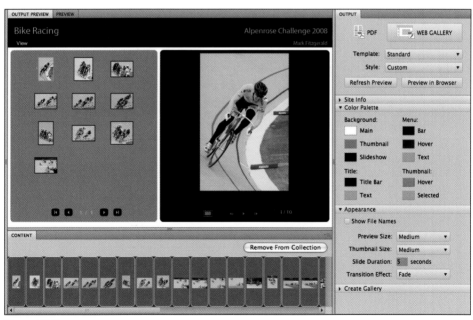

**Figure 14.8**

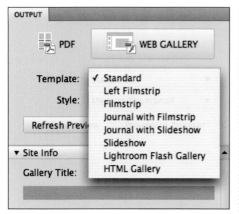

**Figure 14.9**

When you've selected one of these templates, contents of some of the menus options and sub-panels may change to accommodate template-specific settings. For example, when you select the Standard template, the presets in the Style menu directly below the Template menu are Medium Thumbnail and Small Thumbnail. However, when you select the Filmstrip or Slideshow templates, the only option in Template is Darkroom. When you choose HTML, your only choice is Lightroom. But when you choose Lightroom Flash Gallery, the options shown in Figure 14.10 are available.

- **Journal.** This is a list of metadata attached to the file, and includes keywords, creator, and camera settings. Unfortunately, you can't edit this list to omit information that isn't relevant or that you don't want to share online.

- **Slideshow.** When a Slideshow template is used, thumbnails are omitted. The slideshow plays automatically, or navigation controls are used to view specific images.

- **Lightroom Flash Gallery.** Flash is a Web programming language focused mainly on creating a multimedia experience. The company Macromedia, which is now owned by Adobe, developed it. Flash enables a Web developer to make the most of situations that require movies or any kind of animation. That animation ability, combined with the clean-looking layouts created in Flash, makes it perfect for Web galleries.

- **HTML Gallery.** HTML (HyperText Markup Language) is the basic, universal language of Web design. It's used in most of the Web sites you see. This language is not only basic, but it's also very powerful and flexible.

**Figure 14.10**

# note

Adobe Photoshop Lightroom, one of Adobe's newer products, is production software for photographers. It has slideshow and Web gallery modules that work in a similar fashion to AOM, although they are currently more flexible.

Each of the styles shown in Figure 14.10 changes the color palette, as well as the layout of the thumbnails and main image. These presets allow you to quickly pick a style that's close to what you like and then make any specific changes in the sub-panels. Unfortunately, just like the PDF portion of AOM, you can't save templates or style presets for the custom layouts you create.

# Designing a Web gallery

Designing a Web gallery is very similar to designing a slideshow, as you did earlier in this chapter. You choose a template as starting point and then move through the sub-panels to fine-tune the layout. You have so many options in this case that I'll go through the sub-panels one at a time to discuss each of them and how they're affected by Template menu and Style menu changes.

## Site Info

The Site Info sub-panel, shown in Figure 14.11, allows you to customize the information that's displayed on the Web gallery. The Site Title, Collection Title, and Contact Info sections affect the information that appears directly on the gallery. The E-mail or Web Address section provides a link for the Contact name when it's clicked. The Collection Description is visible by clicking the Web Gallery's View menu (that's directly below the Gallery Title), and choosing About This Gallery.

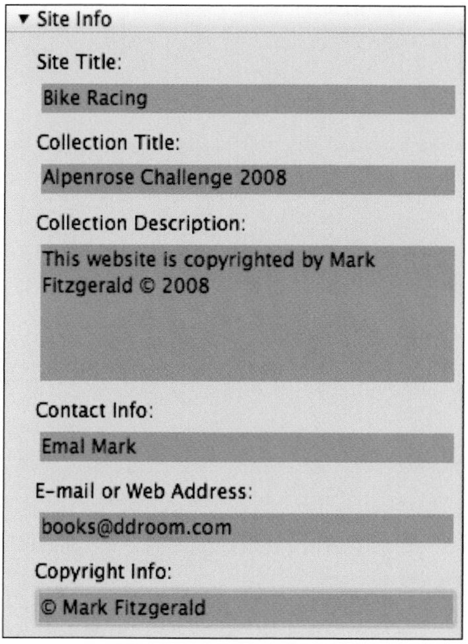

When you select some of the templates, an additional check box appears at the bottom of the sub-panel that hides the Title Bar when you deselect it.

## Color Palette

The options in the Color Palette sub-panel change dynamically to suit the template and style being used. Figure 14.12 shows the Color Palette sub-panel when you've selected the Warm Day style of the Lightroom Flash Gallery template. You click individual color swatches to change their colors with the color picker. This is a good way to make the colors of the Web gallery match the existing color scheme of your Web site.

**Figure 14.11**

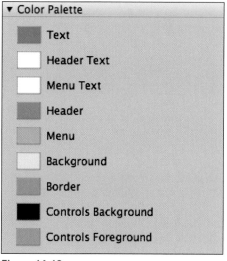

**Figure 14.12**

## Appearance

You use the Appearance sub-panel to change how different Web gallery elements appear. When you use a filmstrip or slideshow style template, the options allow you to control image sizes, slide duration, and transition effect. There's also a box you can check to include the image file names.

When you choose a journal style, as shown in Figure 14.13, extra type controls are added to the sub-panel so you can manage all the type in the journal section of the Web gallery. You also have the option of hiding the journal information by deselecting the Show Metadata option.

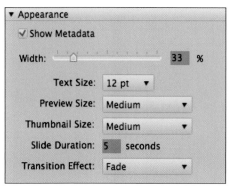

**Figure 14.13**

When you use an HTML template, the Appearance controls allow you to manage the number of columns and rows that are displayed. You can also choose to show cell numbers using the Show Cell Numbers checkbox, much like in the Layout sub-panel in the PDF section.

Finally, when you choose a Flash gallery template, the options allow you to use the Layout menu to change the way the thumbnails are laid out. You can also change the sizes of the preview image and the thumbnails.

# Uploading your Web gallery

After you've designed your Web gallery, it's time to create all the necessary files and upload them to your Web site. You do this using the Create Gallery sub-panel, shown in Figure 14.14. A Web gallery is typically uploaded to an existing Web site. When you upload your new Web gallery, it should be placed into its own folder. Then you provide a link to it from somewhere else on your Web site.

# note

To upload a Web gallery, you need to have a Web site and all the logon information for that site. If you don't have this, contact the company that hosts your Web site.

**Figure 14.14**

The Create Gallery sub-panel gives you two options: You can save all the Web gallery files to a folder on your system (Save to Disk) or you can upload them directly from AOM (Upload). The first option allows you to use your own FTP uploading software. FTP (File Transfer Protocol) is used to transfer files between computer systems.

The Upload option allows you to upload directly from AOM after you set up the Create Gallery sub-panel. Follow these steps to use it:

1. **Click the Upload radio-button and fill in the information for FTP Server, User Name, and Password in the designated fields.** Select the Remember Password option unless you're using a computer that's shared by a lot of people. (You don't want to encourage mischievous Web postings.)

2. **Specify a specific folder to place the Web gallery into using the Folder field.** For example, it's a good idea to have a folder named Web Galleries on the server that stores your Web site. That way when you need to manage your galleries, you know where all of them are.

# caution

When you check the Remember Password box, your password is added to the preset in an unencrypted state. If some nefarious person gains access to your computer, she may be able to find the password to your Web site files.

3. **Click the Save Preset Name button to the right of the Custom drop-down menu.** Custom is the default setting for this menu until you create your own preset. Yes, you finally get to save a preset! I don't know why this is the only place you can save a custom preset in AOM, but let's not look a gift horse in the mouth. If you checked Remember Password, a dialog opens when you click the Save Preset Name button, reminding you that your password is saved in plain text. When you click Yes to continue, the New Preset dialog opens, allowing you to save the name that describes the main Web site that the gallery is being uploaded to and click OK. Click the button and give your preset a unique name. Now your preset will be added to the menu next to the preset button. (Use the Delete Selected Preset Name button to delete an FTP preset.)

4. **Click Upload to upload your new Web gallery.** When the upload is complete, go to your Web site and add a link to the new gallery so that your Web site's visitors can begin to enjoy it immediately.

The Web Gallery options offer a variety of Web gallery designs. You can use one of the presets to quickly build a gallery, or use it as a starting point for your own design. Unfortunately, you can't save your design as a preset. You can only save your FTP settings as a preset. However, don't let this limitation stop you from using AOM to quickly create and share Web galleries of your photos.

# Batch Processing with the Image Processor

I want to tell you about one more thing before you finish this chapter, even though it doesn't directly relate to AOM. Sometimes you don't need a PDF presentation or a Web gallery from a group of images. Sometimes all you need is a bunch of files that are all the same size and file type. For example, say you have a group of raw files from an event and want to convert them all to JPEG files that you can take to your lab for some quick proofs. A really cool feature in Bridge, called Image Processor, allows you to do this and more.

## note

The Image Processor isn't specifically part of AOM; it's part of Bridge. You can launch it from any of the workspaces. (You can also access the Image Processor from within Photoshop by choosing File → Scripts → Image Processor.)

Figure 14.15 shows the Image Processor dialog box. It is divided into four numbered areas, which enable you to control how your files are processed.

Follow these steps to convert a group of files:

**1** Select the photos you want to work with in Bridge's Content panel, and then choose Tools → Photoshop → Image Processor. Because the Image Processor uses Photoshop to process files, Photoshop opens if it isn't already open.

**2** If you need to perform an editing step in Photoshop on the batch of images as they're processed, select the Open first image to apply settings option in the first section of the dialog box. When the Image Processor runs, it opens the first image so that you can apply your editing steps. This adjustment is recorded and applied to every other image as they're processed.

**3** Choose a location to save the files from the second section of the Image Processor dialog box. Normally I don't recommend that you save new, derivative files in the same location as the originals. However, when you choose this option here, a sub-folder is automatically created to contain the new files.

**4** Choose the type of file you want to create from the originals in the third section of the Image Processor dialog box. The options for File Type are JPEG, PSD, and TIFF. You can choose one of these options, two of them, or all three. Special sub-folders are created for every file type you choose, keeping them organized.

## tip

The JPEG file type has a box you can check to convert the color profile to sRGB, which is a good idea if you plan to show the files online or take them to a lab that uses sRGB.

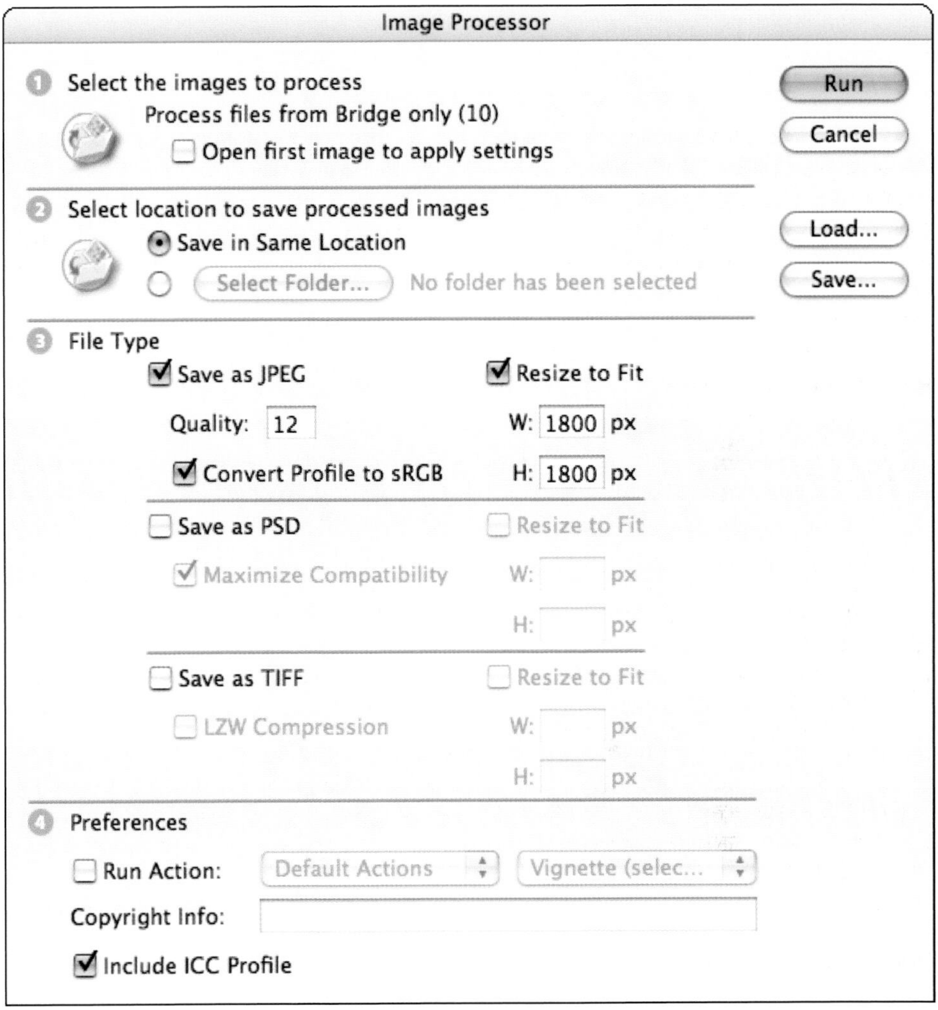

**Figure 14.15**

Each file type has its own saving options. All three offer you the option to resize the files as they're processed. This is extremely convenient. For example, I entered 1800 px into the width and height boxes in Figure 14.15 because my originals are already set to a resolution of 300 ppi (pixels per inch) in ACR. The

1800 px number is derived from the simple math used in calculating resolution: 300 ppi × 6 inches (in) = 1800 px. That means a setting of 1800 px at 300 ppi equals 6 inches.

At first you might think that setting the width and height values to the same number produces a square image.

However, that's not the case here. These boxes are used to limit the length of each dimension, rather than dictate it. This means if the photo is horizontal, it will be 1800 px wide, and if the photo is vertical, it will be 1800 px high.

## see also

Resolution is discussed in detail in Chapter 12.

5 **Use the Preferences in section 4 to add extras onto the files as they're processed.** When you check the Run Action check box, you have the option of executing one of Photoshop's actions. You use the Copyright Info field to add your copyright information to the metadata of each file. Do this if you haven't already added a copyright. It's also a good idea to leave Include ICC Profile checked so that your working space profile is always attached to outgoing files. Otherwise, it can make it more difficult for other software to accurately interpret the color of your files.

6 **Click the Save button or Load button.** Save is used to save a settings file of the current dialog box settings so that you can save different processing scenarios. Use the Load button to load one of these settings files.

7 **Click Run.** The Image Processor goes to work. Each photo is opened in Photoshop, all the dialog settings are applied, the file is saved into a special sub-folder, and then it's closed. Preparing groups of files doesn't get much easier than this.

Placing your work in front of the public is one of the most rewarding aspects of being a photographer. Now that you know more about the different ways you can display your photography, begin to think about how you can use some of these methods to share your work with the world.

# Appendix A: Resources

## Photography Organizations in the U.S.

These organizations tend to cater to professional photographers, but you don't always have to be a pro to join or take advantage of some of the benefits they offer. Additionally, some organizations such as ASMP and PPO sponsor state affiliate organizations that promote the regional exchange of information and professional development through monthly meetings and annual conventions. If you live outside the United States, ask some professional photographers in your area which organizations in your country would be most valuable to someone like you.

### Advertising Photographers of America (APA)

www.apanational.com

This organization works to improve the environment for advertising photographers by promoting mutual cooperation, educational programs, and tools and resources designed to help members excel in business.

### American Society of Media Photographers (ASMP)

www.asmp.org

Established in 1944, ASMP has become one of the world's foremost organizations for professional photographers with chapters in 35 states. Members of ASMP tend to be advertising photographers and photojournalists.

### American Society of Picture Professionals (ASPP)

www.aspp.com

With members from all regions of the United States and ten foreign countries, ASPP promotes an open exchange of ethics standards and business practices to help photographers understand and prosper from new technologies.

### North American Nature Photographers Association (NANPA)

www.nanpa.org

The first and one of the few organizations in North America dedicated to serving the field of nature photography, NANPA promotes the art and science of nature photography as a way of fostering better communication and the appreciation of nature and the protection of the environment.

### Picture Agency Council of America (PACA)

www.pacaoffice.org

A trade organization that strives to foster and protect the interests of stock photography archives of every size, from individual photographers to large stock agencies.

### Professional Photographers of America (PPA)

www.ppa.com

Founded in 1880, this is the world's largest non-profit association for professional photographers with more than 20,000 members in 54 countries. The mission of PPA is to promote education, creativity, and business excellence through worldwide chapters.

## Wedding & Portrait Photographers International (WPPI)

www.wppionline.com

This organization was founded in 1973 to represent wedding and portrait photographers. WPPI's annual trade show and convention is one of the leading sources of continuing education for members and non-members by some of the world's top wedding and portrait photographers.

## Women in Photography International (WIPI)

www.womeninphotography.org

WIPI was founded in 1981 to promote the visibility of women photographers and their work through education, exhibitions, and publications. WIPI serves professionals, hobbyists, and students interested in furthering their technical, creative, and business skills.

# Photography Magazines

With the large number of photo-related magazines, it's impossible to list them all. Here's a list of some of my favorites for amateurs and professionals. Most of these magazines also have an online presence with a wide variety of content.

## After Capture

www.aftercapture.com

This magazine is dedicated to photographic post-production equipment and technology. Articles include product reviews, techniques, and photographer portfolios.

## American Photo

www.popphoto.com/americanphoto/

American Photo features profiles on the personalities behind the lens and their contributions to a wide range of photographic disciplines and styles. Issues feature articles on exhibitions, portfolios, and stories about working professionals. They also publish an annual wedding guide.

## Digital Photo Pro

www.digitalphotopro.com

If I had to give up all magazines but one, this is the one I would keep. Each issue is filled with reviews, articles on techniques and business practices, and inspiring images. It bills itself as the guide to advanced technology and creativity and is aimed at professionals and advanced amateur photographers.

## LensWork

One of the best magazines on black and white photography and the creative process. Each issued, printed on book-quality paper, features articles, interviews and portfolios of some of the best black and white photography being created. www.lenswork.com

## Outdoor Photographer

www.outdoorphotographer.com

Though this magazine is dedicated to all types of outdoor photography, the emphasis is on nature and wildlife photography. Issues cover cameras and accessories, outdoor gear and apparel, ecological concerns, and workshops.

## Photo District News

www.pdnonline.com

This magazine is designed for professional photographers. Issues cover topics such as information on business and marketing, legal developments, new products and technologies, and photographic techniques.

## Photoshop User

www.photoshopuser.com

The magazine of the National Association of Photoshop Professionals, it's intended to serve a wide range of Photoshop users from photographers to designers and animators.

## Popular Photography and Imaging

www.popphoto.com

The product reviews and lab tests in this magazine make it a valuable resource for all types of photographers who want to keep up with the ever-expanding offerings from camera and photography manufactures.

## Professional Photographer

www.ppmag.com

This magazine is published by the Professional Photographers of America. Its purpose is to help readers advance their careers in the photographic industry through well-written articles about the business and artistic sides of professional photography.

## Rangefinder

www.rangefindermag.com

Though this magazine is designed for professional photographers, it has a wide appeal. Each issue typically includes articles on equipment, technical how-to's, marketing, and shooting tips.

## Shutterbug

www.shutterbug.com

Another magazine that covers a range of issues for hobbyist, semipro, and professional photographers. Each issue features tips on products, techniques, and industry trends designed to help photographers advance their craft.

# Photoshop Web Sites

Naturally, the primary Web site for Photoshop is www.adobe.com. This is where you can learn about the latest developments with Photoshop, as well as other Adobe products, and download trial versions of the software. In addition to Adobe's main Web site, there are hundreds of other useful Photoshop Web sites. Here are a few of my favorites.

## Adobe Labs

http://labs.adobe.com/

This Web site covers a range of Adobe products in addition to Photoshop. It allows you to experience and evaluate new and emerging technologies and products from Adobe before they're actually released. At this Web site you'll find prerelease software of upcoming products and technical documentation. Be advised that the products here are not always ready for primetime, but they give you a chance to see what's just over the horizon at Adobe.

## John Nack on Adobe

http://blogs.adobe.com/jnack/

This Web site is a blog by John Nack, the Principal Product Manager for Photoshop. John's blog provides a wealth of information and wit about Photoshop and its development, as well as other interesting digital tidbits.

## National Association of Photoshop Professionals

www.photoshopuser.com

The NAPP Web site is the online source for Photoshop User magazine. It offers a wide range of information and tutorials on all things Photoshop.

## PhotoshopSuport.com

www.photoshopsupport.com

This Web site has a wide variety of tutorials and other resources such as plugins and actions.

# Photography Web Sites

Much like Photoshop Web sites, there are hundreds, if not thousands of photography Web sites. Most focus on product reviews and tutorials to help you improve your photography. Many of them also host forums where you can ask questions of other readers. Here is a small sampling of some of the more popular sites. You could probably spend a lifetime enjoying the wide range of information you'll find on them.

## Camera Labs

www.cameralabs.com

Based in Queenstown, New Zealand, this Web site provides unbiased reviews of digital cameras and lenses. It contains detailed reports and video tours of a range of the latest products, as well as feature articles on how to use them.

## Digital Photography Review

www.dpreview.com

If you want to know about the latest equipment, this is the place to go. It was established in 1998 as an independent resource dedicated to news, information, and reviews about digital photography and digital imaging.

## Imaging Resource

www.imaging-resource.com

Founded in 1998, this comprehensive Web site features reviews of digital cameras and accessories, tutorials, and news affecting photographers and the photography industry. It also features a Photo of the Day Contest that anyone can enter.

## The Luminous Landscape

www.luminous-landscape.com

This comprehensive Web site features a host of tutorials and essays on digital photography products and techniques. The Luminous Landscape also promotes an endowment to fund photographic excellence and advancement, helping to fund a variety of photographic projects.

## The Nikonians

www.nikonians.org

This is the home of a worldwide online community of 100,000 Nikon users. The Web site is not affiliated with Nikon in any way, which is obvious when you begin reading the forums. The Web site feature reviews and tutorials, as well as information on the latest Nikon gear.

## The Online Photographer

http://theonlinephotographer.com/

This Web site describes itself as "all-purpose time-wasting Web site for photo-dawgs of every stripe, age, sex, color, nationality, description, economic stratum, and media preference." New content is published every day covering a wide range of photography topics.

## Strobist

http://strobist.blogspot.com

This blog is dedicated to teaching you how to use off-camera flash to improve your photos. It contains over 1000 articles about lighting products and techniques that appeal to photographers of all abilities.

# Photo Non-Profits

There are lots of photography related non-profits across the country, many of them community-based. I want to share three of my favorites with you. They are all 501c3 non-profits, which means any donation is tax-deductible. I'd like to encourage you to consider supporting one of these groups or seeking out one in your own community.

## Focus on Youth Photography Project

www.focusonyouth.org

This regional non-profit is located in my hometown, Portland, OR. It serves at-risk youth by exposing them to photography and the joy we all experience from it. Professional photographers serve as mentors to the kids, teaching them to shoot photos and print their images in a black and white darkroom, or process them digitally. Some of the success stories from this organization are very compelling. I've volunteered as a mentor for this group and I can tell you that it was a very gratifying experience.

## Now I Lay Me Down to Sleep

www.nowilaymedowntosleep.org

NILMDS is a volunteer organization helping families throughout the country to get through one of the most difficult circumstances they can face — the loss of a baby. They offer their services to create heirloom photographs of these beautiful babies to record their existence and help their families through the healing process. These amazing volunteers selflessly expose themselves to some difficult emotions with the sole intention of helping their community. I encourage you to consider helping NILMDS by volunteering in your community or making a tax-deductible donation.

## Operation Photoshop Rescue

www.operationphotorescue.org

This organization gives you the opportunity to help others with your Photoshop skills. Two photojournalists founded it after the devastation of hurricane Katrina. The mission of the group is to repair photos damaged by unforeseen circumstances, such as natural disasters and house fires. Operation Photoshop Rescue consists of a global network of volunteers who donate their time to help put people's lives back together by restoring their damaged photos. If you don't have time to volunteer, consider making a tax-deductible donation to this worthy organization.

# Photo Sharing Sites

One of the cool things about photography and this wired world we live in is the ability to easily share our photos with the rest of the world through photo sharing Web sites. Most of these sites allow you to upload photos for online viewing and print fulfillment. All of them offer free storage space, with some charging a monthly fee for larger amounts of space. Some even allow you to upload photos directly from your phone. Here's a list of some of the more popular photo sharing Web sites.

## Adobe Photoshop.com

www.photoshop.com

This is the newest kid on the block when it comes to photo sharing Web sites. The Photoshop.com Web site was designed with Adobe Flex, which makes it very visually appealing. You can upload up to 2 Gb of photos and videos for private storage or public sharing for free. You can also use online editing tools to edit photos, though I prefer to use Photoshop to do this before uploading.

## Flickr

www.flickr.com

Flickr is one of the most well know photo sharing sites. A basic account is free and it allows you to easily upload, organize albums and collections, and share your photos and videos. You can also edit photos and add creative effects as well as fonts. You can also take advantage of one of the newer features in the photo sharing world, geotagging. This allows you to drag-and-drop photos onto a map to indicate exactly where they were shot, allowing other users to search for photos by location. Finally, Flickr offers a wide range of output options, including prints, cards, books, and calendars.

## Photobucket

www.photobucket.com

Established in 2003, Photobucket offers the usual photo sharing services, such as online storage and albums. It also offers a Scrapbook Builder for creating online and printed scrapbooks using hundreds of pre-built designs. Another fun feature is the Remix Builder that allows you to put together photos, videos, and music for sharing at Photobucket or on your blog or Web site.

## Shutterfly

www.shutterfly.com

Shutterfly is another well known photo sharing Web site. Storage space is free and Shutterfly claims that they have never deleted any photos because of storage restrictions. One of the fun things it offers is over 400 specialized photo borders with festive and seasonal themes. You can also add free special photo back-printing with a short personalized message when you order prints, allowing you to record information on the prints for future generations.

## Smugmug

www.smugmug.com

Though this family-owned business is one of the smaller players in the photo sharing space, they have lots to offer. One of the main features is an ad-free and spam-free experience for the user. That means you can design an album that doesn't have any corporate logos on it. Smugmug also allows your friends to download full resolution files for printing at home.

# Appendix B: Keyboard Shortcuts

While working your way through this book you encountered many keyboard shortcuts. Because there are so many, they can be hard to remember. I've listed all of the default Photoshop menu and tool shortcuts here as a quick reference guide for you to use when you need to refresh your memory. Note that I did not include shortcuts for the additional menus and tools found in Photoshop CS4 Extended.

## Menu Shortcuts

Some keyboard shortcuts are not cross platform. For example the Mac version of Photoshop CS4 has a Photoshop menu, but the Windows version does not. Some of the commands in this menu are found in the Edit menu of the Windows version. When a shortcut in the list doesn't apply to a specific platform it's marked with N/A.

Remember that you can customize menu, panel, and tool shortcuts by choosing Edit → Keyboard Shortcuts. If you've changed yours, you can see a summary of all shortcuts by clicking the Summarize button on the Keyboard Shortcuts and Menus dialog box that's shown when you choose the Keyboard Shortcuts command.

### Table AB-1
### Photoshop Menu Shortcut Keys (Mac only)

|  | Mac Shortcut | Windows Shortcut |
|---|---|---|
| Preferences → General | ⌘ +K | N/A |
| Hide Photoshop | Ctrl+⌘ +H | N/A |
| Hide Others | Opt+⌘ +H | N/A |
| Quit Photoshop | ⌘ +Q | N/A |

### Table AB-2
### File Menu Shortcut Keys

|  | Mac Shortcut | Windows Shortcut |
|---|---|---|
| New | ⌘+N | Ctrl+N |
| Open | ⌘+O | Ctrl +O |
| Browse in Bridge | Alt+⌘+O <br> Shift+⌘+O | Alt+ Ctrl +O <br> Shift+ Ctrl +O |
| Close | ⌘+W | Ctrl +W |
| Close All | Alt+⌘+W | Alt+ Ctrl +W |
| Close and Go To Bridge | Shift+⌘+W | Shift+ Ctrl +W |
| Save | ⌘+S | Ctrl +S |

| | Mac Shortcut | Windows Shortcut |
|---|---|---|
| Save As | Shift+⌘+S | Shift+ Ctrl +S |
| | Alt+⌘+S | Alt+ Ctrl +S |
| Save for Web & Devices | Alt+Shift+⌘+S | Alt+Shift+Ctrl+S |
| Revert | F12 | F12 |
| File Info | Alt+Shift+⌘+I | Alt+Shift+Ctrl+I |
| Page Setup | Shift+⌘+P | Shift+Ctrl+P |
| Print | ⌘+P | Ctrl+P |
| Print One Copy | Alt+Shift+⌘+P | Alt+Shift+Ctrl+P |
| Exit | N/A | Ctrl+Q |

## Table AB-3
## Edit Menu Shortcut Keys

| | Mac Shortcut | Windows Shortcut |
|---|---|---|
| Undo/Redo | ⌘+Z | Ctrl+Z |
| | F1 | |
| Step Forward | Shift+⌘+Z | Shift+Ctrl+Z |
| Step Backward | Alt+⌘+Z | Shift+Ctrl+Z |
| Fade... | Shift+⌘+F | Shift+Ctrl+F |
| Cut | ⌘+X | Ctrl+X |
| | F2 | F2 |
| Copy | ⌘+C | Ctrl+C |
| | F3 | F3 |
| Copy Merged | Shift+⌘+C | Shift+Ctrl+C |
| Paste | ⌘+V | Ctrl+V |
| | F4 | F4 |
| Paste Into | Shift+⌘+V | Shift+Ctrl+V |
| Fill... | Shift+F5 | Shift+F5 |
| Content-Aware Scale | Alt+Shift+⌘+C | Alt+Shift+Ctrl+C |
| Free Transform | ⌘+T | Ctrl+T |
| Transform Again | Shift+⌘+T | Shift+Ctrl+T |
| Color Settings... | Shift+⌘+K | Shift+Ctrl+K |
| Keyboard Shortcuts... | Alt+Shift+⌘+K | Alt+Shift+Ctrl+K |
| Menus... | Alt+Shift+⌘+M | Alt+Shift+Ctrl+M |
| Preferences | N/A | Ctrl+K |

## Table AB-4
## Image Adjustments Shortcut Keys

|  | Mac Shortcut | Windows Shortcut |
|---|---|---|
| **Levels** | ⌘+L | Ctrl+L |
| **Curves** | ⌘+M | Ctrl+M |
| **Hue/Saturation** | ⌘+U | Ctrl+U |
| **Color Balance** | ⌘+B | Ctrl+B |
| **Black & White** | Alt+Shift+⌘+B | Alt+Shift+Ctrl+B |
| **Invert** | ⌘+I | Ctrl+I |
| **Desaturate** | Shift+⌘+U | Shift+Ctrl+U |
| **Auto Tone** | Shift+⌘+L | Shift+Ctrl+L |
| **Auto Contrast** | Alt+Shift+⌘+L | Alt+Shift+Ctrl+L |
| **Auto Color** | Shift+⌘+B | Shift+Ctrl+B |
| **Image Size** | Alt+⌘+I | Alt+Ctrl+I |
| **Canvas Size** | Alt+⌘+C | Alt+Ctrl+C |

## Table AB-5
## Layer Menu Shortcut Keys

|  | Mac Shortcut | Windows Shortcut |
|---|---|---|
| **New ➜ Layer** | Shift+⌘+N | Shift+Ctrl+N |
| **Layer via Copy** | ⌘+J | Ctrl+J |
| **Layer via Cut** | Shift+⌘+J | Shift+Ctrl+J |
| **Create/Release Clipping Mask** | Alt+⌘+G | Alt+Ctrl+G |
| **Group Layers** | ⌘+G | Ctrl+G |
| **Ungroup Layers** | Shift+⌘+G | Shift+Ctrl+G |
| **Arrange ➜ Bring to Front** | Shift+⌘+] | Shift+Ctrl+] |
| **Arrange ➜ Bring Forward** | ⌘+] | Ctrl+] |
| **Arrange ➜ Send Backward** | ⌘+[ | Ctrl+[ |
| **Arrange ➜ Send to Back** | Shift+⌘+[ | Shift+Ctrl+[ |
| **Merge Layers** | ⌘+E | Ctrl+E |
| **Merge Visible** | Shift+⌘+E | Shift+Ctrl+E |

## Table AB-6
## Select Menu Shortcut Keys

|  | Mac Shortcut | Windows Shortcut |
|---|---|---|
| **Select All** | ⌘+A | Ctrl+A |
| **Deselect** | ⌘+D | Ctrl+D |
| **Reselect** | Shift+⌘+D | Shift+Ctrl+D |
| **Select Inverse** | Shift+⌘+I<br>Shift+F7 | Shift+Ctrl+I<br>Shift+F7 |
| **Select All Layers** | Alt+⌘+A | Alt+Ctrl+A |
| **Refine Edge** | Alt+⌘+R | Alt+Ctrl+R |
| **Grow** | Shift+F6 | Shift+F6 |

## Table AB-7
## Filter Menu Shortcut Keys

|  | Mac Shortcut | Windows Shortcut |
|---|---|---|
| **Last Filter** | ⌘+F | Ctrl+F |

## Table AB-8
## View Menu Shortcut Keys

|  | Mac Shortcut | Windows Shortcut |
|---|---|---|
| **Proof Colors** | ⌘+Y | Ctrl+Y |
| **Gamut Warning** | Shift+⌘+Y | Shift+Ctrl+Y |
| **Zoom In** | ⌘++<br>⌘+= | Ctrl++<br>Ctrl+= |
| **Zoom Out** | ⌘+- | Ctrl+- |
| **Fit on Screen** | ⌘+0 (zero) | Ctrl+0 (zero) |
| **Actual Pixels** | ⌘+1<br>Alt+⌘+0 (zero) | Ctrl+1<br>Alt+Ctrl+0 (zero) |
| **Extras** | ⌘+H | Ctrl+H |
| **Show → Target Path** | Shift+⌘+H | Shift+Ctrl+H |
| **Grid** | ⌘+' | Ctrl+' |
| **Guides** | ⌘+; | Ctrl+; |
| **Rulers** | ⌘+R | Ctrl+R |
| **Snap** | Shift+⌘+; | Shift+Ctrl+; |
| **Lock Guides** | Alt+⌘+; | Alt+Ctrl+; |

### Table AB-9
### Window Menu Shortcut Keys

|  | *Mac Shortcut* | *Windows Shortcut* |
|---|---|---|
| **Minimize** | Control+⌘+M | N/A |
| **Actions** | Atl+F9 | Atl+F9 |
|  |  | F9 |
| **Brushes** | F5 | F5 |
| **Color** | F6 | F6 |
| **Info** | F8 | F8 |
| **Layers** | F7 | F7 |

### Table AB-10
### Help Menu Shortcut Keys

|  | *Mac Shortcut* | *Windows Shortcut* |
|---|---|---|
| **Photoshop Help** | ⌘+/ | F1 |
|  | Shift+⌘+/ |  |

# Tool Shortcuts

Tools that are stacked together have the same shortcut key. I listed them separately here so that you can see each tool in this list. Remember that you can cycle through stacked tools by pressing the Shift key and the shortcut key simultaneously.

### Table AB-11
### Tool Shortcut Keys

| *Tool Name* | *Shortcut Key* |
|---|---|
| Move tool | V |
| Rectangular Marquee tool | M |
| Elliptical Marquee tool | M |
| Lasso tool | L |
| Polygonal Lasso tool | L |
| Magnetic Lasso tool | L |
| Quick Selection tool | W |

| Tool Name | Shortcut Key |
| --- | --- |
| Magic Wand tool | W |
| Eyedropper tool | I |
| Color Sampler tool | I |
| Ruler tool | I |
| Note tool | I |
| Count tool | I |
| Crop tool | C |
| Slice tool | C |
| Slice Select tool | C |
| Spot Healing Brush tool | J |
| Healing Brush tool | J |
| Patch tool | J |
| Red Eye tool | J |
| Brush tool | B |
| Pencil tool | B |
| Color Replacement tool | B |
| Clone Stamp tool | S |
| Pattern Stamp tool | S |
| History Brush tool | Y |
| Art History Brush tool | Y |
| Eraser tool | E |
| Background Eraser tool | E |
| Magic Eraser tool | E |
| Gradient tool | G |
| Paint Bucket tool | G |
| Dodge tool | O |
| Burn tool | O |
| Sponge tool | O |
| Pen tool | P |
| Freeform Pen tool | P |
| Horizontal Type tool | T |
| Vertical Type tool | T |
| Horizontal Type Mask tool | T |
| Vertical Type Mask tool | T |
| Path Selection tool | A |
| Direct Selection tool | A |

*(continued)*

## Table AB-11 *Continued*

| Tool Name | Shortcut Key |
| --- | --- |
| Rectangle tool | U |
| Rounded Rectangle tool | U |
| Ellipse tool | U |
| Polygon tool | U |
| Line tool | U |
| Custom Shape tool | U |
| Hand tool | H |
| Rotate View tool | R |
| Zoom tool | Z |
| Default Foreground/Background Colors | D |
| Switch Foreground/Background Colors | X |
| Toggle Standard/Quick Mask Modes | Q |
| Toggle Screen Modes | F |
| Toggle Preserve Transparency | / |
| Decrease Brush Size | [ |
| Increase Brush Size | ] |
| Decrease Brush Hardness | { |
| Increase Brush Hardness | } |
| Previous Brush | , |
| Next Brush | . |
| First Brush | < |
| Last Brush | > |

# Glossary

**8-bit color** Uses eight bits per color channel to describe each pixel.

**16-bit color** Uses sixteen bits per color channel to describe each pixel. Creates a file that is twice the size of an 8-bit file.

**additive color** Describes the way light waves combine to create color. This is the way humans see things, and it's how most color adjustment happens in Photoshop. This system is called additive because it begins with black (no light). A light source adds wavelengths that have a specific color. Equal amounts of pure red, green, and blue light added together create white. See also *subtractive color*.

**Adobe Camera Raw** Photoshop's raw file converter. See also *raw*.

**artifact** An unwanted visual distortion introduced by the digital process.

**aspect ratio** The relationship of the height of an image to its width. For example, 4 × 5 is the same aspect ratio as 8 × 10.

**banding** Occurs when intermediate tones are lost during the digital process. Because these tones are missing, color graduations show as bands, rather than gentle tonal grades.

**blending mode** Determines how pixels blend with previously existing pixels. Blending modes can be used with some tools, such as the Brush tool, to affect pixel blending for each stroke, or entire layers can be blended with underlying layers by changing the blending mode on the Layers panel.

**Bridge** Adobe Bridge is the file browser that comes with Photoshop. It's named Bridge because it acts as a file browser for all of Adobe's design products.

**burning** The process of locally darkening specific regions of an image without affecting the rest of the image. See also *dodging*.

**cache** A folder that contains hidden information about images that have been viewed in Bridge.

**capture file format** A file format that's used in digital cameras to record captured images. Camera raw and JPEG are the most common capture file formats. See also *editing file format* and *output file format*.

**clipping** The loss of detail due to underexposure or overexposure, or image adjustments to the extreme shadows and highlights. Clipping occurs when a pixel's value is higher than the highest value or lower than the lowest value in the image.

**collection** A virtual group of files created in Bridge. When a photo is added to a collection, it isn't moved or copied. Instead, a visual reference to the photo is placed in the collection. See also *smart collection*.

**color mapping** How individual colors are translated from one color space to another.

**color model** A mathematical model describing colors and their relationships to each other. RGB and CMYK are different color models.

**color profile** A description of the gamut of a particular device, or a document that is attached to a file to describe the color space that was used to create or edit it. See also *editing color space.*

**color profile mismatch** A warning that appears when the working color space in Photoshop doesn't match the color space of the file that's being opened.

**color space** A subset of a color model that contains a specific gamut of colors. Adobe RGB (1998) and sRGB are both color spaces that exist in the RGB color model.

**combing** The effect on a histogram that occurs when image data is expanded by a tonal or color adjustment. It's called combing because the gaps in the histogram look like a comb. See also *spiking.*

**complimentary color** Pairs of colors that are opposite in hue. Red/cyan, green/magenta, and blue/yellow are all pairs of complimentary colors.

**compression** A system used to reduce the size of a file when saving it. See also *lossless compression* and *lossy compression.*

**container keyword** A main keyword in Bridge that contains sub-keywords. See also *keyword.*

**device dependent color space** A color space describing the range of colors that a particular device can see and/or reproduce.

**device independent color space** Color spaces used to describe the range of colors in color editing spaces. These color spaces are not dependent on any particular device.

**digital asset management (DAM)** The system used to identify and organize digital assets such as photos. In Photoshop, Adobe Bridge organizes and adds pertinent metadata and keywords to image files.

**digital negative** A term used to describe raw files. It refers to the fact that a raw file cannot be changed by the editing process, much like the way a negative is unchanged by the printing process.

**DNG** Adobe's Digital Negative file format which is used for storing raw camera data. Proprietary raw files from various camera manufacturers can be converted to DNG for achievability and ease of metadata storage.

**dodging** The process of locally lightening specific regions of an image without affecting the rest of the image. See also *burning.*

**dots per inch (dpi)** Refers to the number of dots per inch that an inkjet printer is capable of applying to a sheet of paper. Generally speaking, the higher the dpi, the better the output. See also *resolution.*

**downsampling** The process of decreasing the number of pixels in an image through resampling. See also *upsampling.*

**dynamic range** Refers to the range between the darkest and the lightest tones in an image or scene.

**editing color space** Describes the total palette, or gamut, of colors available when editing a photo in Photoshop. Also called *working color space.* See also *color space.*

**editing file format** A file format that's used for saving files during the editing process. TIFF and PSD are the most common, though JPEG can also be considered an editing file format. See also *capture file format* and *output file format.*

**file browser** A program that allows the user to visually choose photo files by selecting thumbnails of the images.

**file compression** A system used to decrease the size of a file when it's saved. See also *lossless compression* and *lossy compression.*

**FTP (File Transfer Protocol)** A system that's used to transfer files from one computer system to a remote system. FTP is commonly used to upload files to Web sites and photolabs.

**gamut** A description of the color that a device is capable of capturing or reproducing. The palette of colors it is able to work with.

**GPU (graphics processing unit)** Your system's graphics card. It controls all display functions in your computer.

**grayscale** Another way of saying that the image has no color in it and only tones of gray are used to describe image content. Grayscale is also a color space where only tones of gray are available for editing.

**Hide all layer mask** A layer mask that is all black and therefore hides all content on its associated layer. See also *Reveal all layer mask.*

**image interpolation** When an image is resampled, the color values of new pixels are based on the existing pixels surrounding it. The interpolation method used during resampling controls which type of calculations are used to assign the new colors. See also *resampling.*

**keyword** A descriptive term that's attached to a photo to describe something about it. This term is added to the photo file's metadata so that it can be used at a later date to retrieve the photo. See also *metadata.*

**layer** Discrete segments of image information that are stacked on top of one another. The use of layers is the key to creating a non-destructive workflow.

**layer mask** A system of using black and white paint to hide or reveal specific information on a layer.

**lossless compression** When saving a file, all information is retained during file compression. This means that an image can be resaved and recompressed without compromising image quality. See also *compression.*

**lossy compression** When saving a file, data is permanently removed through compression. Higher levels of compression result in greater data loss. Every time a file is resaved with lossy compression, more data is lost. This cumulative data loss can greatly affect quality. See also *compression.*

**marching ants** Used to describe the moving dashed line that surrounds a selected area because it looks like ants marching in unison.

**metadata** A standardized set of information that describes characteristics of a photo file. Metadata, such as the date of creation and camera settings, is added to a file at the time of its creation. Additional metadata, such as keywords, are added after the file is created.

**monitor calibration** A set of standards that refer to the color temperature, brightness, and contrast for monitor displays. A hardware calibration device measures these qualities in your monitor, and then you adjust your monitor (if possible) to bring it into alignment with the standards. If you cannot adjust your monitor, the calibration device modifies the settings on the computer's graphics card. See also *GPU.*

**noise** Digital artifacts (unwanted leftovers) that often show up as specs that have a grainy appearance. It's usually caused by shooting at high ISO speeds and by underexposure.

**non-destructive workflow** A working system that's designed to prevent permanent changes from occurring to the image. Using a non-destructive workflow insures the greatest amount of flexibility because you can alter or completely undo any previous changes at any time. See also *layer* and *workflow*.

**OpenGL (Open Graphics Library)** A standardized specification developed in 1992 by Silicon Graphics. It consists of a library of standard graphics routines for manipulating images on-screen. OpenGL is used by software manufacturers to speed up and customize the way images are shown on the monitor.

**output file format** A file format that's used for saving files intended for output. The most common output file formats are JPEF and TIFF. See also *capture file format* and *editing file format*.

**Panel menu** A menu you access by clicking the Panel menu button, just below the Close panel button that looks like an X.

**Panel set** Groups of similar panels that are stacked together to save space.

**panorama** A photo that shows a wide view. Panoramas can be horizontal or vertical.

**pixels per inch (ppi)** A term used to describe the resolution of an image. The greater the number of pixels per inch, the higher the resolution. Generally speaking, higher resolution produces better quality when printing an image. See also *resolution*.

**RAID (Redundant Array of Independent Disks)** The simultaneous use of multiple hard drives to improve performance and reliability when backing up data. RAID0, called striping, is used to distribute data across several disks. RAID1, also called mirroring, is used store an exact duplicate of data from one or more hard drives.

**raw** A generic term referring to a digital camera capture format that creates files containing unprocessed data from the camera's sensor. Raw files must be processed with raw conversion software before they can be opened in Photoshop. See also *Adobe Camera Raw* and *DNG*.

**redundancy** A system of storing information across multiple hard drives so that when one hard drive crashes, its lost information is reconstructed from the data on the remaining drives. Also called striping and RAID0. See also *RAID*.

**resampling** Changing the amount of data in an image when resolution or pixel dimensions are changed. See *upsampling* and *downsampling*.

**resolution** A measurement of the detail in an image. Image resolution is measured in pixels per inch (ppi) and printer resolution is measured in dots per inch (dpi). See also *pixels per inch* and *dots per inch*.

**Reveal all layer mask** A layer mask that is all white and therefore shows all content on its associated layer. See also *Hide all layer mask*.

**Scrubby slider** The hand icon with double arrows that appears when you hover the cursor over a numerical input box. When this icon appears, you can click and drag to the left to decrease numerical values, or click and drag to the right to increase numerical values.

**sepia tone** A faded brown color that results from using specific darkroom chemicals to tone a black and white print. Historically this was done to improve the longevity of the print, as well as add a visual element to it.

**smart collection** A smart collection uses standard metadata to sort any range of files. See also *collection*.

**soft proofing** An onscreen preview of the output of a specific output device.

**spiking** The effect on a histogram that occurs when image data is compressed by a tonal or color adjustment, causing spikes to appear in portions of the histogram. See also *combing*.

**spring loaded keys** The ability to momentarily switch to a different tool by pressing and holding its shortcut key. When the key is released, the selected tool springs back to the original tool.

**subtractive color** Describes the way pigments, such as paints, dyes, inks, and natural colorants reflect light. When white light strikes a pigment, the pigment absorbs some wavelengths of light and reflects the unabsorbed wavelengths. The wavelengths that are reflected are the colors we see and what give the pigment its color. See also *additive color*.

**thumbnail** A small graphical representation of a full-sized image used in Bridge to render images more quickly because the original image does not need to be accessed.

**transparency** A gray and white checkerboard that is Photoshop's way of indicating *transparency* — which means there's nothing there.

**twirly** A triangular icon that is used to reveal hidden information. When it points to the side, the information is hidden. When it points downward, the information is revealed.

**upsampling** The process of increasing the number of pixels in an image through resampling. See also *resampling* and *downsampling*.

**virtual memory** The use of empty hard drive space for overflow memory when the system's RAM (Random Access Memory) is full.

**watermark** An identifying mark that's placed on an image to identify something about it or indicate ownership.

**Windows Image Color Management (ICM)** A color management module designed by Microsoft and part of the Windows operating system. It's used to insure accurate color matching between devices.

**workflow** 1) The order in which editing steps are taken to insure that each is executed in the correct sequence. 2) A systematic methodology that insures each step is performed in the correct order. 3) A repeatable system designed to enhance efficiency.

**XMP (Extensible Metadata Platform) sidecar file** A file that's used to store metadata for a camera raw file. The sidecar file has the same root name as the file it is derived from and is stored in the same parent folder as its associated file. See also *metadata*.

# Index

*Continued*

*Continued*

*Continued*